ML
1700
.G29
2006

D0083362

DISCARD

OPERA

THE BASICS

- "Clear and well-organized" —Ellen Rosand, Professor Of Music and Chair of the Music Department at Yale University
- A basic introduction for students and opera lovers
- Covers the entire range of opera from its beginnings to today

Opera: The Basics gives a brief introduction to four centuries of opera, ideal for students and interested listeners who want to learn more about this important genre.   The book is organized in two parts: Terms and Topics; and Genres, Styles and Scores. In the first part, the author traces the origins of opera, introduces the reader to its basic terminology, and considers opera as artistic and social expression. In Part II, the author examines the history of major genres and styles, including serious and semi-serious opera; comic opera and operetta; and vernacular opera. Throughout, sidebars offer studies of key figures and topics relating to opera's rich heritage. The book concludes with a bibliography, discography, and videography.

Opera: The Basics serves as an excellent introduction to the performers, the music, and the styles that make opera an enduring and well-loved musical style.

Denise Gallo is a Senior Music Specialist at The Library of Congress. Previously, she was an Assistant Professor and Co-Director of the Music History Division at The Catholic University of America, where she now remains an adjunct professor. Gallo's other publications include *Rossini: A Guide to Research* (Routledge).

You may also be interested in the following Routledge Student Reference titles:

BLUES: THE BASICS
RICHARD WEISSMAN

FOLK MUSIC: THE BASICS
RONALD COHEN

JAZZ: THE BASICS
CHRISTOPHER MEEDER

ROCK: THE BASICS
WAYNE SHIRLEY

WORLD MUSIC: THE BASICS
RICHARD O. NIDEL

OPERA
THE BASICS

denise gallo

Routledge
Taylor & Francis Group

NEW YORK AND LONDON

Published in 2006 by
Routledge
Taylor & Francis Group
270 Madison Avenue
New York, NY 10016

Published in Great Britain by
Routledge
Taylor & Francis Group
2 Park Square
Milton Park, Abingdon
Oxon OX14 4RN

© 2006 by Taylor & Francis Group, LLC
Routledge is an imprint of Taylor & Francis Group

Printed in the United States of America on acid-free paper
10 9 8 7 6 5 4 3 2 1

International Standard Book Number-10: 0-415-97071-7 (Hardcover) 0-415-97072-5 (Softcover)
International Standard Book Number-13: 978-0-415-97071-6 (Hardcover) 978-0-415-97072-3
(Softcover)
Library of Congress Card Number 2005014489

No part of this book may be reprinted, reproduced, transmitted, or utilized in any form by
any electronic, mechanical, or other means, now known or hereafter invented, including
photocopying, microfilming, and recording, or in any information storage or retrieval system,
without written permission from the publishers.

Trademark Notice: Product or corporate names may be trademarks or registered trademarks,
and are used only for identification and explanation without intent to infringe.

Library of Congress Cataloging-in-Publication Data

Gallo, Denise P.
   Opera : the basics / Denise Gallo.
      p. cm. -- (The basics)
   Includes bibliographical references (p.), discography (p.), videography
(p.), and index.
   ISBN 0-415-97071-7 (hardback : alk. paper) -- ISBN 0-415-97072-5 (pbk. :
alk. paper)
   1. Opera. I. Title. II. Series: Basics (Routledge (Firm))

ML1700.G29 2005
782.1--dc22   2005014489

Taylor & Francis Group
is the Academic Division of Informa plc.

Visit the Taylor & Francis Web site at
http://www.taylorandfrancis.com

and the Routledge Web site at
http://www.routledge-ny.com

This book is dedicated with affection and respect to all of the students in the Johns Hopkins Evergreen Society who asked me to teach them about music.

CONTENTS

INTRODUCTION

In 1702, Abbé François Raguenet published a discourse contrasting French and Italian opera. In addition to a consideration of which language was better suited for singing, he listed specific elements on which operas should be critiqued. Among these was "the composition of the play," or merits of the libretto. Important, too, were "the qualifications of the actors; those of the performers; the different sorts of voices; the recitative, the airs, the symphonies, the choruses, the dances, the machines, the decorations. . . ." (By "symphonies," Raguenet meant the overture or *sinfonia* and any other purely instrumental interludes within the acts. "Machines" refers to the elaborate mechanical stage devices common in Baroque opera.) Finally, he allowed for "whatever else is essential to an opera, or serves to make the entertainment compleat and perfect."

Written about a century after opera's birth in the courts and academies of Italy, Raguenet's essay presents criteria that can still be used when reviewing an opera. However, the scope of the subject is far more imposing today. While he was concerned with only the French and Italian styles, modern writers treat a host of traditions, among them German, Russian, Czech, Spanish, British, and American. And whereas the Abbé had only one hundred years to consider, more than four centuries of musical development and aesthetic change must now be acknowledged.

Not regularly confronted with new compositions as were Raguenet and his contemporaries, today's critics pass judgment on productions of the tried-and-true works of the common repertory, that collection of popular operas such as *Carmen, Don Giovanni,* and *Der Rosenkavalier* that are sure to be included in a number of operatic seasons around the world. They continue to comment on the singers' talent, the director's vision, the conductor's ability, the costume and set designers' art, and, when necessary, the choreographer's imagination. Moreover, they still counsel whether a production is "compleat and perfect," and worth the (usually considerable) ticket price.

In general, a reviewer writes for an audience of readers who are familiar with opera on some level. The task of introducing and explaining it as a genre falls to others who also address the elements explored by Raguenet but consider them in light of opera's historical and cultural development. This literature commonly falls into two categories: scholarly texts and books for general readership. Among the former are music histories, critical editions of scores (see Chapter 11), and specialized studies examining opera as a musical genre, cultural chronicle, social phenomenon, and economic enterprise. However, most general readers with little or no knowledge of music find such volumes intimidating. Based on their own experiences with opera, they seek books that range from the simplest introduction to more comprehensive explorations of composers, stage history, and repertory. Because these two categories are usually mutually exclusive (the authors of one rarely read those of the other), many of these introductory volumes do not reflect the recent scholarship that has revised opera history. Based on similar books from the last century, they reiterate opera's narrative as it once was told.

REWRITING OPERA HISTORY

Late nineteenth- and early twentieth-century scholars wrote the history of opera by examining the resources available to them. In the last quarter of the twentieth century, musicologists working in archives uncovered a plethora of new sources including correspondence, theater records, holographs and autograph scores, and published editions of orchestral scores and piano/vocal reductions. Among these discoveries, for example, were the manuscript scores of Gioachino Rossini's *Il viaggio a Reims* and Giuseppe Verdi's *Stiffelio.* These serendipitous finds allowed scholars to revise the theory that both works had been destroyed because their creators thought them inferior. More important, these operas now can be studied in the context of Rossini's and Verdi's compositional careers. Late twentieth-century research in theater archives also uncovered scores and librettos of well-known works that had undergone significant revisions, signaling the existence of variant versions prepared (some with the composer's participation and some without) specifically to suit local tastes. These archival yields forced scholars to revisit discussions about opera's role in society and reaffirmed the idea that, far from being immutable monuments, opera scores were pliable works changed freely to appease different customs and aesthetics.

With many of the prejudices of earlier histories erased, scholars were encouraged to admit for study the so-called "minor" composers whose works had been dismissed when compared with those of the masters of the operatic canon. Comic opera and vernacular traditions (see Chapters 9 and 10), once thought frivolous and inferior to serious music drama, also became worthy of scholarly discourse. As a result, opera history is undergoing a revision as these new sources continue to demonstrate that our previous understanding of the genre was exceedingly narrow and in many cases simply wrong. Rossini's opera *Otello* offers just one example. Because the libretto veered so radically from the Shakespearean original, Rossini's work traditionally had been lambasted when contrasted with Verdi's rendering of the play. In the late 1980s, scholars discovered that Rossini's opera had not been based on Shakespeare at all but had closely followed the plot of a popular French adaptation of it.

Judgments about Rossini's *Otello* can be attributed to an honest mistake. It is discomforting to discover that something presented as "fact" was really the invention of a well-meaning author ensuring a legacy for a personal hero. Unfortunately, opera history is rife with this "spin doctoring." Bellini scholars, for example, have been sorting out biographical fact from the fiction that his friend Francesco Florimo penned in letters he attributed to the composer. A reevaluation of the patriotic sentiment ascribed to Verdi's music followed an examination of contemporary newspapers indicating that the public's reaction was more post-Unification nostalgia than Risorgimento fervor (that is, patriotism in retrospect). Simply stated, the goal of the ongoing reconstruction of opera history is to present it as it actually was, not as those in the past wanted it to be.

A WORD ABOUT REPERTORY

Throughout this book, readers will find reference to the common or international opera repertory. The creation of this group of works resulted from two issues. First, in the wake of the numerous nineteenth-century revolutions, there were moves to recall tradition by reviving past compositions. On a more practical level, theaters began to keep elaborate productions of large works so they could be mounted again, storing costumes and sets for reuse in future seasons to cut costs. Therefore, many operas became "repertory pieces" simply as a result of economic rather than artistic decision making. Because of the predominance of older works being programmed, the number of commissions for new ones fell drastically below that of prior centuries. In the early nineteenth century, for example, many Italian composers enjoyed four or five commissions annually, whereas some twentieth-century composers produced only one or two operas in the space of their careers. Although opera companies now are including lesser known (but equally worthy) works in their seasons, the repertory pieces keep them in the black during increasingly unstable times for opera worldwide.

ABOUT *OPERA: THE BASICS*

Routledge's *The Basics* series comprises books that introduce broad subject areas, defining terminology and discussing important concepts to prepare readers for more in-depth study. Concise by design, the books nevertheless treat their various topics in a direct and cogent manner. *Opera: The Basics* joins the series as an aid for university students, singers, and adult learners and for opera enthusiasts with some knowledge of and experience with the repertory. Most important, *Opera: The Basics* has been written with an appreciation of the changing approaches to studying opera and with respect for recent scholarship that addresses it as a social and cultural expression. Chapters include as examples the names of operas or of specific selections that readers may already know or to which they can listen to better understand the book's concepts and ideas, but because this volume is intended also for those who might not read music, it contains no score excerpts. Instructors and music students will know where to locate scores to supplement this text; general readers who wish may find them in many libraries or for sale at music stores or Internet websites.

HOW TO USE THIS BOOK

Opera: The Basics is divided into two parts, the first introducing essential terms and topics and the second discussing genres, styles, and scores. Although chapters may be read successively, cross-references make it possible to take them out of order. Chapter 1 introduces the dramatic forerunners of opera and the philosophic and aesthetic theories that inspired the musical innovation that would become its first principal element: monody. Chapter 2 considers musical elements such as overture, recitative, aria, and ensemble, tracing their development within the major national styles. The very crux of opera is the relationship between words and music, the theme of Chapter 3, which examines the libretto's poetic structures and characteristics and the compositional strategies used to set them. Chapter 4 sets out the tasks of the professionals who create and produce operas; Chapter 5, dedicated solely to those who perform it onstage, explores the art of operatic singing and the vocal ranges employed in opera casts. Chapter 6 summarizes opera's history onstage and off, the latter discussion ranging from opera's presence on mechanical instruments and recordings to radio and television broadcasts and webcasting. Part I concludes with a treatment of topics that depict opera as a reflection of society.

Part II includes chapters on serious and semi-serious works and on comic opera and operetta. Because these concentrate primarily on works in the Italian and French traditions, Chapter 10 highlights the so-called vernacular genres of England, Germany, and Spain. The final chapter defines types of scores and editions, differentiating between those used for study and performance.

Just as it is important for an Introduction to explain what a book *will* include, it is equally wise to state what it will *not*. First and foremost, this is a book about opera, not musical theater. Musicologists know the difference between these two genres; a brief explanation at the end of Chapter 9 outlines it for others. Singers, of course, know that one of the major distinctions between opera and musicals is in the vocal production employed for each. Those who wish a demonstration should listen to the original cast recording of *West Side Story* with

Carol Lawrence, Larry Kert, and Chita Rivera, and then to the one made by Kiri Te Kanawa, José Carreras, and Marilyn Horne.

Although *Opera: The Basics* includes a discography and videography, these sections will not suggest which recordings and videos to buy or opine which singers best portray which roles. Although some books offer such value judgments, this volume (and its author) remains solely in the objective realm. The list of sound and video recordings identifies productions of works outside of the common repertory whose composers or librettists have been discussed in the book. The aim is to inspire readers to go beyond their current operatic "comfort level." Similarly, the selected bibliography exemplifies the mission of this volume by including only recent opera scholarship. The bibliographies in these works in turn will lead readers to previously published sources.

A final caveat: *Opera: The Basics* is not for readers who want to understand opera as they always have; it is for those who are willing to take their personal opera odysseys to the next stage and beyond.

ACKNOWLEDGMENTS

Many people devoted their time and energy to assist me with this project, and I would like to thank them here. As always, Professor James Parsons was at the ready to read drafts and return them with constructive criticism; he constantly demonstrates that he is a generous colleague and a devoted friend. Others who took time to read chapters include Deborah Crall and Anne Marie McMahon (two students with great potential), my Library of Congress colleague Catherine Dixon, and my New Oxford, Pennsylvania, neighbor Darryl Reilly. I also thank Dr. Linda Fairtile, music librarian at the University of Richmond, and Debra Evans, director of education at the Metropolitan Opera, for their responses to my (sometimes odd) e-mail queries, and the students in the Smithsonian Associates Italian Opera course I taught in Fall 2004 who willingly tested chapters as their text. Some of the readers mentioned here are musicians; others cannot read music but know opera through performances and recordings. In addition to dutifully catching typos, they also pointed out areas that needed clarification. I have tried to address all of their comments because together they represent the prospective readership of this book.

My special thanks go to Professor Emerita Cyrilla Barr who convinced me to work in opera and to Professor Carolyn Gianturco who suggested I work on Giovanni Pacini. These two fine scholars and teachers started me off. I am grateful, too, to the Washington National Opera, the Baltimore Opera Company, the Washington Concert Opera, and the Summer Opera Theatre Company who continue to invite me to speak to their audiences.

Richard Carlin of Routledge Publishing entrusted me with this project, for which I thank him and all on his staff, especially Marsha Hecht, who assisted in its publication. Finally, I acknowledge my biggest supporters: my husband, Al, who continues to try to show me what computers can do for me; my son, Carmelo, who dodged the bullet on this one by moving to Massachusetts; and my son, Brian, who is closer than ever to becoming Figaro.

TERMS AND TOPICS

THE ORIGINS OF OPERA

Although opera's theoretical origins can be traced back to the late Renaissance, performances were not documented before 1600, the year music historians use to signal the start of the Baroque era. In addition to opera, this period of astonishing creativity inspired the birth and early development of other major musical genres, including symphony, oratorio, and cantata. Yet as the union of music, poetry, art, and dance, all important to seventeenth-century aesthetics, opera represents the ultimate manifestation of Baroque culture.

Style Periods Relevant to Opera History

Baroque:	1600–1750
Classical:	1750–1816
Romantic:	1816–1900
Modern:	1900–1970
Post-Modern:	1970–present

Music historians have used 1750, the year J.S. Bach died, to designate the end of the Baroque era. Similarly, the beginning of Romanticism centers around the life of another musical icon, Ludwig van Beethoven, who in 1816 began his so-called "Third Style" in which radically innovative works such as the Grosse Fuge for string quartet and the Ninth Symphony were created. The post-Modern era began when composers such as John Cage not only challenged cultural authority but also began to investigate and employ elements from non-Western musical traditions.

As logical as style period dates have seemed in past music history narratives, they are nevertheless arbitrary boundaries centered around a handful of Western art music pioneers. Hundreds of other composers made valuable contributions in the prevailing styles. Although organizing history into periods has provided order to the complicated process of understanding musical forms and characteristics, it has eliminated from standard histories composers who in their day were accepted and well-respected. In the early nineteenth century, for example, the operas of Giovanni Pacini were performed with more frequency than those of his younger rivals, Vincenzo Bellini and Gaetano Donizetti. To restore the place of composers such as Pacini in music history, musicologists are rethinking timelines, often preferring to consider musical developments by century rather than style period.

THE DEVELOPMENT OF A GENRE

A study of seventeenth-century music shows that aesthetics varied from one country to another (indeed, from one region or even one city to another). Apart from the most obvious issue—the language of a vocal text—Italian music from this period simply does not "sound" like its French counterpart, and German music doesn't sound precisely like either of those. To a great extent, this can be explained by a proliferation of public and private musical establishments encouraging and supporting diverse traditions. Because most music was commissioned and supported by noble or church patronage, political and religious issues also played a part in generating and maintaining distinct styles. Despite its use in contemporary commentaries and treatises, the widespread criterion of "good taste" by which Baroque compositions were judged could be defined only in terms of a listener's own cultural and artistic experiences.

Nevertheless, certain general characteristics do apply to Baroque music, reflecting the creative environment that encouraged the creation of opera:

- An emphasis on voice, even as a model for instrumental performance
- A move away from polyphony (a musical texture in which multiple independent lines are performed together) to homophony (a melodic line supported by an underlying harmonic accompaniment)
- A tendency to musically represent emotions and passions in order to move the soul of the listener (the so-called "Doctrine of the Affections")
- A penchant for musical ornamentation, embellishment, and improvisation in performance
- An esteem for poetic texts and classical subjects

All of these proved significant in formulating the theory and compositional techniques that inspired the earliest opera composers and singers.

THE FLORENTINE CAMERATA

Renaissance thought flourished in academies (*accademia*, pl. *accademie*), which were societies of intellectuals employing the new "scientific" approach to learning. One such group, referred to as the *Camerata* by composer Giulio Caccini, gathered at the home of Giovanni de' Bardi in Florence, a city long recognized for literary and artistic pursuits. Through their studies and discussions, the *Camerata*'s musicians and accomplished amateurs proposed that Greek drama had been sung rather than spoken. In addition, the importance of the chorus in Greek plays inspired them to try to apply their ideas to the contemporary stage. This connection between ancient Greek drama and opera would resound repeatedly throughout opera's history, inspiring libretto reformers Apostolo Zeno (1668–1750) and Pietro Metastasio (1698–1782) and composers such as Richard Wagner (1813–1883) and Igor Stravinsky (1882–1971).

Several *Camerata* members, most prominently Vincenzo Galilei (father of Galileo) and Girolamo Mei, promulgated the group's theories in their writings. Caccini and Jacopo Corsi, among others, employed them in compositions in a new solo vocal style known as monody. These pieces showcased the dramatic potential in the relationship between music and text, inspiring entire musical dramas (*dramme per musica*). To differentiate them from spoken drama, such works also were called *opere per musica* (sing., *opera per musica*), or stage works set to music. In time, this designation was simply shortened to "opera."

Monody

The polyphonic madrigal, a favorite with musical amateurs and dilettantes, dominated Renaissance secular vocal music. Its texture traditionally featured (often intricate) combinations of several distinct melodic lines that created chordal harmonies when sung together. The Camerata's study of Greek drama led to an appreciation for monody, a single melodic line supported by a simple accompaniment. Musical genres do not disappear overnight, however, especially ones as popular as the madrigal. Thus, although forward-looking composers such as Claudio Monteverdi adapted madrigal poetry to solo settings, he continued to set traditional madrigals, even employing them for choruses in his operas; one of his most dramatic uses of a madrigal chorus is "Non morir Seneca," from *L'incoronazione di Poppea*. Monody gained in popularity in opera, oratorio, and cantata, however, as recitative and aria, both of which will be discussed in Chapter 2.

OPERA'S PRECURSORS

Opera can be traced to several musical, theatrical, and literary genres of the Middle Ages and Renaissance:

- *Intermedio*
- Learned comedy (*Commedia erudite*)
- Italian folk comedy (*Commedia dell'arte*)
- Epic and pastoral poetry
- Church pageants (*Rappresentazioni sacre*)

THE INTERMEDIO

Comprising musical and dramatic elements, *intermedi* were presented between the acts of larger stage works or alone as special pieces for civic celebrations and court festivities such as weddings and birthdays. *Intermedi* did not necessarily have plots; rather, they often consisted of a series of tableaus that were metaphoric representations of noble patrons or of the locale of the court. Because these productions featured lavish sets and costumes as well as music composed and performed by the court musical establishment (*cappella*) or hired musicians, *intermedi* were as much displays of power and wealth as they were entertainment. By the end of the Renaissance, the Medici court in Florence had garnered an unbeatable reputation for *intermedio* productions. Initially, operas were offered as a novel alternative to *intermedi*, but, as surprising as it now may seem, the new genre was slow to gain popularity with audiences who resisted change in their entertainment fare.

LEARNED COMEDY (COMMEDIA ERUDITE)

Humanist intellectuals of Italian Renaissance courts cultivated an appreciation for the comedies of Plautus and Terence. Some of these *literati* even authored their own plays in the classical style. These works were offered regularly in the *accademie*, where members themselves often took part in the performances. Characters in these learned comedies, such as the bombastic soldier or *miles gloriosus*, became stereotypes that made the transition into early opera. Indeed, the *miles gloriosus* took to the stage again much later as Donizetti's Belcore in *L'Elisir d'amore* and Verdi's Falstaff.

ITALIAN FOLK COMEDY (COMMEDIA DELL'ARTE)

The popularity of the *erudite* encouraged troupes of touring players to develop a similar repertory; these professionals polished their portrayals of particular characters so well that they were able to extemporize dialogue within stereotypical skits. Adoption of local dialects helped regional audiences to embrace these stock characters as their own. Recognizable by distinctive masks and costumes, characters such as Arlecchino were presented in productions liberally mixed with song and dance. These characters made the transformation into opera and remained popular until the libretto reforms of the late Baroque temporarily excised comic elements. *Commedia dell'arte* influences were quickly reemployed, however, in time inspiring such memorable roles as Leporello in Mozart's *Don Giovanni* and the characters in Strauss' *Ariadne auf Naxos*.

EPIC AND PASTORAL POETRY

Literary genres that influenced opera include the epic poem and the *pastorale*. Although it was written nearly a century before the first operas were performed, Ludovico Ariosto's epic poem, "Orlando furioso" (published in 1516 and revised in 1521 and 1532), became the inspiration for numerous operatic settings. Its main characters offered the perfect dramatic situation: Orlando (or Roland) is driven mad when the beautiful Angelica spurns him for the Saracen Medoro. The tales of other characters such as Atlante, Ariodante, Ginevra, Ruggiero, Alcina, Bradamante, and Olimpia drawn from the poem's cantos also were chosen as subjects for operas. Among the composers who set plots from this epic are Jean-Baptiste Lully (*Roland*, 1685), Domenico Scarlatti (*Orlando, ovvero La gelosia pazzia*, 1711), Antonio Vivaldi (*Orlando*, 1727), Giovanni Paisiello (*Olimpia*, 1768), Josef Haydn (*Orlando paladino*, 1782), and Ambroise Thomas (*Angélique et Médor*, 1843). George Frideric Handel plumbed the poem for three different works: *Orlando* (1733), *Alcina*, and *Ariodante* (both 1735).

Humanist poets and scholars became fascinated with the notion of untouched Nature. Pastoral poetry, dramatic in tone and lyric in rhythm, became the written vehicle to portray this world. Although the sources of the *pastorale* lay in classical works such as Virgil, significant examples of it were creations of the Renaissance, in particular the dramatic poems *Aminta* by Torquato Tasso (1581) and *Il pastor fido* by Battista Guarini (1585). These two works yielded myriad musical versions, some as madrigal settings and others as *intermedi* and operas. Their stories and characters inspired composers and librettists through the twentieth century.

A brief sampling of operas based on pastoral works includes *Armide* (1686) by Lully; *Aminta* (1703) and *Il trionfo di Armida* (1726) by Albinoni; *Rinaldo* (1711) and *Il pastor fido* (1712) by Handel; *Armide al campo d'Egitto* (1718) by Vivaldi; *Armide* (1771) and *Il pastor fido* (1789) by Antonio Salieri; *Armide* (1777) by Christoph Willibald Gluck; *Armida* (1784) by Haydn; *Tancredi* (1813) and *Armida* (1817) by Gioachino Rossini; and *Armida* (1904) by Antonín Dvořák.

CHURCH PAGEANTS (RAPPRESENTAZIONI SACRE)

Since the early Middle Ages, certain portions of church ritual on feasts such as Easter included musical performances. These solos and unison choruses were chanted in the natural rhythms of speech, usually driven by the patterns of the local pronunciation of Latin. When portions of the performances became too secular, these displays were moved out of the churches; music as sacred dramatic expression, however, was not completely abandoned. Inspired by the missionary efforts of the Franciscans, the *lauda* or song of praise became a popular evangelical tool. These songs were eventually included in religious pageants illustrating scenes from the lives of Christ, Mary, and the saints. This tradition contributed to another Baroque creation, the oratorio, which, although musically identical to opera, presented sacred subjects but without stage sets and costumes. This link between sacred drama and opera would be exploited later in the *azione tragico-sacra*; disguised behind this acceptable genre designator, operas about Biblical subjects or characters were permitted during Advent and Lent when productions would have been forbidden otherwise. This was the tradition behind Rossini's *Mosè in Egitto* (1818) and Donizetti's *Il diluvio universale* (1830).

The First Significant Voice

One of the earliest forces in opera was Claudio Monteverdi (1567–1643). Born and musically trained in Cremona, he later moved to Mantua where he became *maestro della musica* for the powerful Gonzaga family. Initially, his reputation was based on his madrigals, some of which came under attack for ignoring the established rules controlling the use of dissonance. In a response to this criticism, Monteverdi proposed a "Second Practice," or modern style, that permitted better expression of poetry. Demonstrating a sensitivity and appreciation for the expressive potential of music, Monteverdi selected dramatic texts such as verses from Tasso's *La Gerusalemme liberata* and parts of Guarini's *Il pastor fido* to set as madrigals.

Monteverdi's first opera, *Orfeo*, was produced in Mantua in 1607 for the *Accademia degli Invaghiti*. Designated a *favola in musica*, it featured pieces set as monody and madrigals. The libretto, by Mantuan court official Alessandro Striggio, centered on the myth of Orpheus, who influences the gods of the netherworld by playing his lyre. This character, representing the power of music, was the perfect choice for this new genre. In fact, the story had been set twice before (Jacopo Peri's *Euridice* of 1600 and Giulio Caccini's *Euridice* of 1602) and remained a popular subject through later centuries as witnessed in

Gluck's *Orfeo ed Euridice* (1762/revised 1774), Haydn's *L'anima del filosofo* (1791), Jacques Offenbach's *Orphée aux enfers* (1858/revised 1874) and Ernst Krenek's *Orpheus und Eurydike* (1926), to name but a few settings.

Monteverdi's next opera, the tragedy *Arianna*, was composed a year after *Orfeo*. Only the main character's "Lament" remains from this score, commissioned for celebrations surrounding the wedding of Francesco Gonzaga to the daughter of the Duke of Savoy. Leaving service in the Mantuan court in 1612, Monteverdi's next position allowed him to further explore dramatic music. In addition to returning to Tasso's *La Gerusalemme liberata* for a dramatic setting entitled *Il combattimento di Tancredi e Clorinda* (1624), Monteverdi eventually became active in the public theaters of Venice, revising *Arianna* for a production in 1640 and composing three new operas: *Il ritorno d'Ulisse in patria* (1639–1640), *Le nozze d'Enea in Lavinia* (1640–1641), and *L'incoronazione di Poppea* (1642–1643, revised 1651).

Examples of Monteverdi's operatic compositions, such as the aria "*Possente spirito*," the crux of *Orfeo*, demonstrate not only his skill at merging melody with poetry but his able handling of the new monodic style. His later works exhibit how far he had advanced this genre, particularly in the area of musical characterization, seen, for example, in Nerone and Poppea in *L'incoronazione*. Although other contemporary composers contributed to this new musico-dramatic manifestation, Monteverdi's works stand apart, making him the first significant composer in the history of opera.

From its beginnings in the musings of intellectuals, musicians, and cultivated amateurs, opera came to be acknowledged internationally as one of the most significant genres of Western art music. Within its first century, it became a symbol of European culture, and, as such, was a popular export, even to then-obscure corners of the globe. Recently discovered sacred operas in native languages demonstrate that Spanish Jesuit missionaries taught new Christian musicians in South America to compose and perform works in the genre. By the eighteenth century, although most major European capitals boasted opera houses, smaller cities and towns eagerly hosted traveling companies in venues such as town halls. Italian touring troupes brought opera to the new capital of St. Petersburg so that the tsars could Westernize their courts. In the nineteenth century, similar companies braved exhausting and dangerous journeys to perform contemporary favorites for European colonists engaged in trade in China.

In the 1800s, opera was performed in virtually all settled areas of the United States, with productions documented in theaters and in unlikely venues such as boathouses, Odd Fellows halls, and saloons. Although some were sung in the original language, Americans often were introduced to operas in English translation. Works such as Bellini's *Norma* and Donizetti's *Lucia di Lammermoor* were so popular and audiences knew them so well that parodies of them, often performed by minstrels in black face, were common antebellum fare. In Europe, too, operas were translated into the vernacular for new audiences; thus, Wagner was sung in Italian and Verdi in German in an effort to make opera more accessible (see Chapter 3).

By the nineteenth century, opera had gone far beyond its earliest manifestations in Italian, French, and German. Because it highlighted language, song, dramatic plots, scenery, and often dance, opera became the perfect vehicle for nationalist composers who employed it to demonstrate the unique cultures of their own countries (see Chapter 7). Operatic traditions emerged in Russia, Spain, Scandinavia, Central Europe, Greece, England (a rebirth after more than a century of relative inactivity after the death of Henry Purcell in 1695), the United States, and South America. Twentieth and twenty-first century composers added to the operatic repertoire while their audiences experienced opera through various media, including radio, television, recordings, and film (see Chapter 6). One can only imagine the astonishment of members of the Florentine *Camerata* were they to discover how opera developed from their modest discourses into an art form that flourishes on stages the world over.

2

MUSICAL TERMINOLOGY

Any discussion of opera requires an understanding of the special vocabulary used to describe its musical and literary elements. Because of opera's Italian origins, many of its terms derive from Latin roots. Thus, when opera was introduced in Paris, some words were easily adopted into French, another Romance language. *Recitativo*, for example, became *récitatif*. When the French cultivated their own operatic tradition, their unique style and genres required new terms—*tragédie lyrique* (lyric tragedy) instead of *opera seria* (serious opera), for instance. As opera's popularity spread, composers in other countries did as the French had done, either adapting existing terms (*Rezitativ* in German and *recitative* in English) or creating ones to describe their own compositions (such as Wagner's *Gesamtkunstwerk*).

This chapter defines and describes the basic musical forms and structures that make up operas. Certain elements are easily recognizable when heard in performance; recitative, for example, is generally simple to distinguish from aria. The ability to hear whether an aria is *da capo* or *dal segno*, however, requires either an advanced knowledge of music or extensive listening experience and a familiarity with the operatic repertory. For some readers, recognizing one aria form from another will be important; students might be graded on their ability to do so. For others, an understanding that different aria types exist should suffice.

The majority of elements in this chapter are drawn from Italian opera, but most of these are found in other traditions as well. Structures unique to these other conventions either will be mentioned specifically or discussed in Part II.

OVERTURE

Derived from the French word for "opening," an overture is an orchestral number played before an opera's stage action begins. The overture, or *sinfonia* (pl., *sinfonie*) as it is called in Italian, was an integral part of operas through the nineteenth century. From one of its earliest extant examples, the regal toccata preceding Monteverdi's *Orfeo*, the overture expanded in size and significance. Moreover, its development had ramifications beyond the world of opera. When Alessandro Scarlatti and other eighteenth-century composers wrote *sinfonie* in three movements of contrasting tempos (fast-slow-fast), these compositions soon were extracted from their operas to stand on their own merits as concert pieces. (To this day, overtures such as those from Rossini's *Guillaume Tell* and Wagner's *Die Meistersinger* are common fare on classical radio stations). Unwittingly, Scarlatti and his colleagues were contributing to the evolution of another musical genre: the symphony. Furthermore, their efforts to include brass and wind instruments together with traditional strings helped to establish the organization of another creation of the eighteenth century: the orchestra.

Initially, overtures had no musical relationship to the subjects of the works they preceded, a point criticized by those who sought opera reform in the eighteenth century. Concerned composers responded; Christoph Willibald Gluck (or more likely his librettist, Ranieri Calzabigi) explained that in composing the opera *Alceste*, "Ho imaginato che la Sinfonia debba prevenir gli Spettatori dell'azione" ("I thought out the overture so that it would give spectators a hint of the plot."). Composers could employ any one of various ways to relate the overture's music to the action that followed. If an opera had a happy ending, its overture could preface that with joyful themes. Another strategy introduces musical themes and motives from the opera; a particularly dramatic example of this foreshadowing is heard in Mozart's overture to *Don Giovanni* when the ominous chords announcing the arrival of the Commendatore's ghost in Act II also open the opera.

Composers in the nineteenth century perfected the connection between overture and opera. Rossini (who, unfortunately, is more often identified with his overtures than with his operas), Bellini, Donizetti, and their Romantic colleagues composed overtures based on themes from arias or ensembles within the opera. The pounding Druid war chorus as well as the heroine and Pollione's duet, "In mia man alfin tu sei," are quoted in the overture to Bellini's *Norma*. Giacomo Meyerbeer's grand opera *Les Huguenots* prefaces the drama about the Catholics' massacre of French Protestants with an overture that cites Luther's chorale "Ein feste Burg." Of the many remarkable overtures from nineteenth-century works, several are worthy of special note. Carl Maria von Weber foreshadows Nature's violent responses to the diabolic forging of the bullets in the Wolf Glen scene in the overture to *Der Freischütz*. One of the most dramatically conceived overtures (or as Verdi called this one, a *preludio*) belongs to *La traviata*. The composer characterizes Violetta by prefiguring episodes in her life, but in reverse order. The sobbing string figures of Act III begin the piece, leading next into "Amami Alfredo" from Act II. The flighty ornamentation that accompanies the second statement of that melody reflects the vibrant vocal style in which Violetta performs in Act I, an appropriate transition into the party scene onto which the curtain opens.

By century's end, composers eschewed overtures, opting for a rapid start of the dramatic action. Although Verdi's *Aida* (1871) has a prelude, his *Falstaff* (1893) does not. Neither do the operas of Puccini. A brief, fugal opening sets the scene for the hectic action of *Madama Butterfly*'s first act, whereas the chords associated with the villain Scarpia immediately set the tone as the curtain rises in *Tosca*. For the most part, composers in the twentieth century followed suit, as did Alban Berg in *Wozzeck*, Carlisle Floyd in *Of Mice and Men*, and André Previn in *A Streetcar Named Desire*, to name but a few. When its golden age in opera ended in the late nineteenth century, the overture migrated to a position of prominence in the scores of musical theater.

TYPES OF OVERTURE

Over the centuries, different traditions developed unique types of overtures, which reflect separate musical styles.

FRENCH OVERTURE

With its musical origins in courtly dance, the French overture features two distinct sections of music. The first is slow and stately, punctuated by characteristic dotted rhythms; the faster second section, different in rhythm and meter, is often followed by a repeat of the first. After Lully began to employ this form for his operas and ballets, it became the standard musical introduction to that nation's operatic works. Because of the cultural connections between the courts of France and England, overtures in the French style also appeared in English compositions, including Henry Purcell's opera *Dido and Aeneas* (1689). By the mid-eighteenth century, the French overture had fallen out of fashion, but its form inspired later composers to begin overtures with slow introductions.

PRELUDIO

Because of the symphonic nature of overtures through the early 1800s, some composers concerned with the overall drama of their operas later opted for "atmosphere" pieces that would more effectively set the tone of the work. By mid-century, Verdi and others began to use the term *preludio*, diminishing—at least semantically—some of the independent musical stature an overture might have had from the work it preceded. It is impossible to distinguish aurally between an overture and a *preludio*; because the distinction is in the mind of the composer, the only way to be certain which term is correct is to see how the piece is identified in the score. Knowing the date of a work and a composer's preferred terminology helps us make an educated guess, though. For instance, in the score of *Stiffelio* (1850), Verdi was still using the term *sinfonia*; beginning with *Rigoletto* (1851), he used *preludio*.

VORSPIEL

Although one finds the German term *Ouvertüre* in Richard Wagner's early operas, by the mid-1840s, he had begun to employ the word *Vorspiel*. Basically a German translation of the word "prelude" ("pre" and "vor" both mean "before" and "lude" and "spiel" both mean "play"), Wagner attempted to differentiate these later overtures, at least philosophically, from his earlier ones. In essence, this is what Verdi intended by adopting the term *preludio*, but for vastly different reasons. Because of Wagner's attempts to develop opera that reflected the culture and aesthetics of the German people, he created specifically German terms that would distance his music from what he perceived as the domination of the Italian and French traditions. He even abandoned the word "opera" because of its foreign connotations, instead describing his works as "music dramas." Works before *Tannhäuser* (1845) have an *Ouvertüre*; those after have a *Vorspiel*.

RECITATIVE

Early Baroque treatises describe a modern style of vocal performance referred to variously as *"stile recitativo," "recitar cantando," "cantar recitando,"* and *"cantar recitativo."* The theorists who coined the phrases, among them members of the *Camerata*, were envisioning a singing style that would emulate the declamatory techniques of spoken drama. By combining *recitare* (to recite) with *cantare* (to sing), they in essence proposed "sung dramatic speech." Singer/composer Jacopo Peri made use of this new style in his opera *Euridice* (1600), describing it in the work's preface as midway between speech and song. A year later, Giulio Caccini published examples of this type of monody and instructions for performing it in *Le nuove musiche*. Recitative developed into a distinct poetic and musical component of operas, employed until composers eventually abandoned it in the nineteenth century.

RECITATIVE'S DRAMATIC FUNCTION

Because Humanists closely allied music with language and poetry, early Baroque composers were careful to make recitative not only imitate the natural rhythms of speech and the rise and fall of the voice, but also to respect the proper accents and stresses of the libretto's poetic text. Furthermore, by scoring recitative with descriptive consonant or dissonant harmonies, composers were able to heighten the drama and move their listeners. The recitative "Ahi caso acerbo" in which Sylvia describes Euridice's death in Act II of *Orfeo* offers an example of how Claudio Monteverdi depicted an emotionally charged episode.

Although recitative originally was employed for great dramatic moments, by the 1700s this distinction was saved for the aria, a shift resulting in no small part from the rise of the professional singer and audiences' enthusiasm for virtuoso performance. As monologues or dialogues, recitative became the vehicle for plot development; in contrast, arias generally were reserved for moments of reflection, reaction, or emotional expression. Through much of the eighteenth century, opera scores were comprised of alternating recitative passages and arias, with the occasional duet or chorus added for dramatic or comedic interest. Toward the end of the century, composers and librettists began to break this structural pattern when they experimented with the theatrical possibilities of ensembles, numbers featuring several characters, sometimes with the addition of chorus.

In the nineteenth century, composers of comic operas for the most part retained traditional recitative. In serious works, however, recitative regained dramatic weight when it was subsumed into the *scena* (pl., *scene*), a musico-dramatic construct comparable to a scene in a stage play. *Scene* included a fluid mixture of recitative and instrumental passages that led into arias, duets, or larger ensembles. In Act I of Rossini's *Semiramide*, for example, the enmity between the characters Arsace and Assur is established in an animated *scena*. Thus, recitative again became an essential part of establishing an opera's dramatic thread rather than simply serving as a bridge between lyrical numbers. This renewed attention to setting dialogue in flexible musical structures eventually inspired composers to abandon recitative altogether in favor of continuous melody. Wagner rejected recitative (along with aria) as too "Italian" for his German music dramas. Verdi also shed it in his late works; one hears the startling contrast between Verdi as nineteenth-century traditionalist in *Oberto*, his first work, and Verdi as musical pioneer in *Falstaff*, his last. In the twentieth century, the occasional inclusion of recitative by Neoclassical composers served as a musical allusion to an earlier age, as is the case in Igor Stravinsky's *The Rake's Progress*.

MUSICAL ELEMENTS OF RECITATIVE

Baroque singers performed recitative by controlling its tempo, speeding up the line to reflect a character's passion or agitation and slowing it down for expressions of despair or tranquility. Delivering narrative sections and simple dialogues at a normal pace provided the needed contrast to set off moments of dramatic intensity. Because recitative in early seventeenth-century works was not as melodically distinct from aria or arioso passages as it would become in the next century, singers were able to embellish it with ornaments imitative of affective gestures such as sobbing or sighing. By the following century, however, ornamentation ceased to be a dramatic device, instead becoming a means to demonstrate vocal agility. Thus it was transferred to the more lyrical aria.

Unlike their predecessors who had carefully set passages of recitative to match their poetry and dramatic intent, composers in the classical era employed predictable harmonic patterns that featured frequent modulations within the dialogue. This minor task of composing might even have been relegated to students. Recitative's harmonic significance certainly was less than that of an aria; rather than ending firmly on a tonic or home key, recitative in operas from the eighteenth through the early nineteenth centuries generally concluded with a cadence that led into the key of the following aria. Although the advent of the *scena* gave recitative more rhythmic interest, to a great extent harmonies still were conservative and dependent on the tonality of the next number.

RECITATIVO SECCO (FR., RÉCITATIF SEC)

Secco or "dry" recitative is accompanied by a keyboard instrument such as a harpsichord, often with the support of a few sustaining bass instruments such as cello, double bass, and bassoon (collectively known as the *continuo* group); by the late eighteenth century, the fortepiano had replaced the harpsichord. *Secco* accompaniment features simple chords that punctuate the recitative passages. Generally, the singers set the tempo.

RECITATIVO ACCOMPAGNATO (FR., RÉCITATIF ACCOMPAGNÉ)

By the late eighteenth century, composers were beginning to experiment with the dramatic effects of setting portions of recitative with the accompaniment of the orchestra's string section. Although "accompanied recitative" also can imply full orchestral support, that setting is often referred to as *recitativo obbligato* (Fr., *récitatif obligé*) or *recitativo stromentato*. By the mid-nineteenth century, composers still employing recitative favored this richer sound, usually reserving *secco* accompaniment for comedy.

RÉCITATIF MESURÉ (MEASURED RECITATIVE)

In French opera, recitative is generally notated without specific rhythms to suggest the natural flow of the language and the poetry (*récitatif simple*). For added musical and dramatic interest, composers devised a form of recitative in which the rhythms subtly shift to create a more flexible link into the aria or ensemble that follows. Although it is somewhat like *arioso* style (that is, a style midway between recitative and aria), *récitatif mesuré* really has no equivalent in Italian opera. Both styles of recitative can be heard in "Le perfide Renaud me fuit," in Act V, scene 5 of Lully's *Armide*.

RECITATIVE VS. SPOKEN DIALOGUE

Although recitative served to develop an opera's plot, audiences often found it tedious, demonstrating far more enthusiasm for arias, especially those performed flamboyantly by a reigning *divo* or *diva*. The British, for instance, barely tolerated recitative, considering it a useless interruption; Catherine the Great, an opera enthusiast and librettist herself, decreed that as little of it as possible be performed in productions at her court. Nevertheless, Italian composers continued to employ recitative, as did composers of French operas for the serious stage. Vernacular traditions such as *Singspiel*, *opéra comique*, ballad opera, and *zarzuela*, on the other hand, eschewed recitative in favor of spoken dialogue (see Chapter 10).

ARIA

An aria is a lyrical number, usually for solo voice. Derived from the Latin for "air," the term was applied to music as early as the fourteenth century to refer to the manner in which a piece was performed rather than to the piece itself. Although aria also could mean instrumental music, in time the term became identified solely with song, in particular the settings of stanzaic poems. Once identified with song and poetry, arias came to be set as monody along with recitative. Although in the earliest operas, little distinction can be heard between certain passages of recitative and aria, in general, the former simulated patterns of speech, whereas the latter's rhythms followed the scansion of verse.

Originally, recitative had been the true musical innovation, but aria soon surpassed it in significance and appeal. Because long sections of recitative could become tedious, an aria, with its melodic potential, was far more engaging. Furthermore, singers were better able to showcase their vocal talents in arias; as music history demonstrates, virtuosi performers demanded these of composers. Rival *divas* Faustina Bordoni and Francesca Cuzzoni supposedly even stooped to counting the number of notes in the arias Handel composed for them, complaining when the other was given more to sing. Most important, because composers came to use melody, rhythm, tempo, and harmony as tools to set text, arias provided the perfect vehicle for dramatic expression.

ARIA'S DRAMATIC FUNCTION

Unlike theatrical works in which the action is driven by continuous spoken dialogue, operas include moments of stasis when dramatic action is temporarily stopped to accommodate a musical number such as an aria, duet, trio, or large ensemble. In theory, recitative leads logically into an aria in which a character comments on his or her situation or expresses emotions and passions. In some arias, the character states a problem and solves it before the end of the piece, thus leading directly back into the dramatic flow. Unfortunately, not all opera texts are so well-written; in fact, many present the barest thread of dramatic connection between the recitatives and arias. A case in point is the *pasticcio*, or pastiche, in which arias from several operas are simply strung together with bits of recitative. Although the result is musically satisfying, the libretto's text is often senseless.

On the most basic level, recitative develops the plot, whereas arias allow more reflective glimpses into characters and situations. In this way, an aria is akin to a theatrical monologue or soliloquy in which a character speaks directly to the audience to express his or her thoughts. Such solo speeches are generally employed sparingly in plays, though. Quite the reverse is true in opera where arias occur with some frequency; in fact, some seventeenth-century operas feature as many as fifty arias within their scores.

As with recitative, the function of aria changed with time. When dramatic significance shifted from recitative, poets such as Apostolo

Zeno and Pietro Metastasio suggested reforms that established a pattern for arias that would maintain the poetic and dramatic integrity of the text. Of course, librettists could dictate what they wished, but after arias came into the hands of singers, they were performed as the singers wanted, usually displaying their ability to embellish a vocal line. Although musical reformers such as Gluck attempted to rein in singers and control their vocal abuses, performers' predominance in opera is demonstrated by the fact that, until the middle of the nineteenth century, composers only wrote arias after hearing the voices of those singing the lead roles. Arias, then, were suited to individual talents. In *Die Zauberflöte*, Mozart composed The Queen of the Night's "Der Hölle Rache" for his wife's sister, Josefa Hofer, giving her a *tour de force* that highlighted what her voice could do naturally. Subsequent productions of operas often required new arias to be composed to accommodate different cast members' specific abilities.

MUSICAL ELEMENTS OF THE ARIA

The aria is opera's most recognizable musical component. Even people with little or no knowledge of Western art music most likely have had some exposure to an aria or could at least identify the term as belonging to the realm of opera. Popular performers such as Andrea Boccelli perform arias on network television, and films such as *Moonstruck* and *Pretty Woman* included arias in their soundtracks. Because it is a closed form—that is, a piece with a distinct beginning and end—an aria can be easily extracted and performed outside of its original context.

By the mid-nineteenth century, dramatic expression of both the libretto and its musical setting became a more critical concern. Giuseppe Verdi, for example, decided to abandon traditional operatic structures and experiment with more fluid musical settings. Even though *Falstaff* is a score of continuous music, Verdi's Fat Knight does have an aria, "Quand'ero paggio." Unlike the closed form arias of previous centuries, however, it merges neatly with the music that precedes and follows it. Wagner, of course, avoided aria because it was reminiscent of non-Germanic traditions; thus even though Siegmund's "Winterstürme" in *Die Walküre* begins like an aria and can, in fact, be performed as a tenor solo, it does not fit the conventional mold. Puccini included arias in his works but presented them in a unique manner, signaling them with a distinct change in accompaniment; a good example of this technique can be heard by listening to the dramatic rise and fall of the orchestral activity in the two Act I arias in *La bohème*, Rodolfo's "Che gelida manina" and Mimì's "Mi chiamano Mimì."

TYPES OF ARIAS

STROPHIC ARIA

The earliest operas featured strophic arias. As with hymns in which all verses are sung to the same tune, strophic arias employ the same melody for all stanzas of text. To create musical interest, composers often added variations to the accompaniment; similarly, singers often performed each strophe with different vocal ornaments. An early strophic aria of great significance is "Possente spirito," placed by its composer, Monteverdi, at the very heart of *Orfeo*. Strophic arias are easily remembered because of their melodic repetition; for that reason, they became common in popular vernacular operas such as *Singspiele* (see Chapter 10). As an example, one might cite one of the most memorable entrance arias in opera history: Papageno's "Der Vogelfänger bin ich ja" from Mozart's *Die Zauberflöte*.

DA CAPO ARIA

An examination of arias from the mid-seventeenth to the late eighteenth centuries shows that their texts were relatively short poems. Composers would expand arias by repeating sections of music. One such manifestation, the *da capo* aria, became both common and popular in the eighteenth century. In simplest terms, this type of aria features two sections of poetic text set to different, usually contrasting sections of music. In musical analysis, these two sections are traditionally labeled A and B. The words *da capo* ("from the top") would be written into the score at the end of the B section as a signal for the singer and the orchestra to return to the beginning of the piece. Not only did this conserve paper, but it also eliminated the tedious task of recopying large portions of the score. Composers often distinguished the A from the B sections by using different keys, tempos, or meters; as a dramatic touch, the A section might be in the major mode and the B in minor (or vice versa).

Generally, when a *da capo* aria is sung, the A and B sections are first performed as written; the B section may end in a cadenza, a musical stopping point at which a singer is free to improvise without orchestral accompaniment. This display then is followed by more virtuosity as the singer repeats the A section from the beginning (*da capo*), this time ornamenting its melody to demonstrate vocal agility and stamina. Because of this embellishment, the return of the A section (often marked A', or A prime) can be quite exciting. Because seventeenth- and eighteenth-century singers were accustomed to improvising trills and runs, composers simply notated the basic melody and trusted the singer to decorate it. Because this art was lost by the late nineteenth century, singers on early twentieth-century recordings generally did not embellish the return of A because the scores lacked notated ornaments. Late twentieth-century musicological studies of Baroque and classical singing treatises, however, have encouraged more historically informed performances by singers such as Marilyn Horne, Emma Kirkby, and David Daniels, who ably demonstrate how such intricate passagework can sound.

Early *da capo* arias often feature a *ritornello*, an orchestral section that, as its name implies, "returns" after introducing the aria to divide its sections and then conclude it. In its most simplified form, a *da capo* aria with *ritornello* (R) could be diagrammed as RARBRA'R. To extend the piece, of course, the A and B sections could be repeated; to shorten it, vocal sections or statements of the *ritornello* could be eliminated.

During the last quarter of the eighteenth century, the *da capo* aria, a veritable staple of the operatic repertory, fell into disfavor. Even though it invited exciting virtuosic performance, as composers and librettists became more attuned to the dramatic possibilities of the aria, the predictability of the *da capo* form was seen as hackneyed. Newer, more flexible musical settings were devised.

DAL SEGNO ARIA

A *dal segno* aria is similar to a *da capo* in that it repeats music and text but not in their entirety. The reentry occurs *dal segno*, "at the sign" (𝄋) written into the score where the return is to begin. This type of aria came historically before the *da capo* but was, in general, less popular. Nevertheless, some eighteenth-century composers employed it as an alternative form. An example of a *dal segno* aria is "Non è si vago e bello il fior nel prato" from Act I of Handel's *Giulio Cesare*.

THROUGH-COMPOSED ARIA

Whereas the *da capo* and *dal segno* arias feature repeats, the through-composed aria employs different music for each line of text, freeing a composer from employing a strict form. Furthermore, through-composition eliminates some of the dramatic quandaries posed by the *da capo* structure. For example, if a problem is stated in the A section text but then solved in the B stanza, its restatement when the A text returns is dramatically nonsensical. Granted, these issues are more troublesome today, for as historian John Rosselli has demonstrated, audiences in the eighteenth century generally were far too concerned with a singer's virtuosity (or with who was doing what with whom in the next theater box) to pay close attention to an aria's text.

Although examples appear in the eighteenth century, arias with distinct, nonrepeating musical phrases and harmonic accompaniments became the norm when nineteenth-century composers such as Wagner and Verdi began to approach the libretto as a dramatic vehicle. A powerful late twentieth-century example of a through-composed aria is Blanche's "I want magic" in Previn's *A Streetcar Named Desire*.

RONDÒ

Popular in the late eighteenth century, the *rondò* features two tempos, the first slower than the second. The thematic material of the faster section is often a variation of that of the first. Because *rondòs* are generally technically difficult, they were traditionally reserved for principal singers and often were showcase pieces at the end of acts. Mozart satirizes this virtuosity when he assigns the *rondò* "Bester Jüngling" to one of the two rival *divas* in *Der Schauspieldirektor*. This type of aria was expanded in the nineteenth century; one of the classic examples is "Nacqui all'affanno e al pianto" from Rossini's *La Cenerentola*. The term *rondò* should not be confused with *rondo* or *rondeau*, both of which normally apply to instrumental music.

CAVATINA

Cavatina (pl., *cavatine*) has two definitions: (1) a single movement aria and (2) in the Italian tradition, a main character's entrance aria (also known as a *sortita*). The term, with the first definition only, appears in French as *cavatine* and in German as *Kavatine*. One eighteenth-century example, the Countess' aria "Porgi, amor" in Mozart's *Le nozze di Figaro*, fits both definitions. By the nineteenth century, especially in the Italian tradition, *cavatina* more routinely referred to a main character's entrance number. This designation created some difficulty, however, because a protagonist's initial aria also was often the first in a double-aria pair. Some writers, therefore, linked *cavatina* with *cabaletta*, the second movement of the two. However, because the term *cavatina* was not used in this sense in the nineteenth century, the preferred term for the first-movement aria is *cantabile*.

CANTABILE

As a general musical term, *cantabile* means a piece written in "singing" style. As previously noted, in the nineteenth century, the *cantabile* was the first movement of a double aria, most probably because traditionally it was slower and more lyrical than the second movement in the pair. Just as the *da capo* aria's text reflected two different ideas, the text of the *cantabile* was dramatically distinct from that of the *cabaletta*. Bellini's *Norma* provides a notable example, with "Casta diva" as the *cantabile* and (separated by a brief choral interlude) "Ah! bello, a me ritorna" as the *cabaletta*. The texts of these two arias, written by librettist Felice Romani, offer an example of the dramatic diversity between the two. In the first, Norma sings the ritual prayer as her "public" self, the Druid priestess; in the *cabaletta*, on the other hand, she allows the audience to glimpse her "private" self, the lover of Pollione, enemy of her people. Toward mid-century, the musical differences between the two aria types became less obvious.

CABALETTA

This second movement of a double aria is generally faster and more rhythmically animated than the *cantabile*. Because of the drama inherent in its quick rhythms, the *cabaletta* also was employed as the final movement of the *scena* and duet, with each singer performing the music in a key appropriate to his or her vocal range.

By mid-century, Verdi would state his intention to abandon *"cabaletta"* opera, for, as he noted, librettos often did not provide an appropriate point for the necessary change in tone from the *cantabile*. Thus, as styles changed, the *cabaletta* fell out of fashion. In the early nineteenth century, however, they provided exciting and energetic musical moments, especially because singers took the same opportunity to embellish them as their predecessors had the *da capo* returns.

COUPLET

From its origins in the *opéra comique*, the *couplet* became an important element in nineteenth-century French *grand opéra* (see Chapters 8 and 9). Similar in many ways to a strophic aria, the *couplet*, however, features two different stanzas of text followed by a common refrain. Often, after the refrain is sung by the character to whom the aria is assigned, the chorus repeats it. One familiar *couplet* is "Votre toast," the so-called "Toreador" song from Georges Bizet's *Carmen*.

> Escamillo's and the chorus's refrain from the couplet *"Votre toast"*:
>
> Toréador, en garde!
> Toréador! Toréador!
> Et songe bien, oui, songe en combattant
> qu'un oeil noir te regarde
> et que l'amour t'attend,
> Toréador, l'amour, l'amour t'attend!

ENSEMBLES

Just as in stage plays, characters in operas interact. They generally "speak" to each other in recitative or arioso passages, but when such conversations delve into the realm of intense personal expression or involve rapid plot development, these dialogues can be arranged as ensembles. A duet, for instance, is the common setting employed for passionate conversations between two lovers; similarly, the jealousy of a romantic triangle is aptly depicted in a trio. Ensembles not only offer rich vocal textures as multiple voices merge together harmonically, but they also provide musical variety when interspersed with recitative passages and arias. Most important, they can depict dramatic action in a unique way, because although it is impossible to have several actors speak simultaneously in a stage play (and remain intelligible), multiple singers can perform their individual lines at the same time. In such instances, they are repeating lines of text they have already sung as solo dialogue, so the audience is familiar with their significance. Often reserved for climactic act finales, large ensembles are especially effective for depicting communal confusion, dismay, surprise, or celebration.

Large ensembles were popular until early eighteenth-century *opera seria* reformers deemed them frivolous and distracting (see Chapter 8); for a time, the most common ensembles in serious works were duets and the occasional trio. Comic operas, however, continued to feature larger ensembles, for their musical and theatrical settings permitted just the right element of humorous mayhem (see Chapter 9). By the end of the eighteenth century, ensembles, especially those including the chorus, again became a focal point in serious opera because of their dramatic potential. In the nineteenth century, composers and librettists not only employed various types of ensembles but also built them into complex multipartite structures that facilitated dramatic pacing and led to boisterous, dynamic closing movements.

A word of caution: the presence of multiple singers onstage does not always signify an ensemble. In fact, all of the characters and the chorus may be present, but if only one is the musical and dramatic focus of a complete number, that selection is considered an aria, not an ensemble. For example, the whole Druid community is present when Norma sings "Casta diva," and even though they participate briefly, their intervention is more an element of the accompaniment. Confusion over how to characterize an operatic number can be dispelled by consulting the score to see what designation the composer has given it.

TYPES OF ENSEMBLES

DUET (IT., DUETTO; FR., DUO; GER., DUETT)

The most common operatic ensemble is the duet. Librettists have written texts for two voices, for instance, to depict encounters between lovers, friends, enemies, or masters and servants. Duets generally begin with one character "speaking"; the second character then "responds" alone or joins in with the other. Unison duets were particularly common in early French operas because of the importance ascribed to the text; thus, two characters sang the same words simultaneously to ensure comprehension. Various possibilities exist, however, when duets feature alternating solo sections. At times, the second singer echoes precisely what the first has performed; in other cases, the second has the same melody but different words. If the plot features conflict between two characters, the second may be given a new melody as well as new text, thereby musically underscoring their differences. Although composers may have the singers perform in turn, they generally include sections like elaborate cadenzas in which the two sing in harmony.

As with arias, duets can be strophic, *dal segno*, *da capo*, or through-composed, and can range from a few measures to lengthy multi-movement musical structures that dominate the action of an entire act. Single-movement duets were commonplace in the nineteenth century outside of Italian and French opera. In those traditions, four-movement duets had become the norm. Generally beginning with a *scena*, they contain these sections:

- *Tempo d'attacco*: a fast movement performed by one or both singers
- *Cantabile*: a slower, more lyrical section than the two surrounding it
- *Tempo di mezzo*: a quick transition section
- *Cabaletta*: a rapid, energetic conclusion

The compositional decision of where to end one of these sections and begin the next was not arbitrary. The librettist would furnish the composer with dialogue that lent itself dramatically to the necessary shift in tempo; the onset of an argument, for example, would warrant a faster pace, whereas emotional reflection would suggest a slower one.

Of the myriad four-movement duets in the nineteenth-century repertory, one in *Rigoletto* can serve as an example of the structure: the *Scena* and Duet between Gilda and the Duke (Scene 12 in Act I). Gilda begins the *scena* with a brief recitative dialogue with her chaperone, Giovanna: "Giovanna, ho dei rimorsi." The music then moves to the *tempo d'attacco*, "Signor nè principe io lo vorrei," only to be interrupted by the Duke ("T'amo! T'amo, ripetilo"). He performs the *cantabile*, "È il sol dell'anima, la vita è amore," after which he is joined by Gilda, and both conclude this second movement with a harmonized cadenza. The *tempo di mezzo*, "Che m'ami, deh! ripetimi," is a dialogue between the Duke and Gilda. Other characters interrupt, however, before the tempo quickens for a lively *cabaletta*, "Addio, speranza ed anima," that ends as the soprano and tenor, in harmony, exploit the uppermost reaches of their vocal ranges.

As helpful as it can be to describe structures in terms of patterns, there always will be exceptions. The duet between Rigoletto and Gilda that immediately precedes this one follows the model until the final movement when Verdi eschews the *cabaletta* for the more lyrical "Veglia, o donna, questo fiore." When it better served the drama, composers such as Verdi were willing to break the mold.

Possible Duet Constructions

"Son risoluto insomma" from *L'incoronazione di Poppea*: Of the many duets in this early work, perhaps the most dramatic sets the willful Nero against the reasoned Seneca. Their constantly accelerated musical responses depict the rapid-fire retorts of an angry debate.

"La ci darem la mano" in *Don Giovanni*: A duettino, or brief duet, in which Giovanni presents the melody first, followed by Zerlina, whose new texts responds to his. The duet concludes as, in harmony, they introduce a new musical section.

"Bei Männern, welche Liebe" from *Die Zauberflöte*: Papageno and Pamina perform this strophic duet, alternating solos with harmonized sections.

"Sì, fino all'ore extreme" in *Norma*: One of two duets in the opera in which Norma and Adalgisa's close harmonies demonstrate their friendship. Similarly, "Au fond du temple saint" from *Les Pêcheurs de perles*, employs harmony to underscore Nadir and Zurga's sacred vow of friendship as they renounce the woman they both love.

"Cheti, cheti, immantinente" from *Don Pasquale*: Heir to a long line of comic ensembles, this duet highlights the *parlante* or "patter" style of *opera buffa* (see Chapter 9). Pasquale initiates the duet; Malatesta then repeats the melody with new text. Finally, in unison, each sings his own text as rapidly as possible.

"O sink hernieder, Nacht der Liebe" in *Tristan und Isolde*: In this Act 2 duet, the lovers engage in an array of vocal and harmonic activity. Although they share some lines and conclude in harmony ("O ew'ge Nacht"), the majority of the duet is conversational.

TRIO OR TERZET (IT., TERZETTO; FR., TRIO; GER., TRIO)

The three-voice ensemble has been an integral element of opera since the mid-seventeenth century. Although the duet provides compositional possibilities, the addition of a third character permits even more structural flexibility. For instance, although most three-voice ensembles conclude with all characters singing, a composer may single out any one or combine any two to vary musical texture or enhance the drama. These are among the reasons why trios were popular in French opera, especially in eighteenth-century *opéra comique* productions (see Chapters 8 and 9). In the Italian tradition, multi-movement trios often served as act finales.

Trios can portray the thoughts of like-minded characters. In the Prologue of Monteverdi's *Il ritorno d'Ulisse in patria*, for example, the personifications of Time, Fortune, and Cupid agree on the weaknesses of human nature. The Three Boys' close harmonies calm and guide Tamino, Papageno, and Pamina through their trials in *Die Zauberflöte*. Brünnhilde, Gunther, and Hagen join to plot against Siegfried ("Welches Unholds List liegt hier verhohlen?") in Act 2 of *Götterdämmerung*. Three voices also can be employed to depict two characters in conflict with another. In the third-act trio "Sortez de l'esclavage," from *Castor et Pollux*, Rameau pits the spurned Phoebe against Pollux and Telaira, and in the concluding fifth-act trio of Meyerbeer's *Robert le diable*, "Robert, qu'ai-je entendu?", Alice and Bertram attempt (unsuccessfully) to save Robert from damnation. Finally, trios can define individual characters. Although George, Lennie, and Candy join together in the refrain "I believe we just might swing her" in *Of Mice and Men*, they express their own dreams for the ranch they plan to own.

Il trovatore offers an example of a trio that serves as an act finale. In the first movement, "Qual voce!", the jealous Count faces Leonora and Manrico. Not only do the lovers sing together, setting the Count musically apart, but they have their own text and melody. To further depict the Count's emotional isolation, Verdi underscores his part with different agitated rhythms. Ending in the fast-paced movement (*stretta*, pl. *strette*) "Di geloso amor sprezzato," the finale climaxes as the two men go off to fight a duel. Even more than duets, trios and other larger ensembles can incorporate plot development and dramatic action.

QUARTET (IT., QUARTETTO; FR., QUATUOR; GER., QUARTETT)

Although there are examples of four-voice ensembles in seventeenth-century opera, they did not become a common feature in serious works until the last quarter of the eighteenth century. One explanation for their absence may be that influential librettists such as Pietro Metastasio preferred arias and smaller ensembles that would allow audiences to better comprehend their poetry. Equally influential singers may have balked at performing group numbers that would disguise their individual talents. Comic opera standards differed, however, and quartets are found in *opera buffa*, moving from there easily into operas in the *semiseria* (semi-serious) tradition (see Chapter 8). In France, quartets were common in *opéra comique*.

Four-voice ensembles often begin with solo passages for each character, after which the composer may alternate the singers in various ways, even combining them in smaller ensembles. Two couples, for instance, may perform two duets simultaneously (a double duet), as in the third-act finale of *La bohème* when lovers Mimì and Rodolfo are countered by Marcello and Musetta's bickering. A trio texture may be set against the fourth singer, as in the second-act finale of *Così fan tutte*. In "E nel tuo, nel mio bicchiero," Fiordiligi, Ferrando, and Dorabella sing a three-voice canon as Guglielmo comments to himself in musical asides. Perhaps the most famous—and most dramatic—example of a quartet is "Bella figlia dell'amore" from *Rigoletto*. Although the characters are combined into pairs (Rigoletto reveals the Duke's true nature to his broken-hearted daughter, Gilda, as they watch him attempt to seduce Maddalena), each character's vocal line depicts his or her *persona*. Maddalena's flirting laughter is especially effective against Gilda's anguished sobs.

OTHER ENSEMBLES

Although they offer the widest range of vocal textures, larger ensembles are set less frequently than duets, trios, and quartets because they are reserved for significant moments when the participation of most or all of the characters is necessary. If the actions or reactions of the community also are depicted, the principals will be joined by the chorus. This added dramatic weight provides some of the most exciting moments in opera, and modern productions generally emphasize the spectacle inherent in such numbers. Because of their musical complexity, large ensembles demand the added precision of soloists and choristers alike.

Some Examples of Larger Ensembles

Quintet (Fr. *quintette, quintuor;* Ger. *Quintett;* It. *quintetto*):

- "Sento, o Dio"—*Così fan tutte*
- "Ti presento di mia mano"—*L'Italiana in Algeri*
- "Nous avons en tête une affaire"—*Carmen*

Sextet (Fr. *sextuor;* Ger. *Sextett;* It. *sestetto*):

- "Questo è il fin di chi fa mal"—*Don Giovanni*
- "Quest' è un nodo avviluppato"—*La Cenerentola*
- "Chi mi frena in tal momento"—*Lucia di Lammermoor*

Septet (Fr. *septuor;* Ger. *Septett;* It. *settimino*):

- "Tout n'est que paix et charme"—*Les Troyens*
- "Colla cenere disperso"—*Stiffelio*
- "En mon bon droit j'ai confiance"—*Les Huguenots*

Because they generally depict critical encounters or important revelations, ensembles occur at climactic points of the plot. Thus quintets, sextets, and septets often are included in act finales.

FINALE (FR., FINAL)

Although "finale" may mean the actual end of an opera, the term also can refer to a continuous chain of numbers concluding an act. All acts will have a finale of sorts, but the most significant will occur in the penultimate act when the plot's climax is reached. The finale, then, reveals significant new plot developments and registers the reactions and resolve of the characters. From that point on, the story, often predictable, concludes as the actions in the final act (or denouement) tie up loose ends.

The structure of the multi-movement finale is similar to that of the multi-movement duet or trio. Often preceded by a chorus, the first section is the *tempo d'attacco.* In finales, the next movement is a *pezzo concertato,* or "concerted piece," a multi-voice ensemble, generally in a slow tempo (*largo*), that features a combination of soloists

DISCARD

GARDNER HARVEY LIBRARY
Miami University-Middletown
Middletown, Ohio 45042

simultaneously performing individual lines with different texts. This movement can also be called a *largo concertato*. The third movement, or *tempo di mezzo*, is the transition section that connects the *pezzo concertato* with the concluding movement; in a finale, however, the *tempo di mezzo* is generally more complex than one in a duet or trio. The conclusion of the finale is the *stretta*, a rapid movement often performed at breakneck speed. In dramas, the *stretta* generally reflects the characters' agitation, anger, or stupefaction. In comedies, it depicts the utter confusion and lack of control at the turn of events. One of the most delightful comic *strette* is "Mi par d'esser con la testa" in *Il barbiere di Siviglia*.

The sextet from *Lucia di Lammermoor* (Act 2, scene 2) offers a good example of how a composer can set a larger ensemble in the finale. After the chorus "Per te d'immenso giubilo" (with brief intervention by Arturo), Arturo and Enrico sing a brief section of recitative and the *tempo d'attacco*, "Se in lei soverchia è la mestizia," begins. When the chorus interjects a comment, the tempo changes to a pulsing andante ("Piange la madre estinta") sung by Enrico, Arturo, and Lucia. The shocked chorus announces the arrival of Edgardo and the tempo slows to *larghetto* for the *largo concertato*, the sextet "Chi mi frena in tal momento," with the participation of Edgardo, Enrico, Arturo, Lucia, Raimondo, and Alisa. The *tempo di mezzo*, "T'allontana, sciagurato," follows. Amid rising musical tension, Edgardo's curse sets off the furious *stretta*, "Esci, fuggi il furor che m'accende," sung by all soloists and the full chorus.

Acts, of course, can conclude with arias, duets, or trios, but by the late eighteenth century, the *finale concertato* was gaining popularity; by the following century, it had become standard fare. In fact, it was so common that Verdi's decision to omit a *stretta* from the Act 2 finale of *La traviata* seemed a radical departure. Always the dramatist, the composer realized that ending the act with the *largo concertato* "Di sprezzo degno se stesso rende" was more powerful and indeed more sensible. Although traditional structures were important and, to a great extent, pleased the public who had come to expect them, it took a composer of great courage to determine that, in some cases, they simply would not work.

CHORUS (IT., CORO; FR., CHOEUR; GER., CHOR)

The term "chorus" is used for the largest operatic musical ensemble as well as for the group of singers that performs it. A chorus is usually set in four-part harmony (soprano, alto, tenor, and bass), but, should a libretto call for an all-male or all-female ensemble, the relevant ranges may be subdivided into combinations of first and second tenors, baritones, and basses or first and second sopranos, altos, and contraltos. The chorus singers might depict a specific group such as priests (*Die Zauberflöte*), prisoners (*Fidelio*), wedding guests (*Madama Butterfly*), or a ship's crew (*Billy Budd*). Often, however, as in Greek drama, they represent the community, as in *Semiramide*, *Lucia di Lammermoor*, and *Guillaume Tell*; choral texts then express general reactions of the populace such as joy, fright, horror, or outrage.

As musical numbers, choruses usually are set homophonically, with all voices singing the same text and blending in chordal harmony. Exceptions exist, of course, as in the polyphonic madrigal choruses of Monteverdi's operas. Works composed during the libretto reform period of the early eighteenth century rarely included more than a chorus in the final act because emphasis was placed on arias and small ensembles. Later in the century, though, choruses became an inherent part of the action, and, as previously discussed, in the nineteenth century they played a significant role in multi-movement finales.

Choruses also are employed in opening sections called *introduzioni* (sing., *introduzione*). The singers in the chorus generally begin such a section, but they may be joined by either a secondary or a principal character, who will be given a solo. *Nabucco*, for instance, opens with the Israelites singing "Gli arredi festivi"; the prophet Zaccaria responds with a traditional *cantabile-cabaletta* pairing: "D'Egitto là sui lidi" and "Come notte al sol fulgente." Dramatically, the *introduzione* informs the audience of the plot and some of the conflict. Theatrically, it serves to draw them into the production with an element of musical spectacle.

In the French tradition, choruses were among the musical numbers in sections called *divertissements*. A compilation of vocal music and dances inserted into larger works such as *tragédies lyriques* or *opéras comiques*, these reflected the spectacle inherent in the French tradition, but often were only marginally related to the plot (see Chapters 8 and 9). Examples of *divertissements* with choruses occur in the last act of *Atys* and at the end of the Prologue of *Castor et Pollux*. The heritage of the *divertissement* continued in France, eventually manifesting itself in nineteenth-century *grand opéra*, as in Act 3 of *Robert le diable* when the debauched nuns' spirits dance.

Some Well-Known Choruses

Although it is difficult to single out choruses from the many powerful ones in the repertory, this list offers some worthy examples.

- "Ahi caso acerbo, ahi fato empio e crudele!"—*Orfeo*
- "Come away, fellow sailors"—*Dido and Aeneas*
- The Furies Chorus—*Orfeo ed Euridice*
- "O welche Lust!"—*Fidelio*
- "Lasst lustig die Hörner erschallen!"—*Der Freischütz*
- "Guerra! Guerra!"—*Norma*
- "Chi del gitano i giorni abbella?"—*Il trovatore*
- "Slava"—*Boris Godunov*
- The Humming Chorus—*Madama Butterfly*

Of course, music does not stand alone in opera. Chapter 3 considers how these forms and structures relate to their sung text: the libretto.

3

MUSIC AND TEXT RELATIONSHIPS

Composers had been writing vocal music since the Middle Ages, but the discussions that inspired the development of opera in the late sixteenth century proposed something quite different: a musical setting that would enhance a secular dramatic text. In theory, words and music would contribute to the dramatic effect equally; over time, however, poets and composers debated which element was more significant. It should come as no surprise that librettists such as Ranieri de' Calzabigi placed emphasis on the text, suggesting that the function of the music was to support the words. Mozart, on the other hand, spoke for composers when he maintained that a libretto's poetry was "the obedient daughter of the music." Many nineteenth-century composers, following the example of Hector Berlioz and Richard Wagner, ensured the importance of both components by writing and setting their own librettos. No matter how poets and composers defended their singular contributions, they knew that although drama (or comedy) might be inherent in an opera's text and music, it was realized more fully in their union.

This chapter explores the relationship of musical forms to the dramatic and poetic structures of librettos.

LIBRETTO (IT., PL., LIBRETTI; FR., LIVRET; GER., TEXTBUCH; ENG., LIBRETTO, PL., LIBRETTOS)

Meaning "little book" in Italian, "libretto" refers to the actual booklet that contains the text of a large vocal work such as an opera, oratorio, or cantata, and by extension to the text as well. First and foremost, the libretto provides the composer with the words to be set; up through the nineteenth century, its specific verse forms often dictated the musical structure of the score, as will be seen shortly. Its secondary purpose is to allow audiences to read the plot as well as familiarize themselves with the words, some of which might be lost in singing. Audiences also can use the libretto to follow the text or its translation during the performance. Even the earliest operas had published librettos; those for public performances were sold at locales near the theater or at the theater proper. Although they had relatively few pages (generally between twenty and thirty), some librettos were large enough to accommodate elaborately engraved illustrations or score excerpts. Conforming to the contemporary notion of portable literature in the eighteenth and early nineteenth centuries, some of these booklets were made small enough to slip into a man's coat pocket or a woman's reticule.

Opera houses still sell librettos, but surtitles projected atop the stage or on seatback screens have made them redundant. Audience members who wish to study an opera before a performance can find librettos of common repertory works at many large public libraries. Opera texts and translations also are easily accessible on a number of web sites. Moreover, liner materials in audio recordings generally include a copy of the text, and videos and DVDs often are subtitled. Librettos linked to productions, however, may not faithfully represent the original text. Constructed for a specific performance or cast—or made to fit into the allotted time of a recording medium—they may well feature cuts, substitutions, or rearranged scenes. Nevertheless, whether linked to historical performances or contemporary ones, variant texts prove useful in documenting an opera's production history.

SETTING THE LIBRETTO

Certain composers and librettists collaborated as teams (see Chapter 4). Others never even knew each other and hence had no influence on each other's work. In France, for instance, a libretto was subjected to a dramatic reading before an artistic committee; only when it was approved could it be passed on to a composer. Elsewhere, a libretto generally was commissioned from a theater poet (see Chapter 4) and a composer then was engaged to set it. Some composers and librettists made private arrangements to work together, and then one or the other would use his or her connections to find a theater that would agree to premiere their work.

Because the whole text had to be approved first, only in France could a composer be certain of beginning a score with a complete libretto. Financial need forced most poets to take on several projects at a time, so they often submitted their work to composers in parts. If the whole text did arrive, the composer still might not set it in order but choose to begin with an internal number he or she found inspiring. Of course, there were also cases when parts of the libretto were decidedly uninspiring or simply could not be set for a variety of musical reasons. Often under commission deadlines themselves, many composers were loath to ask for changes because precious time could be lost by returning the libretto and waiting for revisions. In many cases, they either set exactly what they were given or revised the words themselves. Others did not hesitate to request changes. Verdi, for instance, was notorious for demanding that librettists give him precisely what he wanted. Nor was he above giving a libretto to a second author if he felt the first had not revised it satisfactorily; such was the case when Verdi turned over Francesco Maria Piave's libretto for *Macbeth* to Andrea Maffei.

LIBRETTO AS HISTORICAL DOCUMENT

Just as librettos are artifacts of performance history, the cross-outs, erasures, and paste-overs found in revised librettos document the compositional phase of an opera. Any notations, especially in the hand of the librettist or composer, give a libretto special historical significance. Even without special markings, printed librettos are important as sources of production and theater history. As with today's theater programs, they contained a variety of information about the production; preceding the text would be a title page with the name of the work, its composer and librettist (although one or both of these have been known to be omitted), the venue and year of the performance, and, if applicable, the event the opera celebrated.

The libretto generally listed the singers, often identifying them as well by role; significant backstage personnel, including the costume and set designers; and the choreographer and his dancers, if there were a ballet in addition to or within the opera. If presented at an important public theater, there might also be information identifying the *impresario* (see Chapter 4). A new libretto generally was issued for each subsequent production, reflecting the change in theater, cast members, and any textual revisions or musical substitutions.

Librettos of productions with significant court support generally included some encomium for the patron. Disclaimers also were common; librettists, for example, protected themselves by publishing statements explaining that even though their characters were pagans and sinners, they themselves dutifully obeyed the laws of the Church. In fact, in areas with stringent religious censorship, librettos were required to have an imprimatur, a statement that Church authorities approved of their content.

To economize, librettos for operas with spoken dialogue (see Chapters 8, 9, and 10) often contained only the text for vocal numbers; in fact, some theaters hoping to make a greater profit from these works included score excerpts of the most popular ones. In the nineteenth century, music often was included in generic librettos sold by theaters and music publishers; printed with the original libretto (alongside a translation, if the opera were in a foreign language), these magazine-sized booklets commonly featured the vocal lines or even piano-vocal arrangements of one or more popular arias. These publications often were supported with advertisements for local music dealers and instrument makers.

When scholars employ librettos as primary sources for research of performance histories, they compare all autograph and published versions to see the changes made (many without the composer's knowledge) when an opera was produced at new venues; this information is crucial for scholars preparing critical editions of scores (see Chapter 11). Although today's habit of preparing librettos and compositions on computer may be more efficient, future scholars will only be able to study an opera's genesis if its creators are wise enough to save various versions in separate files.

Librettos also have helped to trace the careers of important singers and document the history of operatic production at specific courts and theaters. In addition to those in theater archives, many collections of librettos, once the possessions of private collectors and opera enthu-siasts, have been purchased by or donated to important research libraries where they remain a rich resource for ongoing study.

THE LIBRETTO AS LITERATURE

The subjects of the earliest librettos were inspired by classical literature (see Chapter 1). Although the Church frowned on the glorification of these pagan tales, a character such as Orpheus made an elegant symbol for the power of music, the very idea behind the theories that inspired opera. Noble patrons did not seem to mind these associations either, because opera's characters represented them; to be seen as Apollo clearly spoke to one's cultivation of the arts. Operas with classical themes, of course, appealed to a limited audience familiar with these dramatic and poetic elements; in fact, their very exclusivity made them the perfect subject for parodies such as those performed at the fair theaters in Paris (see Chapter 9).

With the rise of a literate middle class in the late eighteenth century, fashionable contemporary literary genres such as the novel became libretto sources. In the Romantic era—a term derived from the French word *roman*, or novel—other literary models such as stage plays and long dramatic poems provided subjects and themes for operas. Nationalism (see Chapter 7) inspired compositions that expressed and even nurtured exclusivity, appealing to groups of people linked by common languages and history. A reaction to the domination of the Italian and French traditions, nationalism inspired librettos that drew on folklore and popular culture.

Librettos in the late nineteenth and early twentieth century reflected the various "-isms" of contemporary literature, art, and drama; among these were *verismo*, Symbolism, and Expressionism. Begun in Italy and used to describe works such as *Cavalleria rusticana* and *I pagliacci*, veristic opera (see Chapter 8) treats characters from the lower elements of society who are trapped in their environments and whose dilemmas are resolved through brutality and violence. Linked with musical Impressionism, Debussy's *Pelléas et Mélisande* is an example of Symbolism; as a work of art, it is completely static (that is, there is no significant plot or character development) and hence was intended to have no meaning beyond the confines of its libretto and score. Berg's *Wozzeck*, in which painful emotions are internalized and true communication is impossible, epitomizes the discomfort and pain of Expressionistic art. Late twentieth-century works also employed literary models, but current events and politics also provided subjects, as in Philip Glass' *Einstein on the Beach* and John Adams' *Nixon in China*.

Literary genres inspired a host of operas from the eighteenth to the twentieth centuries.

Novels: *Pamela* (*La buona figliuola*), *The Recess* (*Elisabetta, regina d'Inghilterra*), *The Bravo* (*Il bravo*), *The Bride of Lammermoor* (*Lucia di Lammermoor*), *Yevgeny Onegin*, and *La vie bohème* (*La bohème*)

Novellas and short stories: "Billy Budd," "Cavalleria rusticana," "Der Tod in Venedig" (*Death in Venice*), "Madame Butterfly," "Owen Wingrave," "Le rosier de Madame Husson" (*Albert Herring*), and "The Vampyre" (*Der Vampyr*)

Poems: "Norma" (a verse tragedy); "The Borough" (*Peter Grimes*); "The Corsair" (*Il corsaro*); "Don Carlos, Infant von Spanien" (*Don Carlos*); and "The Lady of the Lake" (*La donna del lago*). The epics *Das Nibelungenlied* and the *Edda* were sources for *The Ring Cycle*. "Gerusalemme liberata" and "Orlando furioso" inspired myriad works (see Chapter 1).

Stage plays: "La folle journée, ou Le mariage de Figaro" (*Le nozze di Figaro*); "Le barbier de Séville, ou La précaution inutile" (*Il barbiere di Siviglia*); "Giulietta e Romeo" by Scevola (*I Capuleti e i Montecchi*); "Bertram, ou Le pirate" (*Il pirata*); "Beatrice di Tenda"; "Hernani" (*Ernani*); "Saffo"; "Le pasteur, ou L'évangile et le foyer" (*Stiffelio*); "Le roi s'amuse" (*Rigoletto*); "La dame aux camélias" (*La traviata*); "La Tosca" (*Tosca*); "Boris Godunov"; "Riders to the Sea"; "Její pastorkyňa" (*Jenůfa*); "Le viol de Lucrèce" (*The Rape of Lucretia*); "Electra" (*Elektra*); and "Salome." Shakespeare's plays and their adaptations were popular sources, especially in the nineteenth century.

Some librettos became sources for others: *Il barbiere di Siviglia* (*Almaviva*, which became Rossini's *Il barbiere di Siviglia*); *Il califfo e la schiava* (*Adina*); *Don Giovanni, ossia Il convitato in pietra* (*Don Giovanni*); *Agatina, o La virtù premiata* (*La Cenerentola*); *L'italiana in Algeri* (setting by Mosca; libretto revised for Rossini); *Il turco in Italia* (setting by Seydelmann, revised for Rossini); *La somnambule, ou L'arrivée d'un nouveau seigneur* (*La sonnambula*); *Gustave III, ou Le bal masqué* (*Un ballo in maschera*); *Le duc d'Albe* (*Les vêpres siciliennes*); *Medea*; and *Ser Marcantonio* (*Don Pasquale*)

Because librettos share many of the elements of prose and drama (plots and subplots, characters, symbols, and themes), there is always the temptation to subject them to similar literary analysis. Some librettos are indeed worthy of such exploration because their authors intended them to stand on their own merits as literature. Most prominent among these, of course, are those of Metastasio, which were published as texts meant also for dramatic readings. Richard Wagner's librettos for the *Ring Cycle* are perhaps the best known examples.

Before Wagner composed the four works in the *Ring*, he read their librettos as dramatic texts on numerous occasions. In his attempts to create truly German opera, he turned to medieval literature for inspiration, adopting *Stabreim*; used in epic medieval Germanic poetry as a memorization device, it emphasizes internal alliteration rather than end rhyme. Wagner's application of it demonstrates the importance he placed on language and sound in these works. In the first act of *Das Rheingold*, for example, the giant Fasolt sings the following line: "Freia, die Holde, Holde die Freie." The alliteration occurs as the initial letter of each word of the first half of the line is repeated in reverse in the second half. Although an excellent example of *Stabreim*, the line, however, makes little sense and indeed is a bit of a grammatical quandary (in English, the text translates as "Freia, the Fair One, Fair One the Free"). Freia, whom the giants Fasolt and Fafner have come to take as payment for their work on Valhalla, is indeed a beauty, but she is hardly free if she is to become their possession. Wagner was willing to make a semantic sacrifice to obtain the sound of the ancient literature he was imitating.

For each libretto with significant literary merit, there are many with little or none. Most librettists (and composers, for that matter) assumed that their works would be short-lived. Thus texts were generally written hastily to meet commission deadlines. Even librettos that were returned for revision may not exhibit significant literary quality because, in many cases, the changes would have been made to improve the musical setting, not the poetic text.

Furthermore, before applauding a librettist's genius, it is important to know the true source of a work. One libretto that has been dissected regularly as a literary work is Lorenzo Da Ponte's text for *Don Giovanni*. An excellent poet, Da Ponte plumbed not only folk sources for the tale of Don Juan but also knew the text of Molière's *Dom Juan*. His main source, however—and one from which he liberally and literally borrowed—was a libretto by G. M. Bertati entitled *Don Giovanni, ossia Il convitato in pietra*, produced in Venice several months before the premiere of *Don Giovanni*. Hence, one could study *Don Giovanni*'s libretto as a pastiche of sources, but not as a work demonstrating Da Ponte's literary genius. His only original libretto for Mozart was *Così fan tutte*, a tale that from its premiere raised questions about how it should be interpreted on the stage and on the page.

LITERATUROPER

Some composers chose to adapt the texts of important literary works as librettos. Because these operas' literary significance was considered to be as great as their musical interest, these works were labeled *Literaturoper* (literature opera). Operas in this category include Debussy's *Pelléas*, Vaughan Williams' *Riders to the Sea*, Berg's *Wozzeck*, and Strauss' *Salome* and *Elektra*. Because they are so true to their sources, *Of Mice and Men* and *A Streetcar Named Desire* also belong to this category.

TEXT-MUSIC RELATIONSHIPS

When discussing the composition of an opera, credit goes unfailingly to the composer. One never hears mention of Solera's *Nabucco*, Lemaire's *Samson et Dalila*, or Sonnleithner's *Fidelio*; more often than not, the librettist's contribution is overlooked. Nonetheless, even though many of them did not compose music, librettists knew contemporary musical forms and wrote texts that could be set appropriately. In fact, until the mid-nineteenth century, the verse patterns in librettos often dictated which parts should be recitative, arias, or ensembles, leaving the composer's decisions to a selection of melody, harmony, key and tempo. These predictable structures explain why librettists and composers could work so quickly and why it was so easy to substitute texts for self-borrowing (see Chapter 4) and parody (see Chapters 9 and 10).

In the following sections, the principles of versification in Italian and French opera through the nineteenth century will be introduced.

ITALIAN VERSIFICATION

Analyses of Italian verse consider two issues: the syllable on which the final accent falls and the number of syllables in a line. The most common line, called *verso piano*, ends with a word that has its accent on the penultimate syllable: ri-TOR-no. If the accent falls on the last syllable, co-SÌ, the line is called *verso tronco*. The final type, *verso sdrucciolo*, features the accent on the antepenultimate syllable: can-TA-bi-le. Determining the number of syllables in a line (the second criterion for analyzing verse) can be challenging because consecutive vowels within a line are often elided, thus making one syllable out of what might appear to be two.

Italian poetry employs lines that range from three to eleven syllables. Although all of these appear in librettos, the more common ones are the seven-syllable line (*settenario*) and the eleven-syllable line (*endecasillabo*). Recitative was written as *versi sciolti*, free unrhymed lines that alternate in length between *settenari* and *ende-casillabi*. Often these lines can be broken up between characters, as the following recitative between Eusebio and Ernestina in Scene iv of Rossini's one-act farce *L'occasione fa il ladro* demonstrates:

Eusebio:	Non lo permetto.
Ernestina:	Il mio dover....
Eusebio:	Scusate;
	Dell'urbano trattar so la maniera.
Ernestina:	Ma in questa casa io son per cameriera.
Eusebio:	Il caso vostro esige

The brief exchange between the two characters in the first three lines is actually an *endecasillabo* that has been divided (the elided vowels are underlined):

Non/ lo/ per/ me/ tto Il/ mio/ do/ ver/ Scu/ sa/ te

Two more *endecasillabi* follow. Eusebio's next line, the last in this example, is a *settenario*, again, featuring a syllable with elided vowels:

Il/ ca/ so/ vo/ stro e/ si/ ge.

Recitative featured lines of varying lengths but only occasional rhymes, such as "maniera" and "cameriera" in the passage above. Aria texts always rhymed, however, and generally employed lines of similar length. The Metastasian aria text featured two strophes of three or four lines; perfect for the *da capo* aria (see Chapter 2), the first strophe forms the A section and the second, the B. The text of "Va tacito" from Act 1 of Handel's *Giulio Cesare* serves as an example. In the following sections, the upper case letters refer to the musical sections of the *da capo* aria and the lower case letters diagram the poetic rhyme scheme.

A SECTION

Va tacito e nascosto	a
Quand' avido è di preda	b
L'astuto cacciator	c

B SECTION

E chi è mal far disposto	a
Non brama che si veda	b
L'inganno del suo cor	c

(Here, the A section returns in performance)

The rhyme scheme is the same for both strophes: a b c. Scanning the lines demonstrates a pattern of *settenari*:

Va/ ta-/ ci-/ to e/ na-/ **sco-**/ sto
Quand'/ a-/ vi-/ do è/ di **pre-**/ da
L'a-/ stu-/ to/ ca-/ cia-/ **tor**
E/ chi è/ mal / far/ di-/ **spo-**/ sto
Non/ bra-/ ma/ che/ si/ **ve-**/ da
L'in-/ga-/nno/ del/ suo/ **cor**

As previously, the underlined sections indicate where consecutive vowels have been elided to form a single syllable. The accented syllables in each line are in boldface. The first two lines of each strophe are *versi piani*, the accent falling on the penultimate syllable. The third is *verso tronco*, with a final stress. This text may seem exceedingly brief for an eighteenth-century *da capo* aria, but with instrumental ritornellos (see Chapter 2) and vocal embellishments, its performance time is just over six minutes.

Before these verse patterns had been established, seventeenth-century composers examined libretto texts for verses that could appropriately be set as arias; some scholars suggest the term "cavare," or "dig out" is the root for "cavatina" (see Chapter 2). When these predictable verse structures reigned, however, composers could easily write music even before they had seen the text. By the nineteenth century, librettos still featured *versi piani, tronchi,* and *sdruccioli,* but composers sought more irregular line lengths to obtain greater flexibility for their vocal lines. Hence, the Metastasian ideal gradually was abandoned for more natural sounding texts that encouraged through-composition (see Chapter 2). By the end of the nineteenth century, the libretto's verse patterns became secondary to its drama.

FRENCH VERSIFICATION

Although the spoken stage inspired many aspects of French opera, composers (beginning with Lully) and librettists decided that the traditional *alexandrins* (12-syllable rhymed couplets) of classical French drama would be too restrictive. A brief example, taken from Oreste's opening speech in Act I of Racine's *Andromaque,* demonstrates the "square" pattern of this verse:

> Oui, puisque je retrouve un ami si fidèle,
> Ma fortune va prender une face nouvelle;
> Et déjà son courroux semble s'être adouci,
> Depuis qu'elle a pris soin de nous rejoindre ici.

Instead, French libretto texts are set in *vers libres,* a free mixture of lines of varying length. Eight- and ten-syllable lines (*octosyllables* and *décasyllables*) were employed most frequently for recitative, whereas airs were written with greater variety of line lengths. French syllable counts are determined by the number of syllables *pronounced.* The only exception is when the *e muet* (or silent e) occurs at the end of a line; although it is pronounced, it is not counted as a syllable. Lines that end with an *e muet* are (like Italian *versi piani*) often called feminine endings; those without (like *versi tronchi*) are masculine.

A passage from Quinault's libretto for Lully's *Atys* offers an example. In Act I, scene 8, Cybele has just made a spectacular descent onto the stage in a chariot:

RÉCITATIF

> Je reçoy vos respects; j'aime à voir les honneurs
> dont vous me presentez un éclatant hommage
> mais l'hommage des coeurs
> est ce que j'aime davantage.

Lines one and three have rhyming masculine endings (*honneurs* and *coeurs*), whereas two and four, ending in *e muets*, are rhymed feminine endings (*hommage* and *davantage*, pronounced "o-ma-juh" and "da-van-ta-juh"). The first two lines are *alexandrins*, the third has six syllables, and the last eight. Because they are internal, the *e muets* at the end of *hommage* in line three and *j'aime* in line four are counted as syllables.

The *Air* that follows Cybele's *récitatif* exhibits a different pattern:

Vous devez vous animer	a
d'une ardeur nouvelle, (nu-vel-luh)	b
s'il faut honorer Cybele, (Cy-be-luh)	b
il faut encor plus l'aimer.	a

The rhyme scheme is a-b-b-a, with rhyming lines having the same type ending (one and four masculine and two and three feminine). Lines one, three and four have seven syllables, whereas line two has five. As in the *récitatif* passage, all of the *e muets* are pronounced because *d'une* is within the line, it is actually elided with the following vowel (see underlined text).

As in Italian, French verse patterns were often broken up among characters when employed as *récitatif*. This brief dialogue from Act I scene iii of Rameau's *Castor et Pollux* offers an example:

Castor: Ah! je mourrai content, je revois vos appas.
Telaïre: Prince, osés-vous encor me parle de tendresse?
Castor: On permet nos adieux.
Telaïre: Eh! ne deviés-vous pas
Les épargner à ma foiblesse?

The first two lines are *alexandrins*. Castor's next comment and the first half of Telaïre's reply make up a third *alexandrin*, a combination of two half-lines known as a *hémistiche*:

On/ per/ met/ nos/ a/ dieux/ Eh!/ ne/ de/ viés/ vous/ pas

The final line has eight syllables (*octosyllable*). The rhyme scheme, hidden when the lines are separated, is *appas/ pas* and *tendresse/ foiblesse*.

The two most important French versification rules, stressing the pronounced syllables and rhyming in patterns, lasted until the end of nineteenth century, when, as did their Italian colleagues, composers sought to experiment with longer lines to achieve the sound of a more conversational flow.

A BRIEF WORD ABOUT GERMAN VERSIFICATION

Early German verse forms were analyzed in two ways: by counting the syllables or by counting patterns of stressed and unstressed syllables. The latter proved more reasonable; in fact, German verse generally can be scanned by counting feet, or units, of stressed and unstressed syllables as English verse can. An interesting example from Act I of Mozart's *Die Entführung aus dem Serail* demonstrates that Mozart and his librettist Gottlieb Stephanie the Younger were associating the character of Konstanze with heroines from the Italian tradition. On the other hand, her maid Blonde fits squarely within the German *Singspiel* heritage. The text of Konstanze's Act I aria "Martern aller Arten" may be compared below with Blonde's aria "Welche Wonne, welche Lust":

Martern aller Arten	a
Mögen meiner warten,	a
Ich verlache Qual und Pein.	b
Nichts soll mich erschüttern.	c
Nur dann würd' ich zittern,	c
Wenn ich untreu könnte sein.	b
Lass dich bewegen, verschone mich!	d
Des Himmels Segen belohne dich!	d
Doch du bist entschlossen.	e
Willig, unverdrossen,	e
Wähl ich jede Pein und Not.	f
Ordne nur, gebiete,	g
Lärme, tobe, wüte,	g
Zuletzt befreit mich doch der Tod.	f

These lines, set as an aria in the elaborate style of Italian opera, vary in length and have a more intricate poetic rhyme scheme; Blonde's text for the most part follows a pattern of four poetic feet of stressed/unstressed syllables (DA-da), or trochaic tetrameter:

> Welche Wonne, welche Lust
> Regt sich nun in meiner Brust!
> Voller Freuden will ich springen,
> Ihr die frohe Nachricht bringen;
> Und mit lachet und mit Scherzen
> Ihrem schwachen, kranken Herzen
> Freud und Jubel prophezeihn.

THE LIBRETTO IN TRANSLATION

Libretto translations serve two very different purposes: to render the meaning of the text as closely as possible or to provide a performance text in another language. Because the former is strictly for comprehension, little attempt is made to follow the original language's stresses and rhythms. Therefore, it will not match the musical setting, not even for recitative, although it can be used for spoken dialogue in vernacular genres (see Chapter 10). On the other hand, while translations made for performance respect vocal rhythms as much as possible, the meaning often becomes secondary.

Two English-language versions of Arsace's aria "Ah! quel giorno ognor rammento" from Act I, scene v of Rossini's *Semiramide* demonstrate the two distinct purposes for translating a libretto text. The first, an almost literal translation done for an 1854 performance in London, appeared in a dual-language libretto sold in England and the United States:

> Ah! That day I e'er remember,
> Of my glory and great content.
> When I could from the barbarians
> Both preserve her life and honor.
> In these arms I bore her off
> From the vile oppressor's grasp,
> And I felt against my heart
> The quick throbbings of her own. . . .

The rhythm of the poetic line is trochaic tetrameter: "AH! that DAY i E'ER reMEMber." Problems occur in the two lines that include "the," which in English would never be stressed: "THE barBARians" and "THE quick THROBbings. . . ." Although the meaning is salvaged, the words are unsingable.

The same text from an undated English-language performing edition maintains the aria's musical rhythm but strays from its original meaning.

> Live this day, in mem'ry shining,
> All its glories for aye enshrining;
> When from barb'rous foes insulting,
> I thy honour, thy life did wrest,
> From th'oppressor, when I tore thee,
> In my arms I fondly bore thee
> 'Gainst my heart, wildly exulting,
> Thine responded joy opprest. . . .

In the aria, Arsace is recalling how he saved Azema, to whom he refers in the third person: "her life and honor" and "I bore her off." The translation shifts to second person by using "thy," "thee," and "thine," suggesting a new method of address. Most noticeable, however, is the translator's need to compensate for the shift away from a foreign language by employing "foreign" or stilted sentence structures ("When from barb'rous foes insulting") and archaic vocabulary ("aye" and "wrest"). However, he keeps the text's trochaic pattern by eliding the offending syllables ("th'oPRESsor") or dropping them ("'GAINST" rather than "aGAINST").

Throughout the nineteenth century, English-speaking critics and audiences complained that performance translations were distortions; even though they did not understand the words, they preferred hearing opera with its original text. The next best solution was to attend adaptations of contemporary works from the Italian and French repertories made expressly for British and American stages. Among the works mounted were *The White Lady* (Boieldieu's *La dame blanche*); *The Libertine* (also *Don Juan*) and *Tit for Tat* (Mozart's *Don Giovanni* and *Così fan tutte*); and *The Turkish Lovers* and *Cinderella* (Rossini's *Il turco in Italia* and *La Cenerentola*).

Many composers and musicians earned their reputations by adapting foreign works; two adapters famous on both sides of the Atlantic were Henry Rowley Bishop and Michael Rophino Lacy. Although Bishop's works are now commonly considered hack jobs, he answered the needs of the contemporary stage with adaptations of operas by Mozart, Rossini, Boieldieu, and Weber, among others.

As musical director of Covent Garden from 1810 to 1824, his works, along with those of his contemporary, Lacy, remained staples in that theater's repertory until the 1840s. Lacy was not a composer but a theater musician and actor. From 1827 to 1833, he worked between Covent Garden and Drury Lane, translating texts and arranging scores he adapted. Another author whose adaptations became famous was W.S. Gilbert, who transformed foreign operas into English burlesques or "travesties." His first was *Dulcamara, or The Little Duck and the Great Quack* (1866), a parody of Donizetti's *L'elisir d'amore*. Among others that followed were *Robert the Devil, or The Nun, The Dun, and The Son of a Gun* (Meyerbeer's *Robert le diable*) and *The Pretty Druidess, or The Mother, The Maid, and The Mistletoe Bough* (Bellini's *Norma*).

MINSTREL PARODIES

Blackface minstrel troupes often arrived on the heels of opera companies traveling across the United States, offering audiences parodies of operas they had just seen days before. Among the minstrels' repertory were works such as *The Virginian Girl* (Balfe's *The Bohemian Girl*), *Shin-de-Hella* (on Lacy's English adaptation of Rossini's *Cinderella*), *Lend-her-de-Sham-Money* and *Lucy-do-lam-her-more* (Donizetti's *Linda di Chamounix* and *Lucia di Lammermoor*), and *The Gas Ladder* (Rossini's *La gazza ladra*). The popularity of these works suggests that audiences were not only amused by the dialect songs and stage business but were also familiar enough with the operatic originals to understand the satire.

SOME FINAL POINTS

CUTS

Local tastes often dictated cutting sections of a libretto. The English, for example, never liked recitative; hence, many performances of Italian works featured mainly arias. Even though a printed summary would fill in elements of the plot, the musical structure of the work was harmed because removing musical numbers left scores that did not segue correctly. Hence, new musical bridges had to be composed to merge the sections around the number that had been removed. The habit of cutting all recitative is extreme; quite frequently, though, composers would omit setting a few lines in long passages of recitative. The complete text would appear in the printed libretto with eliminated sections bracketed off.

Today, directors often remove scenes or numbers to trim performance time; also these cuts are made because members of the cast or the chorus may not be able to perform the music. Another habit is to cut an aria from one section of text and move it elsewhere. This nipping and tucking must be done with care, for the overall dramatic and musical design of the work can be harmed.

REPEATED TEXT, ARCHAIC WORDS, AND THE UBIQUITOUS "AH!"

Composers often choose to set lines more than once to stress certain aspects of the drama or reiterate certain musical phrases. These repeats are strictly musical; hence, although they are in an opera's score, these lines will not be repeated in a printed libretto or in surtitles, which are momentarily suspended until one character begins a line of new text.

The vocabulary in librettos can pose problems for translators. In line with the original notion of the language of opera (that is, words elevated above common speech), poets sought particularly elevated words. Use of a dictionary to translate is often futile because many of these terms are now obsolete. Some Italian examples include *brama* rather than *spada* (sword), *speme* instead of *speranza* (hope), and *aura* for *tomba* (tomb). This archaic vocabulary often confuses translators with less-than-expert language skill. Hence, one might find line translations that vary radically from one another.

Librettists often included seemingly senseless interjections such as "Ah!" in the midst of their lines. Just a few of many possible examples from *Norma* demonstrate:

> "E tu pure, ah, tu non sai. . . "
> "A lui cedi, ah, cedi a me!"
> "Vieni in Roma, ah, vieni, o cara. . . "
> "Che ascolto? Ah! Deh parla!"
> "Ah! No, giammai, ah, no. Ah, pria spirar!"

Less-than-brilliant poets might have employed interjections such as "Ah!" to arrive at the correct number of syllables in a line of verse. A more practical explanation is that in a highly dramatic text, this kind of interjection demonstrates a character's highly charged emotional state and allows the composer to give the singer a chance to express that emotion by momentarily stopping the vocal line to sing the interjection, often with embellishments.

The rhythms of speech and the syllabic stresses of words give language an inherent musical quality. A poet who explores the possibilities of the sounds of words and a composer who respects their rhythms forge a powerful link between text and music. Chapter 4 discusses the roles of those who create the music and the text for operas and also the tasks assumed by those who mount their creations on the stage.

4

PROFESSIONS

The musicians in the orchestra strike the overture's final chord, and the curtain rises on an elaborate replica of a seventeenth-century village square. Singers in period costumes promenade onstage, performing the opening chorus. Among them are supernumeraries, non-singing volunteers who help populate crowd scenes. As the number concludes, the lights sweep stage left onto the tenor, who begins his entrance aria. When he finishes to enthusiastic applause, the curtain falls, only to rise again in the proverbial blink of an eye to reveal a lavish salon where the *prima donna* sits, reading a letter. Of course, opera boasts spectacular "snafus"—Tosca bounces back up from her suicidal leap, Brünnhilde's stallion bolts, a chorister's feathered hat ignites after brushing against a lit candle. But when all goes well, the months of planning and preparation result in a seemingly effortless spectacle.

Major opera houses schedule productions as far as three years in advance to engage the best singers and conductors; dependent on annual budgets, smaller companies work on tighter deadlines. After a season is programmed, administrators decide if there are funds to design new productions; if not, they arrange to rent scenery and costumes from other companies (generally out of their geographic area so shared audiences will not see the same production twice). As the opening draws near, the crew builds the set. Then technical rehearsals with the cast and orchestra give the stagehands practice moving backdrops and props during the brief intervals between scenes. These rehearsals are equally important for the singers because they need to learn to move, often in elaborate costumes, around the set. If the opera includes dancers, they, too, must practice in the relatively small area of the stage not populated by singers.

Before cast members set foot onstage, they gather for "seated rehearsals" (Ger., *Sitz-Proben*) to work through the score with an accompanist and, if necessary, vocal and language coaches. Then the director explains each scene's "blocking," or stage movement. Because the cast and crew must be paid for their time, full rehearsals in the theater are extremely costly; furthermore, contracts and union regulations generally limit overtime. Rehearsals are even more constrained in larger houses that run more than one production at a time. So when a theater rehearsal is called, everyone from the *diva* to the lowliest stagehand is expected to be prepared. The final rehearsal, or "dress," is so close to a real performance that many opera houses open them to donors and VIP guests.

This abbreviated overview sketches how the cast and crew prepare for a performance. The following sections outline the tasks and responsibilities of those who create and produce opera.

COMPOSER (IT., COMPOSITORE; FR., COMPOSITEUR; GER., KOMPONIST)

Most of the operas in today's international repertory were composed during the eighteenth and nineteenth centuries, but occasionally companies still commission new works. Although the tools have changed radically, with high-tech notation software replacing quills and inkwells, a composer's primary task remains the same: to create an accompanied vocal setting of the text of a large-scale dramatic work.

UNDERSTANDING THE VOCAL IDIOM

Unlike musical instruments, which can have a span of multiple octaves, the human voice has a limited range in which it can perform effectively (see Chapter 5). Untrained voices generally do best with stepwise melodies that lie in the middle of this range; opera singers, on the other hand, train not only to extend this compass but to negotiate melodic lines that can feature large leaps and elaborate embellishments. Throughout history, composers have understood these special voices and exploited their abilities. In the eighteenth and early nineteenth centuries, it was standard practice to listen to singers before writing an opera's arias; as Pacini wrote, composers would fit music to the voice as tailors would fit clothes to the body. If an opera succeeded and were produced elsewhere, the composer might have been asked to write substitute arias if the originals did not suit the new cast members. Today, composers are rarely called on to create roles for specific singers, so, in addition to writing works that demonstrate their own genius, they craft roles suited to vocal ranges. For example, Rossini created the role of Semiramide for his wife, Isabella Colbran; had he composed it in the twenty-first century, he simply would have written the part for "soprano."

On a practical level, composers must bear in mind that singing is a physical act, and arduous vocal lines tax the voice and sap the performer's energy. In the past, it was common to give each singer strategically placed arias in a variety of styles so that they could pace themselves while still demonstrating vocal agility, lyrical interpretation, and dramatic rendering. Because performers tended to embellish vocal lines (as do today's singers trained in historical performance practice), composers often constructed less intricate melodies that invited improvisation. Moreover, as exciting as elaborate arias might be for an audience, some composers reserved such numbers for highly dramatic moments.

UNDERSTANDING THE ORCHESTRAL IDIOM

Many composers in the seventeenth and eighteenth centuries learned the principles of orchestration through experience. As musicians playing in ensembles themselves, they were able to observe firsthand how their contemporaries employed instruments in the orchestra. Another method of self-instruction was to copy out and study other composers' scores. By the nineteenth century, most promising composers attended music schools and conservatories to study with prestigious *maestri*; for example, Donizetti studied composition in Bergamo with one of the most influential opera composers in the era between Mozart and Rossini: Johann Simon Mayr. Other important composers with noted pupils include Antonio Salieri (Beethoven, Schubert, Meyerbeer, and Hérold), Niccolò Zingarelli (Bellini and Mercadante), Anton Rubinstein (Tchaikovsky), and Amilcare Ponchielli (Puccini). Denied entry to Milan's conservatory—at nineteen, he was deemed too old—Verdi studied privately with Vincenzo Lavigna who had connections to La Scala.

In addition to understanding the orchestra as a body, composers must understand its individual components. Each instrument has its own "voice" (tone) and "color," with high-pitched instruments described as "light" and low ones as "dark." When writing accompaniment for the voice, the composer must weigh whether it is better to use the whole orchestra (*tutti*, It.) or to isolate certain instruments or sections for their unique qualities. In the nineteenth century, for instance, composers attuned to the dramatic possibilities of single wind instruments often paired a flute or oboe with the soprano in a "mad" scene to highlight the character's lonely, discomfited state.

To employ an instrument efficiently, the composer has always needed to be aware of its limitations and the demands on its player. Such knowledge was critical before technical changes in the nineteenth century produced modern instruments. Before horns had valves, players had to add or remove lengths of tubing to change keys; thus, composers had to remember to omit the horns for enough measures to accommodate the shift. Other instruments simply could not produce certain notes. Now, these technical issues only concern those editing historical scores for modern performance. Today's composers decide whether to accompany voices with a traditional orchestra or explore last century's trend of looking beyond the standard ensemble. Glass' *Einstein on the Beach*, for instance, features amplified instruments and a synthesizer. Such innovation requires careful reevaluation of acoustic balance so that traditional instruments and, more important, the singers' voices will not be overpowered.

UNDERSTANDING LANGUAGE AND TEXT

What takes precedence when composing an opera: the music or the words? This query has sparked debate from the genre's earliest days. Originally, the music was envisioned as the medium for the expression of poetry and drama, but, less than a century into its history, the emphasis had shifted to the music. Virtuoso singers demanded arias that they, in turn, embellished to show off their talents. Furthermore, a preponderance of librettos of poor literary and dramatic quality only provided the performers with words to sing. By the eighteenth century, influential poets such as Apostolo Zeno and Pietro Metastasio had proposed reforms. One composer to address this issue was Gluck, who, in the preface to the revision of his opera *Alceste*, suggested that a thoughtfully composed score could eliminate musical excess and best serve its libretto.

Born in Bohemia in 1714, Christoph Willibald von Gluck began his career as an organist in Prague. As did many composers interested in theater, he went to Italy, where he premiered his first opera in 1741. After traveling throughout Europe, he settled in Vienna in 1752. In time, he became a composer for the Habsburg court, the same post Mozart would assume—at less than half the salary—when Gluck died in 1787.

In Vienna, Gluck collaborated with librettist Ranieri de' Calzabigi. Together, they produced the first of Gluck's so-called "reform" operas: *Orfeo ed Euridice* (1762). The second, *Alceste*, premiered in Vienna in 1767 and was revised for Paris in 1776. In the latter's preface (often attributed to Calzabigi), Gluck elucidated his reforms, prompted by singers whose self-serving embellishments distracted from the music and by composers whose complaisancy resulted in tiresome and formulaic works. His new style would not only respect the poetry, but also ensure that the music reflected the libretto's dramatic content. Arias would be placed where necessary, not where expected, and vocal lines would facilitate delivery of the text, not distract from it. Every note of the score—even of the overture—would relate to the plot. His aim, he stated, was "noble simplicity."

Although some composers adopted Gluck's reforms wholesale (or chose from them selectively), others in time would propose different solutions to the question of how to balance the demands of text and music.

In addition to the significance of words, composers are concerned with their sounds. Every language has a natural rhythm determined by the patterns of its stressed and unstressed syllables. For the text to make sense when it is sung, the composer must carefully set it to analogous musical rhythms. Generally, composers working with texts in languages in which they are fluent sense rhythmic patterns instinctively; when dealing with less familiar languages, they must either have a good ear or work closely with someone who will indicate awkward passages. Composers adept at setting text in several languages include Mozart (German and Italian), Rossini (Italian and French), Meyerbeer (German, Italian, and French) and Stravinsky (Russian and English).

Through much of the nineteenth century, librettos featured texts in predictable poetic patterns, greatly simplifying the composer's task (see Chapter 3). Instead of poetry, modern librettos, such as those in American English, generally feature conversational language that exploits the natural rhythms in verbal expression. However, composers have always had to understand subtle linguistic nuances, especially when texts were in dialects or particular idioms. In this respect, Pergolesi's task in setting the Neapolitan in *Lo frate 'nnamorato* can be likened to Strauss' handling of the concocted Viennese dialects of *Der Rosenkavalier* and Previn's treatment of Tennessee Williams' drawls in *A Streetcar Named Desire*.

UNDERSTANDING SOCIETY

No opera was ever created in a cultural vacuum, and composers have always had to be culturally involved and abreast of aesthetics, society, and often politics (see Chapter 7). Should one set a work in a proven musical style or risk public disapproval with something novel? Although now monuments in the repertory, the most popular works of Verdi and Wagner broke current compositional molds, often premiering to confused or hostile audiences. Should the work pander to societal mores or dare to offend? Stalin named Shostakovich an enemy of the Soviet state after seeing a performance of *Lady Macbeth of the Mtsensk District*. Should the music be facile on the ear or an abrasive reflection of a perplexing society? Everyone loves to hear Mozart and Puccini, but it is the discerning soul who perceives *Wozzeck* as a brilliant reflection of its time.

Who's better, Mozart or Puccini?

Each composer works with the musical tools available. In the century that separated Mozart from Puccini, myriad changes occurred. The orchestra assumed more players and the tone qualities of instruments improved.

Also, musical harmony was redefined; hence, Puccini could employ lush chords that would have been blasphemous in the more conservative tonal system of Mozart's day. Their audiences, too, were different. Mozart's crowds enjoyed a happy ending, hence, the rollicking—though moralistic—fugue that concludes *Don Giovanni*. Puccini's audiences preferred to mourn the deaths of suicidal or sickly heroines.

It is often said that music "progressed" from the time of Mozart to Puccini, but "progress" is a subjective term. Did nineteenth-century musicians appreciate the better tones of their new instruments? In fact, most complained about learning new playing techniques. And what of the singers who initially faced those new, improved sounds? Having to sing more loudly was problematic for voices already under constant strain. If one insists that music progressed from the seventeenth to the twenty-first century, why are audiences not more enthusiastic about so-called "modern" works?

Faulting one composer because he or she did not have the same cultural environment or musical tools is unfair. Although one may prefer Donna Elvira to Tosca, such a judgment is subjective. Neither Mozart nor Puccini is the "better" composer. They are simply "different," one from the other.

METHODS OF COMPOSITION

In general, a composer is presented with a libretto that he or she then agrees to set. The offer may come as a commission, a legal contract that binds the composer to complete a work for a specific venue and production date. In the eighteenth century, many composers were attached to courts and were already under obligation to write operas for their patrons' entertainment; one of Haydn's main responsibilities as *Kapellmeister* for the Esterházy princes was the creation and production of operas. In the nineteenth century, when fewer composers were under court patronage, commissions were issued directly by theaters or handled through impresarios (see Impresario later in this chapter) or music publishers. A commission guaranteed financial remuneration, so many composers learned to worked quickly to earn more money. In fact, Donizetti's nickname was "Dozinetti" because he had penned dozens of scores.

Many composers were free agents, able to seek and accept commissions on their own. Others worked for theaters or impresarios; while

Rossini was under contract in Naples, he required permission to accept commissions for theaters in other cities. Of course, composers have always been free to decide to write an opera and go in search of a libretto themselves. Mozart wrote frequently to his father of his hunts for suitable opera texts. Wagner went a step further by writing his own librettos for the *Ring* and then seeking the necessary financial assistance to build a theater to produce it (see Chapter 6).

Each composer has a preferred work method. Bellini seems unique in the intriguing habit of composing melodies as a musical exercise and then later fitting them to words. The usual method of writing an opera is to set the text to a vocal line and then sketch out an accompaniment. Full orchestration begins only after the composer is satisfied with the results of this early stage. Such sketches are important for scholars, who study them to document an opera's compositional history and a composer's work habits. Even if some of the numbers drafted were not included in the final work, many composers retained them for future use. The recent discovery of some Verdi sketches demonstrates that *Rigoletto*'s famous "Caro nome" had actually been intended (with a different text) for *Stiffelio*.

Some composers began their task with a complete libretto in hand; such was the case in France, where a composer would only be able to begin setting a text after it had passed a series of readings to ensure its literary quality. In nineteenth-century Italy, however, a composer often knew the opera's plot but received sections of the libretto as the poet completed them. Hence, some operas were composed an act or even a number at a time. Even when they arrived in installments, librettos were not always delivered in a timely fashion. Verdi waited months for the text of *Il trovatore*, only to discover in the newspaper one morning that his librettist had died (a new one was quickly engaged to complete the task).

Because theaters often required composers to travel, some operas were written in transit. Studies of the watermarks on the score paper Mozart used demonstrated that parts of his operas were composed at different times in different cities. Because of professional pressures, composers often gave their students or assistants some of the lesser compositional tasks; one such duty was the scoring of recitative (see Chapter 2). Because Lully had codified a standard for French orchestration, he often relegated this straightforward chore to others. Young composers also were engaged to copy out orchestra parts, a tedious task that nonetheless came with a small stipend and invaluable experience in studying instrumentation.

REVISIONS

Opening night often proved less than auspicious. Sometimes, it was the presence of a claque, audience members paid by rivals to hiss or whistle; such a crowd greeted the initial performance of Bellini's *Norma*. In other cases, the audience and the critics simply did not like the work. This latter reaction caused Puccini to withdraw *Madama Butterfly* immediately after its premiere.

If, after consideration, a composer sees no merit in reworking a score, it may be put aside permanently. Otherwise, pieces of it may be salvaged for later operas, or the work as a whole may be revised. Alterations may include reorchestration, composition of new music, textual changes, or the restructuring of entire acts. After the composer is satisfied with the new version, the work will be presented to the public again. Successfully revised operas include *Fidelio*, *La forza del destino*, and *La rondine* (although Puccini eventually decided that he liked the original of the three versions best).

Even compositions with successful premieres also may undergo revision. Italian works going on for production in Paris, for example, generally necessitated change to suit French tastes. Aware of their dislike of castratos on the operatic stage, Gluck rescored *Alceste*'s male lead to a tenor role for the Parisian debut. Also, because French opera routinely featured dance, Italian composers revised their scores to include ballet, as Verdi did for the Parisian debut of *Macbeth* in 1865.

SELF-BORROWING

Linked to the issue of revising a work is self-borrowing, the practice of a composer taking music from one work and reusing it in another. One oft-cited example is Rossini's use of the same overture (with minor changes) for *Aureliano in Palmira*, *Elisabetta, regina d'Inghilterra*, and *Il barbiere di Siviglia*. Because of the frequency of his self-borrowings, Rossini suffered criticism in his own day and in early valuations of his work, but, in reality, self-borrowing was a common practice. Vivaldi and Handel did it routinely. Donizetti borrowed music from five of his operas for *Anna Bolena*. Given the competition for commissions and the time allotted to complete scores (in some cases, weeks, if composers' accounts are credible), it would seem logical to employ successful music again or to take perfectly acceptable music from a less-than-stellar production.

Today, audiences can hear self-borrowings in recordings or stage productions. However, in Rossini's day, the risk was quite small that an audience in Naples would recognize an aria from another opera that had premiered in Venice. Generally, self-borrowing brought little more than criticism. What brought legal action was "borrowing" from the works of another composer. Such activity was prevalent enough in the nineteenth century to make large publishing houses like Ricordi hire agents to ensure that music was not illegally appropriated or produced without permission.

LIBRETTIST (IT., LIBRETTISTA; FR., LIBRETTISTE; GER., TEXTDICHTER)

As with a playwright, the librettist creates a serious or comic theatrical work, generally divided into acts and scenes. This text, however, will be set wholly or in part to music; hence, it must be constructed in sections that can accommodate operatic numbers such as recitative passages, arias, and multi-character ensembles. The librettist, therefore, must pay particular attention to dramatic pacing; for example, arias should be placed where action can be stopped temporarily because their texts generally indicate moments of reflection or reaction (see Chapter 2). Even though the goal is a musical setting, the librettist should still be concerned with the quality of the text and the drama, for, as *Camerata* members proposed, a libretto should constitute elevated language made more meaningful through musical expression. In reality, however, opera history is rife with examples of wordsmiths who produced lackluster texts and nonsensical plots. Through much of the eighteenth century, many librettos included the names of everyone involved in a production from the dance master to the costume designer, but quite often there is virtually no clue about their authors—perhaps with good reason.

Librettists were generally poets, some amateur and some professional. Alessandro Striggio, who wrote the text for Monteverdi's *Orfeo*, was by occupation a diplomat for the Gonzaga family of Mantua. Although active in the musical world, Jacopo Ferretti, a favorite with Rossini and his contemporaries, worked in the tobacco industry. Others actually held posts as poets for noble patrons or public theaters. One of the most influential librettists of all time, Pietro Metastasio, had an appointment at the Imperial Court in Vienna; his compatriot Caterino Mazzolà held a similar post at the court in Dresden. Felice Romani, author of Bellini's *Norma* and *Beatrice di Tenda* and librettos for Mayr, Rossini, Pacini, and Mercadante, worked for a time at La Scala. At Venice's La Fenice was Francesco Maria Piave, who wrote for Verdi and myriad other contemporaries. In the seventeenth and eighteenth centuries, many clerics became librettists, for their education afforded them the necessary experience with languages and classical literature. Lorenza Da Ponte, who replaced Metastasio at the Habsburg court and later worked with Mozart, boasted of such a background. By far the most famous cleric-librettist was Giulio Rospigliosi; author of one of the earliest Roman comedies, *Chi soffre speri* (1637), he later became Pope Clement IX. Even "enlightened despots" such as Frederick the Great and Catherine the Great wrote for the operatic stage.

Because musical training was a significant element in a proper education up through the nineteenth century, many librettists knew how to read music and many were able to compose. Leading examples include Hector Berlioz, Richard Wagner, and Arrigo Boito, who wrote librettos that they themselves set. Although knowledge of music is a plus, at the very least, librettists must have the ability to hear musical elements in words and phrases, carefully selecting vocabulary that not only fits rhythmic patterns but also has "singable" sounds. Some consonants, for instance, prove difficult because the lips must close to pronounce them; on the other hand, the singer's mouth remains open on vowels, allowing unrestricted sound. Bearing sound in mind, the librettist also must choose words with appropriate significance.

Whether they themselves are composers or not, librettists need to know the current musical forms. For instance, the *da capo* aria text needed to reflect some dramatic shift for the B section. Similarly, to mirror the obvious musical difference between a *cantabile* and a *cabaletta*, the text of the second had to express a contrasting thought or tone (see Chapter 2 for explanations of aria types). In addition to current musical styles, librettists need to be aware of culture and aesthetics, specifically, the type of subjects that will appeal to audiences. Those writing in the seventeenth and early eighteenth centuries exploited mythology and history for characters that would metaphorically represent opera's noble patrons. With the rise of literacy, librettists chose tales based on literature.

Pietro Metastasio was born Pietro Trapassi in 1698. The son of poor parents, his education was secured first by his godfather, Cardinal Ottoboni, and then by his patron, Gian Vincenzo Gravina, whose legal career he was to follow. Gravina introduced the young man to society and encouraged his earliest literary efforts. Influenced by ancient models, Trapassi published his first collection of verse, with Gravina's support, under the classical rendering of his name: Metastasio.

After his patron's death in 1718, Metastasio moved to Naples, where local aristocrats quickly recognized his poetic talents. There, he met the castrato Farinelli, with whom he would enjoy a lifelong friendship. Metastasio's first libretto, *Didone abbandonata*, was set in Naples in 1723. By the end of the decade, he had become famous enough to warrant an invitation to join the Habsburg court in Vienna as its poet, providing texts for operas and court celebrations. Settings of his *opere serie* librettos delighted the Viennese until fickle imperial tastes turned to French opera, Italian comic works, and the native German *Singspiel*. Although less active in the final years of his life, the sheer number of musical settings of his librettos demonstrates the international respect accorded to his work. After Metastasio's death in 1782, Lorenzo Da Ponte, Mozart's collaborator for *Le nozze di Figaro*, *Don Giovanni*, and *Così fan tutte*, assumed his post but never equaled his fame.

Metastasio's works were as much literary masterpieces as operatic texts. In the spirit of reform, he established a model that would standardize *opera seria* until the early nineteenth century. The typical Metastasian libretto featured six or seven characters of noble birth who faced a series of challenges together. As they worked through these problems, they demonstrated their strength and virtue as a moral example. Generally, the plot would resolve happily, leaving the audience with a sense of trust in their own noble leaders (for whom these characters were transparent representations). Structurally, the operas had three acts, each with a dozen scenes; musically, the text was laden with recitative and peppered with arias that occurred just before characters left the stage (hence the term "exit aria"). Climactic scenes at the ends of the second and third acts warranted larger ensembles. Although Metastasio claimed to know nothing of music, he was able to write verse that captured the natural rhythms of the Italian language and hence was easy to set. Perhaps the most popular librettist of all time, his texts were employed throughout the operatic world virtually hundreds of times for more than a century, the last settings dating from the 1830s.

Some librettists never met the composers who set their words. Others worked in a theatrical environment with numerous composers. Opera history boasts several composer-librettist teams that worked successfully on operatic projects; among these are Lully and Philippe Quinault, Gluck and Calzabigi, Galuppi and Goldoni (see Chapter 3), Mozart and Da Ponte, Bellini and Romani, and Puccini and Luigi Illica (who drafted the text) and Giuseppe Giacosa (who set it into verse). Some of these collaborators made significant contributions to contemporary musical theater; for instance, Meyerbeer and Eugène Scribe established the characteristics and standards of *grand opéra* for the nineteenth-century French stage (see Chapter 8) and influenced opera productions internationally.

IMPRESARIO (GER., SCHAUSPIELDIREKTOR)

Originally, operas were commissioned by noble patrons and produced at their courts by members of their musical establishments (see Chapter 7). When Venice opened the first public theater in 1637, opera became a business, and, except for France, where it remained under state control, nobles and wealthy members of the burgeoning middle class began to invest in theaters. However, many quickly discovered that the tasks of theatrical administration were beneath them; others found, after financially disastrous seasons, that the tasks were beyond them. Running a theater meant active involvement in a growing network of professionals who knew which composers were popular, which singers were available, and which operas were successful. By the late seventeenth century, opera had become an international industry, with paying customers from London to St. Petersburg.

The men (and, in rare cases, women) who undertook the tasks of producing operas became known as impresarios, from the Italian "*impresa*," or business. Some impresarios were themselves members of traveling opera troupes that toured smaller towns and cities; others were music professionals with theatrical connections. Although financial arrangements with theater owners and investors varied, basically the impresario received money for an operatic season (see Chapter 7). Out of this sum, he would procure the rights to operas or commission new ones, engage singers (many of whom traveled internationally), hire local musicians for an orchestra, and take care of advertising and production costs. After expenses (and the investors' profits), he was free to keep the remainder.

Some impresarios were business geniuses. Domenico Barbaja, the man who controlled Rossini's every move from 1815 to 1822, rose from obscurity to control almost all of the theaters in Naples. Not only was he wise enough to recognize talented singers and composers, but he also was a savvy investor. His gambling concession in the lobby of the Teatro San Carlo garnered enough profits to rebuild the theater after it was destroyed by fire in 1816. Others were less adept at financial matters. Bartolomeo Merelli routinely went bankrupt; furthermore, his shoddy productions at La Scala in the 1840s drove an angry Verdi away from premiering a work there for more than forty years. Although most composers preferred to remain on the creative side of opera, several, including Handel and Pacini, worked as impresarios.

Italian impresarios often ran seasons throughout Europe. In France, though, the throne controlled the administration of the *Opéra* until the nineteenth century, when business negotiations were assumed by theater managers called *directeurs*. Semi-independent theaters such as the *Opéra-Comique* had their own managers. By the twentieth century, theatrical administration in Europe and the Americas was reorganized, and tasks once handled solely by impresarios were dispersed among various other professionals. The title, however, still applied to high-profile opera administrators such as Oscar Hammerstein I, Rudolph Bing, and Sol Hurok.

CONDUCTOR (IT., DIRETTORE D'ORCHESTRA; FR., CHEF D'ORCHESTRE; GER., DIRIGENT)

An opera conductor is responsible for musical direction during rehearsals and performances. On the most basic level, he or she establishes the beat and maintains a steady tempo, ensuring that the singers and the orchestra stay together. The conductor must also be concerned with orchestral balance so that the instruments never overpower the singers. Even though the musicians and singers, all trained professionals, have rehearsed together, the conductor must focus on both the stage and the pit, for disastrous results would occur if they got out of sync.

The conducting profession is relatively new. Before the nineteenth century, opera orchestras (and instrumental ensembles in general) were directed by the principal violinist or concertmaster (It., *capo d'orchestra*; Fr., *chef d'attaque*; Ger., *Konzertmeister*). This important position still is acknowledged when the first violinist is greeted with applause when entering to tune the orchestra and when the conductor shakes his or her hand to thank the entire ensemble for a good performance. In the eighteenth century, the principal violinist was the only orchestra member with a full score; whereas others played only from their parts, he was able to cue the ensemble and keep time with the rise and fall of his bow. Some principal violinists sat on high stools so that they were more visible, but even in this position, their backs were to the stage. Thus the singers received their cues from another member of the opera orchestra: the harpsichordist.

The harpsichordist (and later the fortepianist) not only played the bass line along with the double basses, cellos, and bassoons (the *basso continuo* group) but also provided the accompaniment for *recitativo secco* (see Chapter 2). In Italian theaters, harpsichords were positioned at the far left and far right sides of the orchestra; in Germany, they were placed at the very center, facing the stage. From either position, the player could cue the singers. Some engravings suggest that the keyboardist also may have beat time on the side of the instrument or gestured with a free hand. This orchestral post was so important that an opera's composer was contracted to sit at the harpsichord for the first three performances of a premiere run.

Iconography demonstrates a different tradition in France. In his day, Lully would beat time with rolled-up paper; by the eighteenth century, a *batteur de mesure* (literally, a "measure beater") kept time by striking a stick against the stage, a distracting practice about which foreign visitors had much to say. In the nineteenth century, engravings depict some musicians using the now-familiar baton, in essence pioneering the task of conducting as we know it today. Other opera composers followed suit; Weber, for example, directed his operas as he conducted them. Other theatrical composers who took the baton were Nicolai, Meyerbeer, Smetana, and later Strauss and Britten. Deserving of special note are Wagner, credited as the founder of the modern school of conducting, and Mahler, lauded as one of the greatest opera conductors in history.

The growing acceptance of Wagner's concept of *Gesamtkunstwerk*, or "total work of art" (see Chapter 8), inspired modern conductors to add another dimension to their task: interpretation. After careful study of a score, conductors develop a vision of how the music should be played. Before rehearsing with the singers, they will work with the orchestra, setting tempos and deciding how best to bring out the subtle nuances of musical phrasing and orchestral color. Because a live performance is "real time," the average audience member would not be able to differentiate between two conductors' renderings of the same work. The contrast is apparent on recordings, however, where even the slightest variation in tempo will create a very different effect. Such decisions—and audience approbation—have created a stable of "star" conductors with fan bases as solid as those of popular singers (the ego of the conductor must merge well with that of the singers, though, or the result is a musical tug-of-war). Among contemporary favorites are James Levine, Riccardo Muti, Riccardo Chailly, Simon Rattle, Pierre Boulez, and Antonio Pappano. Some conductors are especially interested in early music productions and recordings, performed on original instruments from historical scores or scholarly editions (see Chapter 11). Among these are René Jacobs, Nikolaus Harnoncourt, John Eliot Gardiner, William Christie, and Christopher Hogwood.

DIRECTOR (IT., REGISTA; FR., METTEUR EN SCÈNE, GER., REGISSEUR, INSZENIERUNG)

Nineteenth-century Paris was the operatic Mecca. Foreign composers flocked there in hopes of having their works produced or simply to witness the latest theatrical developments. Influenced by the boulevard theaters specializing in spoken drama, French musical theaters adopted the latest in lighting and set design and, more important, in stage direction. Through the early nineteenth century, singers generally sang facing the audience, not each other, even in interactive passages of recitative. Poses were more common than movement, hence the traditional stereotype of the *diva* with one hand on the heart and the other arm extended. Posters for the premiere of *Guillaume Tell* (1828) illustrate a radical change, for singers were depicted facing each other. Commonplace on the French spoken stage, such character action and interaction made their way into opera.

The popularity of opera in nineteenth-century France extended beyond the capital to provincial cities with active theaters. When works were produced at these smaller houses, the score often was sent along with a *livret en mise en scène* (It., *disposizione scenica* or *messa in scena*; Ger., *Regiebuch*), an annotated libretto or production book that included some or all of the following details: stage directions, costume designs, sets, and stage props and their placement. These instructions assisted those directing the piece at the new theater. This concept, perhaps brought back by Verdi, also took a foothold in Italy, and eventually production books were exported along with musical materials to theaters throughout the Western operatic world. When the emphasis of production design shifted to the conductor and director, such materials were no longer needed.

Today, production books are valuable historical tools. Many include illustrations of the costume and set designs from the work's premiere. Also, the stage directions give theater and opera historians a primary-source description of period production techniques. Finally, directors interested in replicating historic performances consult them as a guide. Among the operas with extant production books are *Guillaume Tell*, *Otello*, and *La muette de Portici*.

Stage direction, such as it was, once had been the province of the librettist (and the singer, who moved as he or she pleased). By the turn of the twentieth century, the task fell to the conductor. As they had a century earlier in Paris, developments in stage technology continued to influence opera productions as did modern applications of the Wagnerian philosophy of *Gesamtkunstwerk*. Hence, the sheer complexity of production quickly exceeded the sphere of the conductor, who concentrated mainly on a musical conception of the work. Opera companies turned to directors of the spoken stage, who quickly discovered that they had entered a vastly different realm. Because of the expense, they were allowed limited rehearsal time on stage. Furthermore, they needed to accommodate the extra but all-important element of music in their productions. Some directors adapted well to this new environment, setting what are now considered artistic standards, and, by the end of the last century, audience enthusiasm over the work of certain directors had spawned another manifestation of the operatic "star." A recent production of *I pagliacci* was associated more with Franco Zefferelli than with its composer, Leoncavallo.

Although conductors need to study all aspects of a score, directors should know both the score and libretto thoroughly. Wise directors also study the composer and the cultural environment in which he or she composed, for one can never really "know" an opera simply by hearing it or seeing it performed. After studying the sources, especially scholarly editions that include all versions approved by the composer, directors (and conductors) can make judicious decisions about cutting the score. Failure to take this step can result in careless elimination of critical musical and dramatic links, in essence jeopardizing the whole production's artistic integrity.

A director may decide to update an opera, taking it out of its original temporal setting and (generally) modernizing it. In a recent production of *Giulio Cesare*, for instance, the main character became an American military officer, dog tags and all, who arrived in a tank to battle warriors resembling Al Qaeda militants. Peter Sellars' transfer of *Don Giovanni* from sixteenth-century Spain to the drug-infested neighborhoods of twentieth-century New York offers another example of updating. On a smaller scale, "modernizing" a work can simply mean dressing its characters in contemporary clothes. Generally, such productions add new perspectives to repertory standards; much like updating Shakespeare, they demonstrate that opera's themes are timeless and universal. Some audience members have difficulty dealing with modernizations, though; for them, operas should always feature women in long velvet gowns and men in tunics and tights. The task of preparing audiences for productions, especially explaining a director's new vision, generally falls to a relative newcomer among opera professionals: the educator.

EDUCATION DIRECTOR

During the twentieth century, a veritable chasm formed between audiences of popular music and opera in America. Ironically, a survey of the myriad piano-vocal arrangements sold to nineteenth-century amateur music makers demonstrates that operatic melodies *were* popular music fare (see Chapters 6 and 7), but turn-of-the-century images of the elite in the Met's "Golden Horseshoe" box seats made opera seem inaccessible to anyone but the Vanderbilts. Although European immigrants clung to opera as a part of their linguistic and cultural heritage, their children grew up rejecting connections to the Old World in order to assimilate into their new culture. In short, because of economic and cultural stereotypes, Wagner and Verdi became symbolic of the rich and pretentious. Furthermore, opera was "European" culture, not American.

Over the past twenty years, opera companies have become active in community outreach to ensure the interest of new generations of audience members. Education directors and their staffs target elementary and high school students (and their teachers) by bringing opera into the classroom with workshops and demonstrations. To reinforce these experiences, companies invite schools to attend their technical or dress rehearsals. In the summer, many companies run opera camps in which participants put on operas created especially for children or write and produce compositions of their own. Educators offer talented high school students the opportunity to learn the various aspects of an operatic career in special institutes staffed by professionals in the field.

Opera educators also reach out to adults. Surtitles have eliminated complaints that opera is incomprehensible. In addition to this translation help, companies engage specialists who give pre-performance talks addressing the composer's life and the opera's history. These "informances" also prepare the audience for specific production details such as the ramifications of updating a work. Subscribers generally receive special materials such as study guides with articles on the season's repertory, and now most opera companies maintain web sites that include plot summaries, libretto translations, and essays that help prospective audience members prepare for a performance. Education directors belong to a growing network that develops and shares successful strategies that strip away the myths and stereotypes associated with opera and its audiences.

This chapter has considered the composer, librettist, impresario, conductor, and director—major forces behind the creation of an opera production. Many other professionals work behind the curtain to put an opera onstage: musicians, chorus masters, choreographers and dancers, dramaturgs, vocal and language coaches, set and costume designers, electricians, sound technicians, carpenters, stage hands, and all of the staff employed in theater management and marketing. However, the people in front of the curtain are opera's main attraction, and, as such, warrant special treatment. Hence, the next chapter is dedicated to singers.

5

SINGERS

The profession most obviously associated with opera is that of the singer, because, despite all the labors of others involved in a production, it is the performers onstage who have come to symbolize the genre. Singers bring the characters in the libretto to life, and, together with the musicians in the orchestra, interpret the score. Although some operas feature non-singing roles (Fenella in *La muette de Portici*, Vespone in *La serva padrona*, Toby in *The Medium*, Gottfried in *Lohengrin*, and Guillot in *Yevgeny Onegin*), the voice and its glorification of music and text have been the focus of opera since its origins in sixteenth-century Florence.

Good singers make performing seem effortless. But what makes a singer "good?" On the most basic level, one might describe a good voice as "pleasing to the ear," but such a criterion is extremely subjective. Although it takes a trained ear to distinguish and prefer the sound of a Stradivarius over an Amati violin, the average opera fan finds it quite easy to be opinionated about tenors. Because each human has a voice as unique as his or her fingerprints, listeners, with their own unique tastes, find certain singers' signature timbres, or tone qualities, more enjoyable than others. Although a pleasant voice is among the innate qualities of a "good" singer, excellence in art sets one performer apart from the other in the professional world. In addition to a good voice, then, an opera singer must develop technique, a set of skills acquired through training and practice enabling them to manage and control their voices.

"ATTACK" AND INTONATION

Unlike a piano, which is tuned to play one specific pitch per key, the human voice is able to produce all of the smaller pitches, or microtones, that exist "in the cracks" of the keyboard. One can hear microtones when a violinist slides a finger along a string while bowing; the *glissando* clarinet passage that begins Gershwin's *Rhapsody in Blue* also features microtones. Singers employ a similar technique of connecting pitches (see Phrasing later in this chapter) but they must first concentrate on proper "attack" (hitting the first pitch) and then good intonation (remaining in the key). If they allow their voices to waver down, even by a microtone, they sing "flat"; if they go up, they are "sharp." Correct attack and intonation require a "good ear," the ability to distinguish pitches. Although some singers in opera's history thrived without knowing how to read music, few survived the loss of intonation. Once while singing Norma, the role she had premiered, Giuditta Pasta's intonation deteriorated so badly that the instruments that could not adjust their pitch fell silent, leaving only the strings to accompany her. Shortly thereafter, she retired from the stage.

BLENDING REGISTERS

Every human voice has a range, measured from the lowest note it can produce to the highest. Within each person's vocal range is a "break," that point at which there is a distinguishable difference in tone production; at this "break," the lower register or so-called "chest voice" (It., *voce di petto*) ends and the upper register or "head voice" (It., *voce di testa*) begins. Anyone who has ever sung "The Star-Spangled Banner" has experienced the challenge of moving from one "voice" to another. Most music written for nonprofessional voices has a relatively small vocal compass, allowing the singer to stay within a comfortable middle range. Operatic music, on the other hand, especially from the eighteenth and nineteenth centuries, was composed to exhibit unique vocal abilities. Not only do professionals need to practice extending their ranges on both ends, but they also must learn to negotiate their vocal "breaks" so that one "voice" merges with the other imperceptibly.

PHRASING

Phrasing is critical for a good performance. In addition to enunci-ating clearly, singers must know how to breathe efficiently. Although some have seemingly infinite lung capacity—castratos, for instance, were noted for this amazing trait—others do not. Voice teachers and vocal coaches instruct singers to maximize use of the air in the chest cavity and help them decide the best points to take a new breath without creating an awkward break in the text or melodic line. Proper breathing techniques also enhance *portamento* (the ability to sustain and link notes), whether in passages written by the composer or in sections inviting the singer to improvise ornamentation.

When composers indicate that notes are to be performed *staccato*, singers must produce tones that are crisply distinct one from the other. In opera, though, the majority of vocal lines are *legato*, especially those associated with the so-called *bel canto* repertory. Described as "forth spinning" or "long-breathed," *legato* phrasing requires the singer to connect notes seamlessly. Although this tech-nique requires the singer to hit the microtones, the voice moves so quickly that these interim pitches are heard only as approaches to the next note. One technique employed in the twentieth century necessitates the exaggerated accentuation of the tones between two notated pitches; called *Sprechstimme* by Berg in his opera *Wozzeck*, this style requires the singer to audibly produce the microtones. The unnatural "sing-song" result relates to Expressionism, the concept of personal and societal alienation prevalent in the arts of the early twentieth century (see Chapter 3).

Another issue concerning vocal phrasing is dynamics, or volume. Once again, breathing is the key, enabling the singer to produce a variety of levels of soft (It., *piano*) and loud (It., *forte*) tones. Although the uninitiated stereotype them as frenzied screamers, opera singers face subtle and difficult dynamic challenges such as *messa di voce*, a technique in which the singer gradually shifts from *pianissimo* (very soft) to *fortissimo* (very loud) and back. The development of such skills requires not only study and practice, but also commitment and determination. Technique ensures good musical performance and enhances dramatic interpretation, and, on the most practical level, can determine a singer's future. "Good" professionals can find jobs in choruses or secure roles in smaller opera companies; "great" ones cultivate significant careers.

A Word about Bel Canto

One phrase that is tossed about liberally in discussions of opera is "bel canto," yet no phrase is as ill-defined and misunderstood. Literally meaning "beautiful singing" or "beautiful song," it has been used variously to define periods of opera history and describe pedagogical techniques and vocal style.

Perhaps the greatest confusion is the narrow reference to the nineteenth-century repertory of Rossini, Bellini, Donizetti, and their contemporaries as the "age of bel canto." This application of the term actually began in the late nineteenth century when the flexible vocal style necessary for these early works was contrasted with newer, more heavy dramatic interpretations. Norma's "Casta diva" provides an example of this earlier florid style; the very first syllable ("Ca-") is set over a melismatic phrase (legato passage of numerous notes). Yet such long-breathed, swirling vocal lines, albeit common in this era, are by no means exclusive to it. Works from the seventeenth and eighteenth centuries include similar melismatic passagework; as any singer will agree, Handel and Mozart require equally flexible voices. Their works and those of their contemporaries must also be considered "bel canto."

As far back as the seventeenth century, vocal treatises describe the very techniques ascribed to bel canto singing. In fact, any consideration of the virtuosic style associated with the rise of opera can be linked theoretically with bel canto techniques. Although they never employed the term, the eighteenth-century pedagogues Pierfrancesco Tosi and Giambattista Mancini describe bel canto style. When training singers, Manuel Garcia the Younger (see later in this chapter) called for completely natural, flexible, and effortless interpretation, all characteristics associated with bel canto. In turn, his pupils taught the method to their own students, thus carrying this style into the twentieth century. Furthermore, attempts to link bel canto exclusively with the so-called Italian school of singing fail, for the French and Germans expressed the same ideas about performing. One can not hope to erase all the misconceptions ascribed the term "bel canto." Admitting to its wider significance, however, removes it from the realm of cant.

THE SINGER AS ACTOR

On the most elementary level, opera singers today are expected to demonstrate solid musicianship. Most attend colleges or conservatories, and, of these, a good percentage continues on for graduate degrees or artist diplomas. Although not as common in opera's early history, singers are expected to read both vocal and orchestral scores (see Chapter 11) and have advanced training in music theory (especially necessary in the performance of modern works in which the singer's part is radically different from the orchestra's). Furthermore, they must understand (or at the very least know how to pronounce) a variety of languages, including Italian, French, German, English, Spanish, Russian, and Czech. Because the libretto is perceived as a dramatic script with a plot, it is critical that singers be aware of what they are "saying" in an aria or passage of recitative. In fact, singers are frequently asked to translate what they have sung for an audition; many young performers who did not get a callback have wished they had taken the time to understand the text.

In the seventeenth and early eighteenth centuries, a libretto's drama was portrayed almost solely through the singers' voices, for that was the vehicle thought to move the listeners' souls. By the late eighteenth and nineteenth centuries, composers began to write music that reflected the emotions of the characters, but singers were still generally expected to project them with their voices and accompanying gestures. Only in the nineteenth century, because of the influence of the French dramatic stage, were singers encouraged to act as well as sing, beginning, it is thought, with Rossini's *Guillaume Tell*. During that production, singers actually interacted with each other instead of simply assuming a stance and facing out toward the audience. Last century's great singers also were known as great actors, and today, audiences and critics expect an artist to interpret a character as well as perform the music.

THE ART OF SINGING

Schools specializing in the training of voices have existed since the Middle Ages, but such an institution, known as a *schola cantorum*, was attached to a cathedral, monastery, or convent and specialized in training choir singers. The genesis of opera and the rise of the professional virtuoso resulted in the beginning of vocal pedagogy. Among the first teachers of this new style of singing were Italian castratos (see Castrato later in this chapter) who either taught independently or were associated with secular music schools. Contemporary vocal treatises record what must have been the content of early voice lessons; among these books are Caccini's *Le nuove musiche* (1602), Tosi's *Observations on Florid Song* (1723), Mancini's *Reflessioni pratiche sul canto figurato* (1774), and Bernardo Mengozzi's *Méthode de chant du Conservatoire de musique* (published posthumously in 1804). The first truly physiological study of the voice was the work of Manuel Garcia the Younger, whose experiments with the laryngoscope, a small mirror with which the vocal mechanism could be viewed, brought the art of singing into the world of science. Other singers authored vocal methods for future generations of performers. Such writers include Luigi Lablache, Donizetti's first Don Pasquale (*Méthode de chant*); Lilli Lehmann (*Meine Gesangskunst*, 1902); and Nellie Melba (*Melba Method*, 1936).

Manuel Garcia the Younger was born in Madrid in 1805. The son of two singers (his father, Manuel Garcia, had premiered the role of Almaviva in Rossini's *Il barbiere di Siviglia*), Garcia and his family were part of the first Italian opera troupe to perform in the Americas. The strain of performing took its toll on the young man's voice, and he was forced to retire from the stage in 1829. After the death of his father in 1832, the younger Garcia took over the training of two of his sisters, both of whom became legendary performers: the ill-fated Maria Malibran and Pauline Viardot.

Garcia was appointed to teach singing at the Paris Conservatoire, which, under the direction of Luigi Cherubini, favored the so-called Italian school of singing as taught by castrati such as Girolamo Crescentini. While working in military hospitals, Garcia became interested in the throat and started to study the larynx. His findings, presented to the Paris Academy of Sciences and published as *Mémoire sur la voix humaine*, later were incorporated into his treatise on vocal performance, *Traité complet de l'art du chant*, first published in 1840. The work would be revised and republished in numerous editions and translations until 1872.

Although some contend that Garcia invented the laryngoscope, others maintain that dental mirrors in use at the time may have inspired the tool with which he studied his own larynx. Nevertheless, his findings furthered medical science as well as the instruction and understanding of vocal technique. Garcia published his final work, *Hints on Singing*, in 1894. Retiring from a post at the Royal Academy of Music in London in 1895, he continued to teach privately until his death in 1904. In addition to his sisters, Garcia's studio produced pupils such as Julius Stockhausen (for whom Brahms wrote the baritone solos in the *Deutsches Requiem*), Jenny Lind, and Mathilde Marchesi, who in turn instructed Emma Calvé, Emma Eames, and Nellie Melba.

VIBRATO

Singers employ vibrato to vary or "color" their tone. A violinist gets vibrato by slightly rocking the finger holding the string down on the fingerboard; the result is a gentle waver of pitch. Generally natural to the human voice, some people have a strong vibrato while others have barely any. The absence of vibrato, often called a "white tone," was encouraged in medieval and Renaissance choir music, making all the singers sound homogenous. As professional soloists made careers in opera, however, individuality was encouraged. Furthermore, when performance venues changed from more intimate court settings to large public theaters (see Chapter 6), singers performed with greater volume, which brings out vibrato naturally.

Generally speaking, singers vary the sound of their voices with vibrato to produce richer, more colorful tones, especially when sustaining notes. Too much vibrato can sound ridiculous and indeed is often used in parodies of operatic singing. As with other vocal skills, performers must control vibrato and apply it judiciously.

VOCAL RANGES

Voices are commonly categorized by range. To produce harmony, for example, choruses are generally divided into soprano, alto, tenor, and bass sections. The world of opera recognizes numerous subdivisions within the four basic ranges, and composers, in turn, have used these subtle differences to produce infinite shades of harmony and to offer tonal variety (listening to a whole cast of singers in a single range would be tedious). Vocal ranges also assist in characterization. Villains such as Iago in *Otello* and Scarpia in *Tosca* are depicted by a low voice, adding an ominous tone to their characters. Although singers can be said to be "typecast" by their ranges, some have gone on to capitalize on such characterizations. With training, of course, singers can extend both the lower and upper ends of their vocal compass; some even end up in a different range from the one in which they began. Both Enrico Caruso and Plácido Domingo, two of the greatest tenors in opera history, started their careers as baritones. After struggling as a lackluster tenor, David Daniels went on to become one of the contemporary stage's most prized countertenors. Indeed, the male voice may not "settle" into its correct range until the singer reaches his mid-thirties.

The following table defines the standard limits of the vocal ranges from the *lowest* note to the *highest*. The musical shorthand is interpreted in terms of middle C, the note nearest the center of the piano keyboard. In a musical score, middle C is located on its own ledger line directly between the treble and the bass clefs:

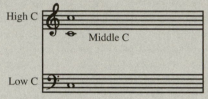

To distinguish one octave from another, musicians employ a type of shorthand (this book uses the symbols in *The New Grove Dictionary of Music and Musicians*). The c below Middle C is written c; Middle C is c′; and the c above middle C is c″. The lowest male voices begin in the octave below c; that note is designated as C. Thus the three octaves in which human voices can sing are:

C c c′ c″

Were we dealing with musical instruments, we would need to include symbols for lower and higher octaves. A piano's range, for instance, goes from A‴ to c″″.

Employing the above shorthand, the "average" vocal ranges are as follows:

Soprano: c′ to a″
Mezzo-soprano: a to g″
Contralto: g to e″
Countertenor: g to d″
Tenor: c to a′
Baritone: A to f′
Bass: F to e′

The remainder of this chapter considers the various vocal ranges employed in operas and the roles associated with them. It is not uncommon to see a specific character identified with one range in one source and with another elsewhere. Guglielmo in *Così fan tutte* is at times labeled a baritone and at other times a bass. This book relies on the casts as listed in the *New Grove*. Readers are simply advised that there are rarely hard and fast divisions between neighboring ranges and that singers frequently cross comfortably from one to another.

SOPRANO (FR., DESSUS, SOPRANO; GER., SOPRAN)

The term "soprano" derives from the Italian word "sopra," meaning "above," for it designated the highest line in polyphonic vocal music. "Soprano" originally referred to a male singer, either a castrato or young boy who sang in this uppermost range; in fact, all the names of the vocal ranges now associated with women—soprano, mezzo-soprano, alto, and contralto—all retain a masculine ending (-o), for they were standard musical terms long before women became professional singers. Although some women were performing professionally in late sixteenth-century court entertainment, opera gave them the possibility to have significant musical careers.

It is often erroneously thought that women's roles in early opera were always sung by male sopranos. Although this was sometimes the case, particularly in Rome where women were periodically forbidden to appear in public theaters, they were associated with theatrical singing by the early decades of the seventeenth century. The popular Vittoria Archilei may well have sung the lead role in Peri's *Euridice* (1600), a work based on the Orpheus myth that predates Monteverdi's *Orfeo* by seven years. In addition to performing their own roles, women were at times cast as men; until Handel was able to import more castrati from Italy, he employed Margherita Durastante for the lead in *Radamisto* and for Sextus in *Giulio Cesare* as well as for female roles such as Agrippina. Durastante's range was more like today's mezzo-soprano, demonstrating that most early soprano roles actually were written lower than those composed in the late eighteenth and nineteenth centuries when the soprano *tessitura* (the median range of a piece) became higher.

Breeches or Trousers Roles
(It., Travestito; *Fr.*, Travesti; *Ger.*, Hosenrolle)

Because the castrato and the female soprano sang in much the same range, opera houses would employ whichever singer was available for male parts. Because sopranos appeared in men's garb, or *travestito* (akin to the English "transvestite"), they were said to be singing "breeches" or "trousers" parts. Furthermore, a woman performing such a role might also be called a *musico*, a term originally applied to a castrato. In certain cases, male roles were generally assigned to women. In Neapolitan comic (*buffa*) works, for instance, the parts of inexperienced youths were given to sopranos; indeed, Mozart followed suit when creating Cherubino in *Le nozze di Figaro*. With the demise of the operatic castrato in the early nineteenth century (see Castrato), women temporarily took over these roles, but the rise of the tenor shortly thereafter put an end to the necessity of "breeches" casting. Yet some composers saw fit to resurrect the tradition. Among later "breeches" roles are Fyodor in *Boris Godunov* (1868), Orlofsky in *Die Fledermaus* (1874), Nicklausse in *Les contes d'Hoffmann* (1881), Hänsel in *Hänsel und Gretel* (1893), Prince Charming in *Cendrillon* (1899), and Octavian in *Der Rosenkavalier* (1911).

Until the nineteenth century, a French soprano was known as a "dessus" to differentiate her from the Italian soprano. Dessus singers had had successful careers creating roles at the prestigious *Académie Royale de Musique* throughout the seventeenth century. Composers such as Lully cast them as lovers, queens, goddesses and mythological heroines, servants, priestesses, countesses, and slaves.

Sopranos thrill audiences because they can reach the highest pitches accessible to the human voice, and composers have exploited this ability to express the height of human passions and emotions. For this reason, sopranos, along with tenors, have come to dominate the operatic landscape, even commandeering roles not originally meant for them. Rossini conceived Rosina in *Il barbiere di Siviglia* for his childhood friend, contralto Geltrude Giorgi-Righetti. Because it is the leading female role, sopranos took it over. It is revealing to hear Cecilia Bartoli or Vivica Genaux perform Rosina (or Cenerentola, also written for Giorgi-Righetti) and contrast their interpretations with Roberta Peters' stratospheric (but fictional) performance of it.

LYRIC SOPRANO (IT., SOPRANO LIRICO; FR., SOPRANO LYRIQUE; GER., LYRISCHE SOPRAN)

Often referred to as the "standard" soprano voice, singers in this category have richly powerful and full tones. Their strong suit is melodic delivery. Roles include the Countess in *Le nozze di Figaro*, Marguerite in *Faust*, and Mimì in *La bohème*.

COLORATURA (GER., KOLORATUR)

Coloratura is often employed to classify a type of soprano; however, as with certain uses of *bel canto*, this term is incorrect. Coloratura describes the florid, ornamented vocal lines of certain operatic roles. Thus it actually concerns a type of music and its interpretation, not the singer who performs it. The notion of the "coloratura soprano" comes from the notoriety of Maria Callas, Joan Sutherland, and Beverly Sills, who all reintroduced roles featuring such music. Music for other vocal ranges features coloratura lines as well: one example is the tenor role of Lindoro in *Il barbiere di Siviglia*.

The true designation for sopranos who excel at coloratura is "light soprano."

LIGHT SOPRANO (IT., SOPRANO LEGGIERO; FR., SOPRANO LÉGER)

Often referred to as "soubrettes," these singers lack the full volume of the lyric soprano but are noted for their ability to sing coloratura (bright florid) passagework. Soubrette roles include Despina in *Così fan tutte*, Nanetta in *Falstaff*, Norina in *Don Pasquale*, and Adina in *L'elisir d'amore*.

DRAMATIC SOPRANO

Such singers possess powerful, energetic voices as well as the dramatic ability to perform roles ranging from Verdi to Wagner. Classic dramatic soprano parts include Lady Macbeth in *Macbeth*, Abigaille in *Nabucco*, Brünnhilde in *The Ring Cycle*, Isolde in *Tristan und Isolde*, and Leonore in *Fidelio*.

MEZZO-SOPRANO (FR., MEZZO-SOPRANO, BAS-DESSUS; GER., MEZZOSOPRAN, TIEFER SOPRAN)

The mezzo lies between the soprano and contralto ranges. As noted previously, most of the roles for soprano created before the late eighteenth century would actually have been deemed for mezzos today; when composers began demanding that women extend their ranges higher, the distinction between the two voices became more apparent. Mezzos were often employed in "breeches parts," filling the need for the high-voiced hero after castratos quit the operatic stage. This mid-range voice became more dramatically important when Verdi employed it for weighty roles such as Princess Eboli in *Don Carlos*, Azucena in *Il trovatore* and Amneris in *Aida*. In the German tradition, mezzo roles include Fricka in *The Ring*, Octavian in *Der Rosenkavalier*, and Brangäne in *Tristan und Isolde*. Perhaps the most famous mezzo role in the operatic repertory belongs to the French tradition: Carmen. Important, too, in French opera is the role of Fidès in *Le prophète*. Despite the slight difference in range, it is not uncommon for mezzos and dramatic sopranos to share the same roles since both voices have a rich, weighty tone.

CONTRALTO (FR., ALTO; GER., ALT)

Used now to designate the lowest female range, the term "contralto" once applied to castratos, who had a comparable vocal compass. Although significant roles have been written for women in this range, it is difficult to find one that is a romantic lead, making the Rossini roles Cenerentola and Rosina, composed for his friend Geltrude Giorgi-Righetti, quite rare. Composers have created contralto leads, however, as did Britten in *The Rape of Lucretia* and Menotti in *The Medium*; generally, however, they were cast as nursemaids or older women. Until the mid-eighteenth century, the range was exploited in comic opera until composers saw the humor in pairing an older man (stereotypically a comic bass) with a younger girl (a soprano)—such as Uberto and Serpina in *La serva padrona* and later Pasquale and "Sofronia" in *Don Pasquale*. Verdi returned the lower female voice to comedy with Mistress Quickley in *Falstaff*.

Contralto parts include Arsace in *Semiramide*, Margret in *Wozzeck*, Sonetka in *Lady Macbeth of the Mtsensk District*, the Princess in *Suor Angelica*, Olga in *Yevgeny Onegin*, and Erda in *The Ring*.

Mezzos whose ranges extend low enough can perform many of the roles written for contraltos. Some even performed "breeches" roles, as did Walt Whitman's favorite singer, Marietta Alboni, who sang the role of Don Carlo in *Ernani*.

COUNTERTENOR

When the casting of castratos fell out of fashion in the early nineteenth century, roles for the high male *tessitura* were assigned either to women ("breeches" roles) or tenors. In the mid-twentieth century, the countertenor, a voice type generally associated with early polyphonic vocal music, supplied another possibility for revivals of these older works. With a compass that overlaps the high extremes of the tenor range and can match those of contraltos and mezzos, the countertenor offered this solution, inspiring the revival of seventeenth- and eighteenth-century operas as well as the creation of new roles such as Apollo in *Death in Venice* and the title role in *Akhnaten*. Countertenors also have participated widely in "early music" performances of operas by Purcell, Lully, and Handel; these productions strive for "authenticity," attempting to replicate the manner in which early operas would have been staged and heard.

Because French audiences found castratos intolerable in stage works, early operas in France feature roles for *haute-contres*, or high tenors, such as Renaud in Lully's *Armide* and the title role in Rameau's *Dardanus*. Some scholars had originally speculated that these men may have been singing *falsetto*, a technique using the "head" voice to produce an artificially high range; when imitating women's voices, for instance, men generally sing *falsetto*. The resulting sound is softer than the full-bodied volume needed for stage singing, though, so current opinion holds that these men's voices were simply unusually high.

CASTRATO (PL., CASTRATOS, CASTRATI)

Historically, women were not permitted to sing in churches (save for convent choirs). Nevertheless, there was a need for voices to perform the soprano or uppermost lines in polyphonic religious music. Boys were generally used to sing these parts, and if a child had a particularly good voice, one worth saving, he would be castrated before his voice "broke." Although this practice was most common in Italy, castratos were employed in church and private musical establishments throughout much of Europe. Educated in the church music schools, they were excellent musicians and prized performers. When noble patrons needed singers for private performances of operas and cantatas, they often turned to church *schole* to borrow or employ castratos; thus, these singers made an easy entrance into the world of opera. Furthermore, as highly trained musicians, many of them (including the previously mentioned Tosi and Mancini) became vocal pedagogues, writing treatises and teaching the first generation of opera singers. Because castratos could have significant success as performers (as did the most famous castrato of all, Farinelli), many parents secretly submitted their sons to the operation in hopes of securing them good futures. Composers employed castratos for the heroic leading roles now associated with tenors. The last castrato role was composed for Giovanni Battista Velluti in the late 1820s, but recordings made in the early 1900s of castrato Alessandro Moreschi document the vocal range. Moreschi was trained for the Sistine Choir and not the stage, however, and his voice should not be considered a good example of how his predecessors must have sounded.

TENOR (IT., TENORE; FR., TÉNOR; GER., TENOR)

Tenors share with sopranos the prestige accorded singers who perform operatic leads. Originally, tenors were assigned the most important line in early polyphonic works. Because the other vocal lines were composed against the tenor (from the Latin "tenere," to hold), it literally held the piece together harmonically. Even early operas recognized the importance of the tenor voice; the roles of Orfeo in both *Euridice* and *Orfeo* were sung by tenors. By the end of the seventeenth century, though, the heroic leads went to castratos, perhaps because they were exceedingly well-trained musicians. It may also have been that the castrato *tessitura*, virtually overlapping that of the female lead, may have been considered more aesthetically pleasing to audiences. Even in France, which generally shunned castratos, leading roles went to *haute-contres*.

By the end of the eighteenth century, tenors were considered more seriously. Mozart alone left a rich legacy for these singers in the roles of Belmonte in *Die Entführung aus dem Serail*, Don Ottavio in *Don Giovanni*, Ferrando in *Così fan tutte*, and Tamino in *Die Zauberflöte*. Their "golden age," just a few decades away, would arrive when the castratos retired from the operatic stage.

Many of the most significant tenor roles come from the nineteenth century repertory; Almaviva in *Il barbiere di Siviglia*, Pollione in *Norma*, Edgardo in *Lucia di Lammermoor*, Alfredo in *La traviata*, the Duke in *Rigoletto*, Manrico in *Il trovatore*, Ernani, Otello, Radames in *Aida*, and Rodolfo in *La bohème* are just a very few from the Italian tradition. In France, tenor roles include Arnold in *Guillaume Tell*, Raoul in *Les Huguenots*, Robert in *Robert le diable*, Nadir in *Les pêcheurs de perles*, Romeo in *Romeo et Juliette*, Werther, and Faust. Beethoven wrote Florestan in *Fidelio* as a tenor; other roles in the German tradition include Max in *Der Freischütz* and Alfonso in *Alfonso und Estrella*. Tenors in Wagner include Siegfried in the *Ring Cycle*, Tristan, Cola Rienzi in *Rienzi*, Tannhäuser, and Lohengrin; always one to break the Italo-Franco bonds, Wagner used tenors for the character parts of Mime and Loge in *The Ring*. Other roles include Lensky in *Yevgeny Onegin*, Grigory in *Boris Godunov*, and both Laca and Steva in *Jenůfa*. The tenor's continued significance is reflected in twentieth-century works: Cavaradossi in *Tosca*, Pinkerton in *Madama Butterfly*, Calaf in *Turandot*, Peter Grimes, Captain Vere in *Billy Budd*, Lennie in *Of Mice and Men*, and Mitch in *A Streetcar Named Desire*.

Although the so-called *bel canto* repertory offered spectacular opportunities for tenors, the works therein presented interesting challenges. Generally, arias included climactic high notes that were simply too high for some singers. One option was to transpose pieces down to a more reasonable key; this, however, creates new problems because the musical sections going from the transposed number to the following piece no longer merge tonally. Thus the subsequent number must be transposed as well or a new musical transition must be composed. The simplest solution, of course, is to cut the offending aria, but this action can have ramifications for the plot. Another option, much to many a soprano's delight, was to have *her* perform the tenor's aria, thus giving her more music. Although some tenors acquiesced, others trained to extend their ranges. As a result, today's tenors amaze audiences with their abilities to take high notes with power and ease. Thus audiences come to hear such pyrotechnics and (often quite vocally) demonstrate their annoyance if a tenor has a bad night. Such expectations are compounded by recordings of "perfect" performances that have benefited from extensive editing in a sound studio.

How then did nineteenth-century tenors sing these roles? Briefly, no one is really sure. Bearing in mind that theaters were somewhat smaller and the instruments of the orchestra could not produce the dynamics they can today, singers simply did not need to sing as loudly. Hence, some of their high notes may well have been sung with the "head" voice or even falsetto. One famed nineteenth-century singer, Gilbert Duprez, is said to have been able to hit a c″ (one octave above Middle C) using his "chest" voice; in theory, this *should* have sounded much like the same note as performed by one of today's great tenors. From Rossini's description, however, the result was exceedingly unpleasant and unnatural.

Dramatically, nineteenth-century tenors' roles generally demanded serious acting ability. Also, their characters generally survived until the end of the opera, whereas their soprano counterparts were either killed or committed suicide before the final curtain. This perceived brutality against women has spurred lively discussion in twentieth-century feminist scholarship.

LYRIC TENOR (IT., TENORE LIRICO; FR., TÉNOR LYRIQUE; GER., LIRISCHER TENOR)

These singers have lighter voices suited for highlighting melodies. Many of the so-called *bel canto* roles such as Lindoro in *Il barbiere* and Ernesto in *Don Pasquale* are suited to these voices. These tenors generally can perform ably in the highest extreme of the range.

TENORE DI FORZA (FR., FORT-TENOR)

With energetic and powerful voices, these tenors fare well in the dramatic roles of the nineteenth-century, such as Edgardo in *Lucia di Lammermoor*, Raoul in *Les Huguenots*, and Don José in *Carmen*.

HELDENTENOR (IT., TENORE ROBUSTO)

This dramatic tenor voice generally is associated with Wagnerian roles, but, with its rich, almost baritonal register, it is equally suited for powerful Verdian roles such as Manrico in *Il trovatore* and Alfredo in *La traviata*. The *Heldentenor* performs with notable energy and endurance.

BARITONE (IT., BARITONO; FR., BARYTON; GER., BARITON)

Although use of the term "baritone" to describe the mid-range of men's vocal ranges was employed in sacred music of the late Middle Ages, it was not identified as an operatic range until the nineteenth century. Before that, roles only bore the assignations "tenor" and "bass." Yet some seventeenth- and eighteenth-century characters definitely are placed within the baritonal compass, among these Aeneas in *Dido and Aeneas*, Guglielmo in *Così fan tutte*, Don Giovanni, and Figaro (who remains a baritone in his incarnation in Rossini's *Il barbiere di Siviglia*). French composers included this mid-range in roles designated *basse-taille*.

Nineteenth-century composers began to cast baritones as comrades or rivals for their tenor leads, thus allowing the possibility of male duets. One of the most inspired of these, "Au fond du temple saint" from *Les pêcheurs de perles*, is a standard in recital repertory as it features both the melodic and harmonic possibilities of this vocal pairing. The composer to whom baritones are most grateful, however, is Verdi, who wrote a succession of dramatically powerful parts, inspiring the designation "Verdi baritone." Among these are Rodrigue in *Don Carlos*, Luna in *Il trovatore*, Germont in *La traviata*, and Iago in *Otello*. Verdi also placed baritones in leading roles such as Nabucodonosor in *Nabucco*, Rigoletto, and Falstaff; he continued the tradition of envisioning tenors as romantic heroes, however. Donizetti employed the baritone, Malatesta, as Don Pasquale's "straight man" and as the traditional tenor rival, Belcore in *L'elisir d'amore*. Puccini used a baritone as a comic lead in *Gianni Schicchi*; other Puccini baritones include Marcello in *La bohème*, Sharpless in *Madama Butterfly* and, clearly in the villainous tradition of Iago, Scarpia in *Tosca*.

Wagner wrote both Wolfram in *Tannhäuser* and Friedrich in *Lohengrin* for baritones, but the designation "bass-baritone" or *Hoher Bass* (higher bass) best describes Wotan, Alberich, and Fasolt in the *Ring*, the Dutchman in *Der fliegende Holländer*, and Hans Sachs in *Die Meistersinger*. In the French tradition, Thomas' *opéra* entitled *Hamlet* employs a baritone for the lead role. With their penchant for lower voices, Russian operas are rife with roles for both baritones and bass-baritones, among these Onegin, Boris in *Lady Macbeth of the Mtsensk District* (high bass), Boris Godunov, and Tomsky and Yeletsky in *Pique Dame*.

As is generally the case, singers with broad compasses often perform roles designated for either a higher or lower range: both tenor Plácido Domingo and bass Samuel Ramey have performed Figaro in *Il barbiere di Siviglia*, for instance. The same is true of the role Don Giovanni; although it has attracted star performers throughout the twentieth century, it was composed for a man who supposedly was barely an adequate singer. Hence, Giovanni's music is less difficult (and less interesting) than Leporello's or Ottavio's.

BASS (IT., BASSO; FR., BASSE; GER., BASS)

Just as sopranos and tenors have been associated with certain parts, basses have accumulated an array of character types; because the lowest male has depicted age and authority, basses are rulers (the Egyptian king in *Aida* and Timur in *Turandot*), fathers (Oroveso in *Norma* and Melcthal in *Guillaume Tell*), gods (Pluto in *Orfeo* and Jupiter in *La Calisto*), spirits and ghosts (Ninus in *Semiramide* and the Commendatore in *Don Giovanni*), and wise men and priests (Seneca in *L'incoronazione di Poppea* and Sarastro in *Die Zauberflöte*). Others have exploited the comic elements of the bass, creating such memorable *buffo* roles as Don Pasquale, Osmin in *Die Entführung aus dem Serail*, Dr. Bartolo and Don Basilio in *Il barbiere di Siviglia*, and Uberto in *La serva padrona*. The dark tones of the range also suggest evil; hence, the Devil is often a bass role, as in *Faust* and *Mefistofele*.

Wagnerian basses are Hagen and Fafner in *The Ring*, King Mark in *Tristan und Isolde*, Heinrich der Vogler in *Lohengrin*, and no less than eight characters in *Der Meistersinger*, just one less than the number of basses in *Lady Macbeth of the Mtsensk District* in the Russian repertory. The Russian predilection for the low voice most likely comes from religious music that features the so-called "octavo bass" whose range reaches a full octave below that of the normal bass. No "octavo" roles appear in opera, however, for it is only possible to chant or sustain such low tones.

Those moments in opera that feature the harmonies of the higher voices are among the most esteemed, but composers also have exploited the beauties of lower ranges as well, as Mozart did by writing a trio for Don Giovanni, Leporello, and the Commendatore as the latter lies dying (Act I). Donizetti did likewise by matching the voices of Pasquale and Dr. Malatesta in the comic duet "Cheti, cheti immantenente" in Act III of *Don Pasquale*.

BASSO BUFFO

Rather than describing a part of the bass range, this term refers to the singers adept at comic Italian roles such as Bartolo in both *Le nozze di Figaro* and *Il barbiere di Siviglia*, Don Pasquale, and Dulcamara in *L'elisir d'amore*. These men excel at techniques like rapid *parlante* ("patter") delivery in which the words are almost spoken rather than sung. Although the same singers may demonstrate lyric ability in serious roles, they downplay this talent in *buffo* parts because the intent is to exploit comic effects (such as making their voices "crack," stutter, or produce a purposefully nasal tone.)

BASSO CANTANTE (FR., BASSE CHANTANTE)

Roles for the so-called "singing" bass lie in the upper end of the range; overlapping the low baritone, these lyrical parts include Escamillo in *Carmen*, Raimondo in *Lucia*, and Gualtiero and Giorgio in *I puritani*.

BASSO PROFONDO (FR., BASSE NOBLE)

The resonant quality of the bass voice often suggests this description. The term describes basses with powerful, rich tones and low range extension (Sarastro in *Die Zauberflöte* and Oroveso in *Norma*). Voices of such depth and strength are referred to in the German tradition as "black basses."

PRIMA DONNA (FEM.), PRIMO UOMO (MASC.)

These singers perform the leading roles in an opera. Employed first in the eighteenth century, the phrase applied to the lead performer in a serious work. Comic leads in turn were referred to as the *prima buffa* and *primo buffo*; because the latter was generally a bass, the term *basso buffo* became a designation in its own right. The term's current connotation derives from the egos that leading ladies tended to cultivate; thus, *prima donna* now implies vanity and self-entitlement.

Singers in supporting leads were known as the *seconda donna* and *secondo uomo*.

COMPRIMARIO, COMPRIMARIA

A singer in a secondary role who was given an aria or part in a large ensemble was known as a *comprimario*. Examples include Monostatos in *Die Zauberflöte* and Giannetta in *L'elisir d'amore*.

FINAL THOUGHTS

Composers often wrote roles for whatever singers were associated with the theaters giving them a commission. Many characters and their music, however, were crafted for specific voices. Mozart, for instance, composed the Queen of the Night for his sister-in-law Josefa Hofer, and most of Rossini's great Italian heroines were written for his first wife, Isabella Colbran. Their arias are as much a witness to these historic singers' talents as are the recordings made by singers such as Luisa Tetrazzini and Enrico Caruso in the early twentieth century.

By the mid-nineteenth century, theaters began to produce older works and a true repertory of operas was formed. Singers then were required to perform a variety of roles that had been created to suit the voices of others. In the early days of opera, if an opera's music did not suit their voices, *divas* (and *divos*) would simply substitute a number from one of their previous successes. Because singers would travel with these pieces, they came to be called "trunk arias." As theater administrations took more control of productions, such "surprises" grew less frequent. Today, singers are required to perform a wide spectrum of roles. Only when (and *if*) they themselves become professional "legends" can they dictate what they will sing.

6

OPERA ONSTAGE AND OFF

Obviously, the best way to experience opera is in a theater, where one is treated to a sensory explosion of sights and sounds. It has not always been possible to attend in person, however. Class was a major barrier until the nineteenth century when social and political revolution made theaters accessible to everyone. Economics has been (and remains) a factor; the cost of the materials and the number of personnel—including major stars—required to produce this opulent art form sets ticket prices at a premium. Fortunately, opera—or at the very least its music—has been made available in a variety of media. In fact, opera has proven itself as adaptable to technological developments as it has to cultural and aesthetic change.

This chapter briefly examines opera's history onstage and then traces its appearance in other guises from the nineteenth-century salon into twenty-first century cyberspace.

OPERA ONSTAGE

During the Renaissance, musical entertainment at courts generally needed little more than a hall large enough to accommodate the performers and the audience. By the end of the sixteenth century, the "marvels" in scenes of more elaborate productions such as the *intermedio* (see Chapter 1) required special technology like levers and winches, so performances were moved into theaters where this equipment was already available and in use for spoken dramas. Stage machinery then became a requisite support for the plots of the earliest operas, especially when hapless humans needed to be saved by gods descending from the heavens in chariots or rising from the depths of the Underworld: the famed *deus ex machina* of classical drama. All of the machines that created these illusions could be placed out of sight (but not always out of earshot) above and below the stage or behind scenic backdrops. When operas developed into full-scale dramatic structures with acts and scenes, other scenic devices were borrowed from the spoken stage; for example, painted panels positioned in the wings could be rolled onstage whenever the plot demanded a scene change. Although this technology pales in comparison to what today's operagoers see when the curtain rises, contemporary accounts confirm that opera's scenographic origins were anything but humble.

THE THEATER PROPER

With designs based on existing theaters, the first opera houses featured stages framed by a proscenium arch, thus physically separating the performance space from the audience. The instrumental ensemble was positioned directly in front of the stage on the ground floor, or *parterre*, but the rest of the floor space was left open so, if necessary, it could be used for elaborate battle scenes or ballets. The audience occupied boxes that fanned out from each side of the stage, with small theaters having as few as three tiers of boxes and larger houses as many as six.

The actual assignment of boxes reflected a rigid class system. Boxes directly facing the stage on the first tier (or the second in some houses) were reserved for nobles and important members of court; consequently, they had the best view of the stage. (Although real nobles had been replaced by "barons" of industry, photographs of the famed "Golden Horseshoe" at the old Metropolitan Opera House demonstrate this configuration.) The nearer one's box was to the stage, the less desirable the view; in fact, those directly next to the proscenium arch could see the full stage only by leaning out precariously over the edge. Similarly, the higher the tier, the poorer the view. Audience members could always see each other, however, and, as social historians have noted, this was perhaps the single most important reason why many subscribers went to the theater—although audiences in northern Germany were reportedly more attentive during performances than those in southern climes (see Chapter 7).

Initially, all of the boxes were held by the aristocracy: the poorest in the top tiers and the wealthiest or most significant in the lower tiers. If the theater was located in a city that had a royal family or reigning noble, the centermost box of the first tier, specially decorated with a coat of arms or symbols of state, would be reserved exclusively for their use; noble offspring or siblings with their own households often would have separate boxes immediately alongside. During the eighteenth and early nineteenth centuries, if rulers were to be in attendance, the performance could not start until they were in their seats, nor could there be applause unless they initiated it. Because these boxes were placed so prominently, they were even more conspicuous when empty, suggesting royal displeasure or disinterest.

In the eighteenth century, the *parterre*, originally left open, was fitted with additional seating; occupants of this area were usually students, soldiers, tourists, and servants with some household status (the lowliest ones were busy serving their masters in the boxes). At the same time, the theater's instrumental ensemble was evolving into the modern orchestra with strings, winds, percussion, and one or two keyboards to accompany recitative. (The French, of course, had the equivalent of an orchestra since the time of Lully; see Chapter 8.) Patrons seated in the front rows often complained because tall instruments such as double basses obstructed their view of the stage. Therefore, when new theaters were built or older ones refurbished, the orchestra was moved into an area, aptly called the pit, below the *parterre* and slightly under the stage. Yet the orchestra still remained prominently between the stage and the audience, a problem Wagner would address in his design of the *Festspielhaus* in Bayreuth (see later in this chapter).

After the revolutionary upsets all over Europe in the nineteenth century, boxes became available to members of the middle class who, eager to raise their social status, replaced impoverished aristocrats. Also, theaters encouraged the sale of individual tickets to a more general public by decreasing the number of boxes and opening up the top two tiers to create galleries with cheap seats. Even though the era saw the demise of the aristocratic system that had dictated theater construction, an element of economic superiority remained, because "good" seats still only went to those who could afford them. Linking these theater designs to the Italian and French traditions against which he was rebelling, Wagner conceived a more democratic plan for his *Festspielhaus* at Bayreuth.

Richard Wagner wanted audiences to understand his works and to have their performances be thought-provoking experiences. Traditional theaters did not permit everyone to have an equally good view of the stage, so he decided to design a special theater. Because the building would be a monument to a new German art form, he sought a town that had no strong ties to the Italian and French operatic traditions. Not only did Bayreuth fulfill his requirements but—realizing that Wagner's promise of packed houses would be bonanza for the local economy—local authorities generously donated the land. Assured of success and support, Wagner laid the cornerstone on 22 May 1872, his fifty-ninth birthday.

Wagner based his design on the theaters of ancient Greece so the seats in the *Festspielhaus* fan out as they would in an amphitheater; thus, everyone in the audience could see and hear well. Wagner kept the proscenium arch around the stage, though, but made it slightly wider and thicker to create the illusion that his characters were as large as the heroic giants of Teutonic mythology they represented. Perhaps the theater's most ingenious effect was its acoustic design. The orchestra was placed underneath the stage, further hidden by a shell-like cover. The sound of the instruments would travel up out of the pit and bounce off the curve of this cover back toward the singers onstage; then, the combined sound of the orchestra and voices would travel unimpeded into the auditorium. Placing the orchestra out of sight ensured that its presence would never distract the audience from their involvement with the drama.

Unfortunately, the cost of building the *Festspielhaus* left Wagner in significant debt, so he was never able to produce the thriving seasons he had envisioned in the project's planning stages. His dream has been realized posthumously, however; every year, Bayreuth attracts thousands of visitors who come to experience Wagner's works at the venue he created for their performance.

Throughout the nineteenth century, theaters lost their connection with courts and became the province of the middle class. In addition to removing many of the barriers inherent in the old social order, theater designers began to cater to a new literate body of consumers who came to see performances rather than be seen at them. Many theaters adopted the more democratic arena-style design of Wagner's *Festspielhaus*, whereas others removed proscenium arches, thereby eliminating the physical and psychological barriers between the stage action and the audience. One of the most significant advancements was in lighting. As the century progressed, chandeliers were exchanged for gaslights and finally for electric lighting, allowing the audiences (and the performers) to see better. First used for stage lights in the 1860s, electricity was employed to illuminate all areas of theaters within twenty years.

The twentieth century saw experimentation with opera in the round and performances in outdoor arenas (some performances have actually been held in Greek theaters in the south of Italy). Scheduled after sunset, these productions provide an enjoyable ambience, as long as the weather cooperates and the wind carries the sound of the voices toward the audience. Boom years for the arts in the 1960s saw the construction of many new houses, some so large that activities on stage are televised on screens around the theater for those too far away to see. In Europe, many communities have engaged private and public funds to refurbish eighteenth-century houses that allow audiences to experience opera as it once was. "Live" opera continues to adapt to its surroundings.

"ACTING" OPERA

Histories of the opera singer generally concentrate on the voice (see Chapter 5). It is also enlightening to consider the singer as actor, for these performers often were critiqued for how well they portrayed their roles. Commentaries of the earliest court entertainment demonstrate that good singers acted as well by gesturing to emphasize the text and using facial expressions to depict emotions and passions. There is every reason to believe that audiences judged singers as actors as well during the seventeenth and early eighteenth centuries. Italian singers were often left to their own devices, but, in France, Lully took personal charge of coaching his singers' every move. Although he wanted to ensure that the King was pleased with his productions, he also wanted to make certain that his operas could compete with the drama of the spoken stage. Certainly, the singer-actor was more interesting to watch and could better command an audience's attention. Not long into the eighteenth century, however, for a variety of musical reasons (not the least of which were the egos of the singers themselves), virtuosity became more important than declamation or dramatic interpretation. In France, when critics bemoaned the decline in acting after the death of Lully, Rameau is reported to have commented that his music required singers, not actors.

Meanwhile, in Italy, the musical patterns dictated by *opera seria*'s librettos (see Chapter 3) had a direct effect on stage direction. Because the action was broken up into distinct scenes, singers simply had to enter and sing their recitatives; one of them would then get an aria, after which his or her character had to leave the stage (hence, the term "exit aria"). The entrance of a new character signaled the beginning of a new scene and the pattern began anew. Dramatic interpretations of arias were simple and stereotypical; the singer would move downstage (the area closest to the orchestra) and perform facing the audience. Generally, the acoustics were best downstage, so audiences (if they were paying attention) would have the best chance of hearing the aria. On a more practical level, eighteenth-century instruments had little volume and sustaining power, so it was easiest for the singer to come downstage to hear the orchestra (or someone who could give the occasional cue, especially necessary if he or she were singing a piece that had been composed just days before). Little movement was necessary; during instrumental *ritornellos*, a singer might move a step or two in one direction but walking about the stage was considered bad form. If other singers were onstage, they were expected to stand as still as stage props (movement, of course, was always a wonderful way to attract attention away from one's rival downstage—hence the meaning of "upstaging" someone). It was also safer for singers to exit from downstage; because the lighting was better there, they were less likely to collide with the sliding scenery flats in the wings.

Opera seria required little acting. Because characters represented nobles, singers simply had to comport themselves as their patrons did. Furthermore, because every opera presented singers with arias that expressed the exact same set of emotions, they simply reproduced pat expressions and gestures while substituting one text for another. Far more important than acting, singers tried to control their bodies during difficult passages of virtuosic embellishment such as those they were expected to perform during *da capo* returns (see Chapter 2). The desired impression was that such vocal pyrotechnics came absolutely naturally and required no effort at all.

By the late eighteenth century, stage directions were often the province of a *corago*, a stage manager of sorts who, among other things, ensured that the singers went on at the right moment and did not collide with sets or with each other as they entered and exited the stage. By the nineteenth century, librettos contained more and more stage directions, so there was greater need to control the movements of the singers. At times, the librettist, particularly if he were employed by the theater, would be tasked with stage direction (see Chapter 4). By mid-century, the French had developed the *mise-en-scène*, a production book filled with detailed instructions on how a particular opera should be produced. These were compiled at first for operas that were to be taken into provincial French cities, but eventually they were found so useful that they were sent along with productions taken outside of France as well. The concept of a production book was quickly adopted by both the Germans and Italians (see Chapter 4). Although these directions dictated what happened onstage, they did little to control individual singers' acting, however.

Ironically, one of the biggest influences on acting in serious opera came from the comic stage. Because *opera buffa* and its corresponding genres in France dealt with real-life characters (and also because comic performers were often less talented singers than they were comic actors), these singers' stage style was more flexible and natural. Furthermore, in the multisectional finales popular in comic works, the usual chaotic chain of events required characters to interact with each other (see Chapter 9). As the chain finale was adopted into serious works, character interaction became essential to the dramatic climax of an act. Still, it took an unusually involved composer to achieve dramatic results. Wagner coached his singers to interact by exhorting them to react to each other; Verdi, too, drilled his singers. The hardest lesson was to get the singer to forget the audience.

It is, of course, unfair to stereotype all singers as disinterested in acting. Many performers in the nineteenth century had stellar reputations as dramatic interpreters. Nevertheless, by the end of the nineteenth century, many others were still relying on the stock gestures they had learned from their teachers; ironically, these very moves made opera singers perfect candidates for the silent film screen. The world of the singer changed radically in the twentieth century; whereas their nineteenth-century predecessors had often refused to rehearse for new productions once they had played a role, with competition and declining audiences it became increasingly necessary for singers to act as professionals and not *divi*. Today, students who plan careers in opera are expected to study various methods of acting; if they cannot bring opera's characters to life, they generally spend their professional lives in the chorus.

THE ROLE OF THE CHORUS

Some singers have had distinguished careers in the spotlights, but others have remained upstage, fleshing out crowd scenes and adding vocal strength to special dramatic or comedic moments in opera. Choruses have played an important part in French opera from the time of Lully. Entering from both sides of the stage and processing to a U-shaped formation behind the singers, the chorus would dazzle in their spectacular costumes. Once onstage, they stood stock-still behind the principal singers, only to move again when it was time for their exit. Chorus members in nineteenth-century *grand opéras*, however, were encouraged to react to each other and to the action onstage, making them individual characters in whatever community the work depicted.

In Italy, choruses were employed for early operas, but *opera seria* librettos concentrated primarily on recitative and aria; only at the end of a work would a chorus be included. The adoption of the chain finale at the end of the eighteenth century allowed for greater use of the chorus. By the following century, operas generally opened with all or part of the chorus onstage to perform the *introduzione* with one of the characters (see Chapter 2).

Composers further made use of the chorus musically by weaving it into solo numbers; Norma's opening aria, "Casta diva" is enriched by the lush harmonies provided by the chorus at its midpoint. Although parts for choruses were included in operas well into the twentieth century, they are no longer the requisite parts of scores that they once were. Composers now determine whether choral intervention is dramatically necessary (or economically feasible).

OPERA AND ART

Literature and the dramatic stage furnished opera with some of its most popular subjects. Similarly, the world of art lent its genius when the prevailing styles of the day found their reflection in set design. For example, the elaborate sets for early Florentine court productions came from the workshops of that city's most famous artists. The spectacle and set designs for which Venetian opera came to be famous in the seventeenth century reflected that city's ornate architecture and festive pomp. Even the sliding sets that featured stock scenes of temples and gardens used as backdrops for *opere serie* were representations of the Baroque and Neoclassical buildings that housed opera's subscribers and patrons.

In the nineteenth century, sets moved away from courtly scenes to depict landscapes, mirroring contemporary art and literature's concern for the conflict between humans and Nature. Later in the century, the urge to depict and experience the exotic balanced with the harsh realities of *verismo* dictated the design of sets. In fact, when rolling flats that would serve from one opera to the next ceased to be useful, set design was entrusted to workshops that specialized in creating scenery for specific productions. In time, all of the artistic schools of the day found their way into twentieth-century set design, among them Expressionism, Futurism, Cubism, and Minimalism. Artists who have lent their names to opera designs include Utrillo, Picasso, Matisse, Gropius, Kandinsky, Dalí, and Chagall.

A reaction to the abstract sets of the second half of the twentieth century were the neo-historical designs used by directors such as Franco Zefferelli in the 1990s. These sets reproduce even the most minute detail of the venue and period in which a given production is placed. Zefferelli's recent version of *I pagliacci* serves as an example. The set recreated a neighborhood of high-rise apartments in Naples, complete with laundry-draped clotheslines and functioning televisions visible inside the apartments. No matter when an opera was composed, directors like Zefferelli can attempt to add a new dimension to a work by taking it out of its usual context and placing it in different surroundings. One may disagree with Peter Sellars' placing *Don Giovanni* in a drug-infested slum, but seeing repertory works out of their traditional garb gives their characters an entirely new dimension.

OPERA IN THE SALON AND THE PARLOR

When members of the merchant class became wealthy enough to enter "society," they began to emulate the training and behavior of the aristocracy. One lesson they learned was that a knowledge of music was critical to their social survival. Owning a musical instrument (generally a keyboard) and learning to play it meant that one could participate in salon soirees in which the guests took turns at the host's pianoforte. These new upwardly mobile audiences also were willing to purchase the opera subscriptions that many nobles no longer could afford, thereby gaining entry into a cultural world that had previously been denied to them. The ability to play and sing as well as a familiarity with the latest operas made these consumers eager customers for some of the most popular music publications of the nineteenth century: piano-vocal arrangements of opera scores (see Chapter 11).

Music publishers marketed piano-vocal reductions of operas just as recording companies in time would promote operas on records and compact discs. Audiences could take the music home to experience it after seeing the performance—or in lieu of seeing it, were attendance impossible. Some of these scores required superior musical ability, but given the importance of nurturing music as a social skill, amateurs had a greater need to practice and were probably able to negotiate the music rather well. For those who sang but not in the opera's original language, translations were generally set just below the original text, even though these versions often distorted the original meaning (see Chapter 3). In addition to books with arrangements of entire operas, including their overtures and choruses, individual arias were available for purchase. Amateurs could also obtain instrumental arrangements of operatic numbers scored so that a flute or violin took the melody line as the piano played the accompaniment. Those extremely fleet of finger could always attempt Franz Liszt's piano paraphrases of operas, virtuosic arrangements that virtually replicate all elements of the original number. One particularly awe-inspiring example of these pieces is Liszt's adaptation of the quartet "Bella figlia dell'amore" from *Rigoletto*.

Simply owning piano-vocal arrangements had social and cultural significance. In many cases, it was probably enough just to leave the score of the very latest opera on top of the piano to send visitors the message that one's family was culturally abreast. Moreover, as many operas passed into the common repertory, their piano-vocal renderings gained renewed significance. The sheer number of opera piano-vocal scores published demonstrates their popularity and importance, and the number that remain extant in libraries, private collections, and antiquarian bookstores suggests that these were cared for by their original owners and passed down as family treasures from one generation to another.

OPERA ON MECHANICAL INSTRUMENTS

Contemporary with the popularity of opera on the household pianoforte, another salon (or parlor) instrument contributed to the diffusion of opera outside of the theater: the musical box. Erroneously dismissed as gadgets, the mechanical boxes constructed in Europe and in America from the nineteenth through the turn of the twentieth century were instruments of superior quality constructed with sturdy soundboards, resonant cases, and tuned combs that accurately produced melodies and complex harmonies. Although early boxes had poor tone quality, advances made through the nineteenth century resulted in machines that could produce as complex a selection as the entire Intermezzo from *Cavalleria rusticana*, true to the original note for note.

The earliest boxes played when a cylinder designed with protruding pins struck the appropriate teeth on a tuned comb. One of the first technical advances of the nineteenth century was inspired by opera: the overture box. Makers constructed longer, thicker cylinders that could accommodate an entire overture or an abridged version of its major sections. Encouraged by the success of these instruments, makers attempted to recreate specific orchestral effects such as strumming. Some boxes included small novelty percussion devices; one instrument played a rousing version of the march from the Act I finale of *Nabucco*, complete with drum rolls and cymbals.

By enlarging the box casings, makers could install longer cylinders that accommodated multiple selections. The next advance was the interchangeable cylinder; some boxes came with as many as six cylinders, offering consumers seventy-two "tunes," as music box selections are called. One of the last developments in the mechanical box industry was the creation of the disk box. Because pinned copper disks were easy to press and inexpensive to sell, manufacturers' catalogues could feature hundreds of selections. These instruments were made with such craftsmanship that those that were not mistreated or stored improperly still play beautifully today.

A survey of tune sheets—repertory labels pasted on cylinder boxes—and disk catalogues demonstrates that opera was one of the most popular genres programmed on mechanical instruments. Verdi's operas, especially *Il trovatore* and *La traviata*, were the overall favorites, followed by Rossini's *Guillaume Tell*. Other composers whose works were made available include Donizetti, Bellini, Gounod, Meyerbeer, and Lecocq (see Chapter 9). Wagner's *Lohengrin* and *Tannhäuser* provided tunes; numbers from the *Ring*, however, were too difficult to extract from their musical contexts. An opera's appearance in the cylinder repertory but its absence in the later disk catalogues suggests that it had fallen out of fashion by the turn of the century; a strong showing of composers and works on both cylinder and disk indicates continued popularity.

In the early twentieth century, an inventor approached one of the most successful musical box manufacturers in the United States and demonstrated a machine that played a disk that reproduced actual musical sounds, not a mechanical interpretation of them. Content with the successful musical box trade, makers foolishly turned him down; his invention, one of the earliest versions of sound recording, put them out of business within a decade.

OPERA RECORDINGS

Although musical boxes offered listeners incredibly accurate melodic and harmonic renderings of operatic selections, they could not produce its most crucial component: the sound of the voice. The gramophone (or Victrola, as it would come to be called by the Victor Company) promised virtual performances in one's home; indeed, that is how the technology was first marketed. Families were pictured in the parlor dressed as they would be for the opera; they were surrounded by miniature figures of contemporary opera stars who would entertain them for the evening. In addition to providing musical entertainment, records were touted as cultural education for Americans, whose sense of "good music" was presumed inferior to that of Europeans. This marketing technique often backfired, though, because it made opera seem too exclusive and distant. Even though almost anyone with a Victrola had a recording of Caruso (indeed, these were given away free to anyone who would come into a gramophone showroom), opera was fast becoming the music of the "haves" while popular music belonged to the "have nots." Nevertheless, the presence of opera on early recordings is noteworthy.

The first recordings were acoustic: sound waves were amplified through a horn onto a wax cylinder. When played back, the results were inconsistent, especially when recording the voice; mid-range notes generally were captured but extremely high and low ones often were not. Because cylinders could hold no more than two or three minutes of music, only single arias could be recorded. Also, because voices needed to project directly into the horn, it was difficult to record more than one singer at a time. As poor as some of these acoustic recordings may sound though, they are now recognized as rare and important historic artifacts. Of particular significance are the few recordings of artists who premiered important roles; Victor Maurel, for instance, recorded "Era la notte," which he sang when he premiered the role of Iago in Verdi's *Otello*. Another acoustic recording demonstrates the voice of castrato Alessandro Moreschi; although he performs sacred selections (he never sang opera but was a member of the Sistine Chapel choir), it is possible to hear the range of his voice (see Chapter 5). Digital remastering has improved the quality of many of these acoustic records by isolating and removing "white noise."

Even though complete operas were being recorded in the early 1900s, the cost of producing them (and, for the consumer, of buying all the cylinders—or, by the 1910s, flat disks) was prohibitive. In the 1920s, acoustic recording was abandoned for the new electric technology. This process produced disks that not only accommodated more music but also more accurately captured the sound of the voice. The earliest records were played on turntables supposedly calibrated at seventy-eight revolutions per minute. Initially these machines were handcranked, causing the speed to fluctuate as the record played. Later, electric-powered record players kept consistent speed. After World War II, the advent of the 33 1/3 long-playing record (or LP) made opera even more available and affordable because as few as four or six of these records, sold in an album, could hold a complete opera. Extra space on a record generally garnered a bonus selection.

Most European countries joined America in the production of records. Composers, too, agreed to the recording of their works, and opera stars saw the potential for spreading their fame by making records. Enrico Caruso was one of the most popular recording stars of the early twentieth century, but even though many people owned his records, they had never been (and probably would never choose to go) to an opera. Conductors, too, such as Arturo Toscanini, spread their repute by making opera recordings. Today, of course, it is possible to purchase recordings of operatic selections by one particular artist, entire operas performed live (complete with applause, coughs, and slightly flat or sharp notes), and operas recorded over several days in a studio (edited to include only the best "takes"). Also, repertory works such as *Don Giovanni* and those of Wagner are available in myriad versions; one can select a production by a favorite singer or conductor. Special recordings offer "historical" or "performance practice" versions played on original instruments and sung with vocal techniques appropriate to the period in which the opera was composed.

Because it is safe to assume that performers sing as they were taught, one of the most interesting areas of current opera research is the study of recordings. Historians compare performances of the same role by different singers to determine if their interpretations come from a learned performance tradition passed from singer to singer or if they are unique. The number of early recordings makes this investigation possible as well for the serious enthusiast, but usually this research must be done using digitally remastered reissues. The advent of the compact disc in the 1980s has, in essence, made records redundant and only those who lovingly cared for their stereo systems still have the sound equipment to play them. In fact, people who wish to dispose of large record collections have trouble donating them to schools or libraries because such institutions have updated their listening technology. Today, portability rules, a trend that started with transistor radios and portable tape recorders. Now, iPods and other compact devices allow enthusiasts to listen to opera wherever they go.

OPERA ON RADIO

The advent of radio initially made the record industry wary; while recording companies were trying to sell music to consumers, radio stations were giving it away for free. Radio did indeed offer opera enthusiasts the opportunity to hear entire works that were not available on recordings—often in live broadcasts. For instance, NBC gave its radio listeners a Christmas gift in 1931 by broadcasting *Hänsel und Gretel* live from the Metropolitan Opera. The next day, Acts III and IV of *Norma* were transmitted over the airwaves. Despite their fears of losing sales, record companies soon found that, after the broadcast was over, fans might seek a recording of the work they had just heard so that they could enjoy it again and again. Happily for the recording and broadcast industries, there was room for them both. Live broadcasts, however, could offer listeners something that a recording could not: an announcer's real-time commentary of the plot and stage action. Indeed, voices such as those of Milton Cross and Deems Taylor of the Metropolitan Opera broadcasts became a significant part of an opera fan's radio experience.

Operas were aired regularly throughout the United States and Europe. In 1940, the Texaco Corporation assumed sponsorship of the Saturday Metropolitan Opera broadcasts, an arrangement that lasted until May 2004. Over the years, this program, broadcast weekly from December to May, garnered some ten million listeners in forty-two countries. In many cases, these weekly broadcasts inspired listeners to attend operas in person and have spurred lifelong interests in the genre. Other cities featuring radio opera include Berlin, London, Chicago, Prague, Rome, and Bayreuth, where a broadcast of *Tristan und Isolde* has become an annual event.

In addition to live broadcasts from theaters, radio stations often brought singers into their studios to air what in essence were concert performances of operas; singers would perform into the microphone without acting out the plot. Composers also began to take advantage of the airwaves to premier new works. One of the first American composers to write an opera for radio was Gian Carlo Menotti, whose *The Old Maid and The Thief* was broadcast on NBC in 1939; always the entrepreneur, Menotti was also one of the first composers to write for the next broadcast medium: television. Meanwhile, local stations with no opportunity to produce their own performances or the financial or technical ability to connect into a relay of a live broadcast often aired recordings of entire operas.

Today, companies are providing subscribers with opera that has been beamed to their radios via satellites high above the earth. If anyone doubts the continued popularity of opera on the air, whether in live or recorded broadcasts, the public outcry when this program-ming is threatened is enough to confirm its appeal.

OPERA ON TELEVISION

Because of the successful presence of opera on radio, television exec-utives on the East Coast of the United States decided to test it on their audiences. The first program, aired in March 1940 by NBC, then the reigning network, was in essence a concert featuring stars from the Metropolitan Opera. In addition to individual selections, the cast performed the quartet from *Rigoletto* and an abbreviated setting of the first act of *I pagliacci*. Reviewers commented on the appearance of the singers in close-up shots, which, of course, was an oddity for, in the world of opera, singers were only seen from afar. Not as successful as opera on radio, the next significant television broadcast involving the Metropolitan Opera was eight years later when ABC aired the opening production of its season: Verdi's *Otello*.

On Christmas Eve 1951, NBC broadcast Menotti's *Amahl and the Night Visitors*. In many ways, this brief work, with its childlike appeal, demonstrated that opera was approachable. In retrospect, it also demonstrated the power of this new medium, because, although Menotti composed far more significant works, it is *Amahl* with which he is still most readily associated. Menotti's was not the only opera to be composed for television; Britten's *Owen Wingrave* claims the honor of having been commissioned for British viewers in 1971. Although opera was present from the television industry's early years, its initial impact was minimal because the average household in America did not own a television set until the late 1940s; World War II and the post-war economy prevented most Europeans from having televisions until well into the 1950s.

As with radio broadcasting, operas can be televised as studio productions or directly from the stage of an opera house. In either case, the program may be live or taped for subsequent playback. In the early years of television when studio productions were the norm, works were generally produced for later broadcasts. Today, however, because relays are easily done via satellite and because audiences want to see opera stars in live performances, studio productions have been all but abandoned. A television broadcast of an onstage performance, however, offers interesting but foreign prospectives for viewers who are accustomed to watching opera live onstage; camera positions will catch action from various angles, whereas the theater viewer sees it straight on (even this is changing, though, for some large theaters have adopted an in-house broadcasting system that flashes close-ups and side shots on special screens).

Although network stations rarely feature opera, it is occasionally broadcast on public television and on some cable networks. It is far easier, however, to find opera on radio than on television.

OPERA ON FILM

Opera has had a presence in motion pictures since the early 1900s. The irony, of course, is that opera is expressed through sound, and the earliest films were silent. Early filmmakers, however, acknowledged the inherent drama in many of the repertory operas and developed creative ways through which theater audiences could experience the music. The simplest, of course, was to provide piano or organ arrangements; because the earliest opera films were merely brief scenes, the theater musician could accompany the movie with the relevant aria or chorus. A more realistic method was to play a recording along with the film. This system worked well when longer film versions of operas were produced; problems occurred, however, if the person running the record player did not observe the precise cue signaling when to begin the music. Although both the film and the recording may have been of the highest quality, if they were out of sync, the result was more comic than artistic. The final solution to bringing opera's music to silent films was to employ a cast of singers and musicians who would perform live in the theater as the film was run. Although this system may have been the most satisfying for the audience, it was clearly the most expensive.

The advent of "talkies" allowed the sound to be incorporated into the film, but recording the voices still presented challenges. Singers generally recorded the soundtrack which then was overlaid onto the film. Here, too, synchronization was an issue. When film microphone systems improved and cameras made less noise while shooting, the voices could be recorded as the film was shot if the stars of the movies were the featured singers.

Many opera singers became popular faces on the screen. Geraldine Farrar and Mary Garden, for example, made silent movies. Indeed, the stock gestures of the opera stage worked well on the silent screen. Among the first to make a name in talking films was Grace Moore, who played the singer Jenny Lind in a feature movie. Other stars included Helen Traubel, who left the Metropolitan in the 1950s to pursue a career in films and television, and Ezio Pinza, who is probably better remembered for singing "Some Enchanted Evening" in the film version of *South Pacific* than for any of his roles on the operatic stage. Stars who used classically-trained voices and made crossovers into musicals included Mario Lanza (who portrayed Caruso on film), Jeannette MacDonald, and Kitty Carlisle, the latter appearing in one of the most popular opera parody films of all time, the Marx Brothers' *A Night at the Opera*. Some composers also became involved in film. Richard Strauss oversaw the shooting of *Der Rosenkavalier*, even composing new music for the film score. Menotti, active as well in radio and television, assisted in the filming of a prize-winning version of his opera *The Medium*.

Filmed operas can either reproduce a production on stage or be shot on location; examples of the latter style include Joseph Losey's *Don Giovanni*, a sumptuous film that uses Venice as its setting, and Franco Zefferelli's *Otello*, a work of impressive cinematography, especially the scene in which Iago sings his "Credo" to dizzying camera movement. Films of productions, often made in conjunction with recording companies, are the products one generally buys when obtaining opera on videotape, laser disc, or DVD. Indeed, opera companies worldwide now offer films of their best productions. Easily available on opera web sites, music web sites, or in stores that sell recordings, these films are perhaps the best way to experience opera if one cannot attend a live performance.

OPERA ON THE INTERNET

Today, almost every opera company hosts a web site on which it announces its season. In addition, many companies, as well as schools of music, simulcast performances over the Internet. In most cases, the quality of the sound will depend on the speakers of the computer that accesses the broadcast, not on the sound equipment from which it is transmitted. Also, the picture may momentarily freeze because of the limitations of the computer server that is feeding broadcast signals to the Internet. Since they can be captured and archived on the host site many of these performances are accessible after the live performance is over, if copyrights permit. A search on the term "opera web cast" will yield the names of sites that currently offer such "cyberformances."

7

OPERA AS A
MIRROR OF SOCIETY

One opera enthusiast asks another to name his or her favorite work. The answer comes without hesitation: "*Carmen.*" The inquirer will understand the response, for it calls to mind a distinct set of characters and melodies. After all, *Carmen* is a classic. But what if the questioner persists, asking, "Which version do you prefer, the original *opéra comique* or the revision for Vienna?" Even if the *Carmen* fan knows of the first version's existence, chances are good that he or she has never seen or heard it, because it is the revision that is generally mounted. If the work *is* produced as Bizet composed it, audiences who know the opera undoubtedly will be confused when they hear spoken dialogue replacing recitative. Although they are tolerant of new productions (that is, new costumes, sets, and a different cast), they expect to hear the *Carmen* they know and love.

In reality, operas were part of a fluid musical tradition that was subjected to constant change for a variety of reasons. The composer and librettist might revise an opera if they (or audiences and reviewers) were dissatisfied with its premiere. Of course, someone other than the work's creators also could make changes. In the case of *Carmen*, for instance, Ernest Guiraud scored the recitative for the work of his deceased friend Georges Bizet, removing it from the uniquely

French tradition of *opéra comique* and making it more accessible to international audiences by revising it in the style of the *Opéra* (see Chapter 8). Nonmusical factors also effected changes. If they wished to succeed, composers and librettists were supposed to appeal to local tastes, conform to social mores, and respect the principles of both Church and state. When they did not, there were problems.

This chapter considers opera as the cultural expression of the people who supported (and often controlled) it.

PATRONAGE

The earliest operas were performed as private entertainment at courts. Librettos were written by poets attached to these households or by talented dilettantes within the patron's family or circle of friends— perhaps even by the patron. The composer most likely would have been the *maestro* of the court *cappella* (pl., *cappelle*), the performing ensemble that provided music for all official civic and religious functions. These musicians, even the *maestro*, were considered servants; in return for a position and job security, they performed at the whim of the court. Kings supported large enough musical establishments for major performances; smaller courts either offered more modest ones or borrowed extra musicians from neighboring *cappelle*. Additional singers often came from the highly trained church choirs within the noble's area of influence.

Composers of these private works needed to please two audiences. The first was the patron himself (or herself). To ensure the satisfactory reception of an opera, the composer generally consulted the patron who selected or at the very least approved its subject. Louis XIV dictated the subjects for several of Lully's operas and certainly sanctioned the content of the rest. The second audience included the noble's family, court officials, and, most important, invited guests who represented other (often rival) noble households. Therefore, an opera needed to be an ostentatious display showcasing the arts and aesthetics cultivated at the host court. Because their librettos extolled the patron's virtues and the spectacle reflected the wealth and bounty of the region under his or her rule, operas were as much a message of power as they were the evening's entertainment. The actual costs of operas under the patronage system varied according to the economic resources available; some productions, especially those at Versailles, were extravagant spectacles that cost dearly. The audience, of course, paid no admission. Members of the court were required to attend; guests were invited for political reasons or because they had curried the patron's favor.

Although operas were offered to the public as early as 1637, noble patronage did not end. Courts continued to offer performances for their guests, even constructing special theaters and commissioning new works or producing operas made popular elsewhere. As *Kapellmeister* for the Esterházy princes, one of Josef Haydn's tasks was the composition and production of operas at the estate theaters, one that featured regular performances and another that produced operas sung by the court singers but acted by marionettes. Even if court opera was an important social and political statement, when a patron was called on to subsidize a military conflict, the money intended for artistic enterprises was rechanneled immediately. With court performances cancelled, audiences attended public theaters.

With the economic, social, and political demise of the aristocratic system in the nineteenth century, wealthy members of the middle class assumed the task of supporting opera by investing in theaters or subscribing to operatic seasons. These new audiences demanded works that reflected their interest in contemporary literature and drama (see Chapter 3). Patrons included normal subscribers as well as wealthy donors whose generosity enabled opera companies to mount productions, a practice especially necessary in countries that lacked substantial government subsidies for the arts. This beneficence was not always without its drawbacks, because donors, much like opera's earliest noble patrons, frequently felt entitled to exert pressure to program works or hire performers that suited their personal tastes. The wealthy women who supported the Metropolitan Opera when Gustav Mahler served as its conductor supposedly drove him to nervous exhaustion with their demands. On the whole, though, most patrons' financial assistance was (and is) given freely. As any opera company will readily attest, such help is essential for survival.

PUBLIC THEATERS

The earliest public opera houses were owned by nobles who dabbled in theater to enhance their reputations rather than to make an investment. In England, groups of aristocrats underwrote theaters, sometimes only to establish a rival to an existing institution; while Handel worked for the Royal Academy under the support of the King, the Prince and others funded the Opera of the Nobility, employing Nicola Porpora to direct it. Although this action was the result of ill will among the nobles, Handel and Porpora were set up in direct competition for the same audience. Whatever their reasons for venturing into theater ownership, many of these high-born proprietors learned the hard way that opera was a business venture. Owners either went bankrupt, merged their interests with other nobles or wealthy members of the rising middle class, or turned to an impresario to manage the theater (see Chapter 4). Another option was to engage a traveling opera company that could present ready-made productions. Generally, however, these touring singers performed in smaller cities or towns that welcomed them at some local venue, whether a real theater or a large room in a municipal building. Companies that toured in the United States performed in a variety of settings, among them Odd Fellows halls, boating clubs, and saloons.

AUDIENCES

Audience members in public theaters paid for admission in three ways: purchasing a box outright (so firm were these arrangements that theater boxes were willed to descendants); subscribing for a season's productions; or purchasing tickets for a single performance. Early opera houses were constructed with several levels of tiers of boxes (see Chapter 6), and those who could afford it generally preferred to buy or rent these private compartments. The level of the tier identified one's social status; the best boxes, saved for the local rulers, were located on the first or second tier, whichever provided the best view of the stage. The higher one went, the lower the social status (and, of course, the worse the view). However, seventeenth- and eighteenth-century box holders, who would have attended every performance, paid more attention to others in the audience than to what was occurring on stage. Curtains allowed them to close off their boxes, and, while servants cooked and served them meals, they could host friends in relative privacy. Only when a favorite singer appeared would they turn to face the stage. In general, opera was perceived as a social event, and for that reason crowds were noisy and inattentive. Silence and attention were phenomena of the nineteenth century.

Seating and pricing based on class distinction demonstrates that public theaters entertained a democratic mix. Aristocrats paid the highest ticket prices and servants the lowest (although they often were admitted without charge if they had come to serve their employers). In the nineteenth century, theaters advertised discounts for soldiers who attended in uniform. By the end of the century, class distinctions had been eliminated; even though the best seats still cost more, anyone who could pay the price could engage them. Today, one would pay the same price for a ticket to *Il barbiere di Siviglia* as for *Tosca*. Up through the nineteenth century, though, audiences not only paid more for dramatic works than for comedies, but they also needed to go to different theaters to see them. It was also common to segregate works from different traditions. Until the end of the nineteenth century, the *Opéra* in Paris only programmed French works; Italian operas were relegated to the *Théâter italien*. The popularity of both is demonstrated by the fact that performances at each theater were scheduled on alternate days.

Subscribers in the seventeenth and eighteenth centuries tended to go to every performance; it was less expensive to entertain in the theater than in their own homes. Even though audience members might only be slightly aware of what was happening on stage, a famous artist's appearance could garner their attention. Also, a clever *divo* or *diva* could attract them with a demonstration of vocal pyrotechnics. These nightly occurrences were basically all they needed until the next opera was produced. Going to a single performance (two, if the work were noteworthy), nineteenth-century crowds attended operas as twenty-first century audiences go to films: to see something new and different. Repetition of the same work generally meant that an opera scheduled to premiere could not be mounted because the composer had not completed it, a bankrupt impresario could not afford to produce it, or one of the singers had fallen ill. In any of these cases, theater administrators would hastily substitute a production from a prior season. Subscribers did not always welcome these reprises if they had paid to see a premiere.

Audience behavior changed radically in the late nineteenth century. Many claim that the source of the change was Wagner, who encouraged complete audience attention during the performance of the *Ring*. Whether or not Wagner gets the credit, at some point audiences generally became more courteous to the artists by ceasing to speak aloud during performances. Announcements now remind audiences to turn off cell phones and pagers and to refrain from recording or videoing performances (this as much for avoiding copyright infringement as for disturbing everyone in the theater). Yet diehard enthusiasts will probably never stop showing their appreciation with shouts of "Bravo!" or "Brava!" for an aria well sung or their disdain with boos, hisses, or whistles when some poor singer has had a bad night.

THEATRICAL SEASONS

Court performances often were scheduled to celebrate birthdays, namedays, marriages, state visits, and military victories; hence, their audience was guaranteed. Public theaters, however, needed to sell seats. If the majority of residents left the city for the more pleasant suburbs in the stifling summer, theaters would be virtually empty (this would change to some degree with increased participation of the middle class who did not go off to country estates). Theaters also could not operate during the penitential seasons of Advent and Lent when the Church ordered them to close. It did not take great business acumen to realize that subscriptions and ticket sales paid bills. Therefore, productions were organized around specific times of the year when the theater would most likely fill. Impresarios also began to engage singers for entire seasons rather than for individual performances; these contracts ensured that performers would be available and, from the singer's point of view, assured them of future engagements. Only unforeseen misfortunes such as state funerals, wars, outbreaks of disease, or an impresario's bankruptcy would interrupt the production plan.

Performance Schedules

Different countries and cities often had their own special performance schedules, but here are the most common seasons.

- Carnival: Beginning on December 26 and ending on Mardi Gras (Martedì Grasso or Shrove Tuesday), the day before Lent began, this season became the most important one for opera productions. Because Easter is a movable feast, the duration of the season (and hence the number of operas that could be scheduled) was dependent on how many weeks there were between Christmas and Lent. A composer who had garnered the commission for the first opera of the Carnival season knew that he had become successful because this production was the theater's biggest draw for subscribers. Examples of operas that opened the Carnival season at La Scala in Milan are Bellini's *Norma* (December 26, 1831) and Donizetti's *Lucrezia Borgia* (December 26, 1833).

- Fair Seasons: Opera productions were scheduled during market fairs popular since the Middle Ages. In France, the Théâtres de la Foire (Fair Theaters) were significant in the development of French comic opera (see Chapter 9). In Italy, the fair or *fiera* season lasted from April to October; one of the most important venues of the Italian *fiera* season in nineteenth-century Italy was Sinigaglia.
- Spring: Starting after the Easter feast, this season ran from April to June, overlapping productions during the Fair season.
- Fall: Beginning in late August, this season ran until the beginning of Advent.

Favorite venues for the summer seasons were spa towns and resorts such as Baden-Baden in Germany and Montecatini in Italy.

Although the Church forbade stage works during Lent and Advent, composers were permitted to offer oratorios, nonstaged works with recitative, arias, and choruses that dealt with Biblical subjects. Because of post-Revolution, anticlerical reactionism in France and in areas subsequently conquered by Napoleon, religious restrictions to opera performances were temporarily abolished, however. And some composers cleverly got around Church bans with a *seria* genre called *azione tragica-sacra*. Although the scores did not differ from those of operas, the religious subjects did. The Teatro San Carlo in Naples regularly programmed this genre during Lent; examples include Rossini's *Mosè in Egitto* (March 5, 1818) and Donizetti's *Il diluvio universale* (February 28, 1830).

Today, when companies present their "season," they also refer to the works they will present. Some companies run performances through the winter holidays, whereas others are cautious of weather emergencies, ending one part of their season in December and beginning again in March. Most large houses do not offer productions in the summer months, a time when special opera festivals run performances. For those willing to travel, though, opera is available year-round.

"LISTENING" TO OPERA

Twentieth-century opera audiences inherited a repertory of bewildering works with improbable plots. Did none of Norma's Druids notice that she had been pregnant twice? Did brother and sister Siegmund and Sieglinde really have an incestuous relationship that produced the hero of a subsequent opera? And what of the singers? The most prized heroes were the men with the highest voices, and the roles of Romeo and Tancred often went to mezzos. What was rational to contemporary audiences gives modern operagoers pause. Most of the subjects of nineteenth-century works made perfect sense to audience members because they were based on popular contemporary literature or stage works. Wagner's characters appealed to German nationalists who were eager to create an operatic tradition beyond the Italian and the French; even non-Germans appreciated the librettos because they created a modern-day mythology in a world that sorely needed one.

Audiences simply suspended belief because opera was about the voice and what it conveyed. Indeed another scholarly approach to studying the genre considers how eighteenth and nineteenth-century audiences "heard" and responded to these works. Some reactions, of course, were national; the Italians and Spanish adored the castrato voice, while the French would not tolerate it on stage. The English approved of the sound but satirized the singers mercilessly. In short, even though operas from other centuries are performed today, they should be understood as products of their age.

THE LIETO FINE

Common in the eighteenth century was the *lieto fine*, or happy ending. Far from implying a rollicking comic-style finale in which characters all "live happily ever after," the happy ending was appended to most Italian *seria* works and French *tragédies lyriques* to reassure audiences that their rulers (whom the opera's heroes symbolized) were proper and good. All of Lully's *tragédies* paid tribute to Louis XIV, and Mozart's final opera, *La clemenza di Tito*, was meant to compliment Emperor Leopold II as an equally just ruler. Even though the characters in these works faced dramatic conflicts, they overcame them with honor and grace, just as one would expect a noble to do.

The object of the *lieto fine* was to have the audiences leave the theater with renewed faith in their government and in their society. Of course, composers and librettists knew that such compliments to their patrons meant security. This artistic propaganda wore thin as the century progressed closer and closer to revolution, first in France and subsequently in Italy and Germany. As soon as the operatic stage was perceived as a platform for civil discontent, authorities began to scrutinize librettos for more than their artistic value.

CENSORSHIP

Generally, any subject that threatened government, religion, or public morality was the target of censorship. The degree to which these topics were deemed offensive and dangerous, however, was not uniform. Thus what might be considered seditious in one place would be allowed in another, and what angered Catholic censors might be permitted by Protestants. Censorship was a function of local government; officials in charge of guarding public morality either worked for the local police, the military, or in special offices appointed expressly to control theatrical activities. Because it is difficult to find offensive references in music (although Rossini's musical citation of the *Marseillaise* in a chorus in *L'italiana in Algeri* certainly was pointed), censors concentrated on librettos.

Plots containing murders or suicides were targeted for including sins against God and society. At times when the restrictive governments were fearful of revolutionaries, librettists were forced to change words such as "oppressors," "freedom," and "liberty." After all, audiences could easily be incited to riot, should the combination of the words and music inspire them. In nineteenth-century Italy, censors in Habsburg-controlled Milan were more lenient than those in the Bourbon kingdom in the south, but police guards attended each performance in Milan, where it was generally felt that a crowd contained in one place could be easily controlled. In Naples and Palermo, however, texts were censored mercilessly. When Verdi tired of the Neapolitan objections to the libretto of *Un ballo in maschera*, which features an assassination, he simply took his opera to nearby Rome, where the opera was allowed with less difficulty. Furthermore, the appearance of characters who were clerics was frowned on; doubly offensive to Catholic Italians was the Protestant minister Stiffelio. Also to be avoided was the exact wording of prayers; one group of censors disallowed "Ave Maria" but found the substitution of "Salve Maria" acceptable.

Long after the days of the Metastasian virtuous noble, censors still were careful to avoid representations of rulers as evil men. Even as early as *Don Giovanni*, Mozart carefully kept this ignoble noble musically distanced from the worthy trio of Donna Elvira, Donna Anna, and Don Ottavio. When adapting Hugo's play *Le roi s'amuse* into what would become *Rigoletto*, Verdi and his librettist Piave had to reduce the rank of the tenor character from king to duke. As foolish as some of these changes may seem today, they were considered absolutely essential for the well-being of the state. In context, they were mere nuisances in comparison to the censorship imposed by the Nazi party and the Soviet state.

NAZI AESTHETICS

German opera at the turn of the twentieth century was dominated by the figure of Wagner. The Expressionist works of Schoenberg and Berg, however, signaled a path different from that taken by Richard Strauss and Erich Korngold. Furthermore, composers such as Ernst Krenek and Kurt Weill toyed with Americanisms like jazz. However, when the National Socialist (Nazi) Party came into power, it stressed the importance of ethnic purity, in essence isolating itself from non-Germanic tendencies. Most radical was its rejection of any music written by or performed by Jews. At the height of its power, the Nazi government collected Jewish musicians who had not heeded the early warning signs and left or who had not managed to escape. Much of the Jewish genius left in Germany was sent to a special concentration camp, Terezin. Ironically, this repressive atmosphere inspired these composers and musicians to express themselves. One of the most significant compositions is an opera, *Der Kaiser von Atlantis*, a work in which the Jews manage to cheat death rather than fall victim to it.

Composers who chose to remain in Germany were made to understand that no avant-garde music would be tolerated. Compositions could only demonstrate the superiority of the German creative genius. Although the Germans had a noteworthy tradition on which to draw, they carefully removed the music of any Jews. Hence the performance of operas by Meyerbeer, for instance, was forbidden.

Although he was not personally linked with the Nazi aesthetic, Wagner came to symbolize its greatest exponent, with writings such as *Das Judentum in der Musik* (*Judaism in Music*) providing a rationale for the proscription of music by Jews. Furthermore, his crusade for the establishment of German opera, a notion he took from Weber before him, gained a significance it never had during his own lifetime. The operas of the *Ring*, particularly the character of Siegfried, supported the theory of the Aryan *Übermensch*. Hitler was a frequent visitor at Bayreuth, although it has been suggested that no other officer in his command appreciated the works as much as he did.

SOVIET AESTHETICS

Two years after *Lady Macbeth of the Mtensk District* had premiered in Leningrad, Joseph Stalin saw a performance of it in Moscow. Within a matter of hours, the state-controlled newspaper *Pravda* had printed an article declaring its composer, Dmitri Shostakovich, an enemy of the Soviet state. Not only did the opera feature (and attempt to get audience sympathy for) an adulteress who murders her husband, but its music did not represent the Russian people. Similar reactions to other composers eventually resulted in the "Resolution on Music," issued by the Soviet Party in 1948. Composers were only to write music that was representative of the masses, avoiding modern techniques and aiming for simple, uplifting melodies. In reality, the "Resolution" was urging composers to write musical propaganda, often in march tempos, that glorified the progress possible in the Union of Soviet Socialist Republics.

Prokofiev also had censorship problems with his opera *War and Peace*, continuing to revise it until he satisfied the Party censors. Because of the dangers inherent in both text and music, most composers simply did not compose operas. One piece that demonstrates the aesthetic, however, is a work whose title translates as *An Optimistic Tragedy*. In it, its composer Alexander Kholminov lauds military heroism. Works such as this were taken to the various republics subsumed into the Soviet Union to encourage similar compositions; when taken abroad to demonstrate the mastery of Soviet music, however, they were deemed incomprehensible.

It is significant that operas that were suppressed during the Soviet era are now being resurrected for performance, allowing Russian audiences to hear (perhaps for the first time) links to their pre-Soviet musical past. Furthermore, composers in once-controlled republics are actively returning to their own ethnic traditions.

OPERA AS NATIONALISM

Just as countries struggled to achieve national governments free of foreign domination, the arts experienced parallel movements. Despite the development of vernacular genres such as *Singspiel*, *zarzuela*, and ballad opera (see Chapter 10), opera composers struggled under the domination of the Italian and French traditions. Following the lead of Weber who preached of the importance of creating an opera for the German people—that is, a serious tradition apart from the popular *Singspiel*—Wagner encouraged German nationalism by writing works that harkened back to the Middle Ages and the "golden age" of Germanic heroes such as Lohengrin, Tannhäuser, and the characters of the *Nibelungenlied*. After studying the older sources, he created *Stabreim*, his version of the alliterative verse found in German epic poetry (see Chapter 3) and employed it in his librettos for the *Ring*. In writings such as *The Art Work of the Future* (1850) and *Opera and Drama* (1852), Wagner spoke out against Italian and French opera, distancing German works from aria and recitative. He even avoided the term "opera" (although he used it for his earlier works), referring to the new German genre as *Gesamtkunstwerke*, or total works of art (see Chapter 8).

In similar attempts to break free of the French and Italian traditions in Russia, Central Europe, and Spain, nationalism exploited these aspects of native culture:

- Language, especially in its inherent rhythms: Bartók's *Bluebeard's Castle* and Janáček's *Jenůfa*
- Use of folk songs and dance rhythms: Glinka's *Ruslan and Lyudmila* and Smetana's *The Bartered Bride*
- Employment of folk tales for subject matter: Rimsky-Korsakov's *The Snow Maiden* and *The Legend of the Invisible City of Kitezh*

- Tales about historic figures and national heroes: Musorgsky's *Boris Godunov* and Szymanowski's *King Roger*

A WORD ABOUT AMERICANS

Nineteenth-century America was interested in opera, but as a nation it rejected its own composers, preferring the works of Europeans. Even composers who trained in Germany and France still bore the stigma of being homegrown. Nevertheless, composers tried their hands at opera. It also proved difficult to get American houses to offer native works. When the Metropolitan Opera opened in 1883, its repertory featured European operas. It was not until 1906 that an American piece would debut on the Met stage: Frank Converse's *The Pipe of Desire*. In 1961, the new Metropolitan Opera House at Lincoln Center opened with Samuel Barber's *Antony and Cleopatra*.

By the middle of the twentieth century, American opera composers had made significant inroads. Among important examples are Virgil Thompson's *Four Saints in Three Acts* (1934) and *The Mother of Us All* (1947), a work about Susan B. Anthony. Although Italian-born, Menotti is considered an American composer, writing librettos and scores for works such as *The Medium* (1946) and *The Telephone* (1947). Menotti also wrote the first opera composed especially for broadcast on American television, *Amahl and the Night Visitors* (1951).

Many opera composers in the United States highlighted American subjects for their works; the first example of a nationalistic subject was *Rip Van Winkle*, composed in 1855 by George Frederick Bristow. Although it is often misidentified as a "musical," Gershwin's opera *Porgy and Bess* (1935) has garnered an international reputation. Composed in 1911 but not performed until 1972, composer Scott Joplin's opera, *Treemonisha*, highlighted the distinctive rhythms of ragtime music. The end of the century saw settings of two great works of American literature: *Of Mice and Men* (Carlisle Floyd, 1970) and *A Streetcar Named Desire* (André Previn, 1998). Although initially dwarfed in popularity by the musical, American operas now stand firmly in the national repertory.

GENRES, STYLES,
AND SCORES

8

SERIOUS AND
SEMI-SERIOUS OPERA

If one were to ask people on the street to describe an average opera plot, chances are likely that it would include passionate characters who face insurmountable challenges, which, in the end, result in the death of one or both of the leads. This skeleton of a plot could be fleshed out into any number of popular works: *Rigoletto, Aida, La bohème, Tosca* or *Carmen,* to name but a very few. A rare response might describe the plot of a comedy such as *Le nozze di Figaro* or *Il barbiere di Siviglia.* Suffice it to say, though, that when asked about opera, the average person thinks in terms of a serious work.

In the Italian tradition, the earliest operas did indeed have serious librettos, as did the French, whose operas were influenced heavily by the tragedies of their spoken stage. As descendants of court entertainment, these operas represented the culture (and exclusivity) of a literate minority. Comedies, often parodies of these aristocratic serious pieces, were the province of the "others" in society. A rise in literacy brought serious and semi-serious operas to public theaters, and by the twentieth century serious operas were well-known enough to become symbolic of the entire genre.

This chapter examines the various manifestations of serious opera in Italy and France and also considers German and English works outside of their vernacular traditions (see Chapter 10).

ITALY

During the eighteenth and nineteenth centuries, *opera seria* ("serious opera") was the dominant style in Italy. Known for their tragic plots and grand singing, these works served as models—both to be admired and also criticized—everywhere opera was produced. By the end of the eighteenth century, however, comic elements— which were previously thought to be unfit for "serious" opera—were incorporated into works that came to be known as *opera semiseria* ("semi-serious opera").

OPERA SERIA (IT., SERIOUS OPERA)

In addition to referring to Italian works with serious subjects, *opera seria* describes a specific body of eighteenth and nineteenth-century operas that follow the conventions of the reforms of Arcadian poets such as Apostolo Zeno and Pietro Metastasio (see Chapter 4). Contemporary composers and librettists rarely used the term, however, preferring to identify their works as *dramme per musica*, or "dramas set to music." Even though Italian *opera seria* was popular throughout Europe, its predictable pattern of alternating recitative and aria made it a perfect target for parody and criticism; indeed, the eighteenth-century British writer Samuel Johnson deemed it "irrational." When composers in the early nineteenth century asked librettists to give them more flexible poetry with which they could experiment musically, the term *opera seria* was used with disdain.

As descendants of court entertainment such as the *intermedio* (see Chapter 1), even the most noble and heroic operas of the seventeenth century contained a variety of elements, including comedy and dance. No doubt stinging from criticism of their librettos leveled by the French, eighteenth-century Italian poet-reformers crusaded to raise their dramatic standards. One strategy was to remove all frivolous elements such as comic scenes and dancing—the latter move certainly a return volley at the French, who considered ballet an integral element of an opera's dramatic action. The aim was to write librettos of a high enough caliber to stand alone as works of literature. Pietro Metastasio's librettos became the exemplar of this new style. With subjects adapted from history, their texts reflected the dignity and optimism of the age. Constructed of prescribed patterns, the text left little control for the composer; alternating unrhymed lines of seven and eleven syllables (*versi sciolti* in *settenari* and *endecasillabi*) indicated recitative, and strophes of rhymed verse (often *settenari* in *verso piano* or *verso tronco*) were arias (see Chapter 3).

The preponderance of an *opera seria*'s text is *recitativo secco* (see Chapter 2). In fact, the Arcadian reformers decreased the number of arias per opera from fifty to no more than thirty (still a startling number of solo pieces by later standards) while expanding the recitative. No matter how elegant the language, long stretches of thinly accompanied sung dialogue are tedious, so passages of recitative were routinely removed during performances. Printed librettos accommodated this practice by providing the audience with the complete text to read. Despite the reformers' literary ambitions, after their words were set to music, they entered the sole province of the singers, who emphasized the arias to demonstrate their vocal strengths.

The chief musical form of *opera seria* is the *da capo* aria (see Chapter 2). The text falls into two sections (A and B) that, for example, state a problem and its solution or demonstrate a character's conflicting emotions. The composer would then set the two sections using different melodic material for each. At the end of the B section, the A section is performed again (*da capo*, or from the top). Dramatically, this often makes little sense; as an emotional expression, however, the *da capo* text stresses a character's internal conflict. The structure's real strength is in its musical setting, a concept discovered and exploited by singers who embellished the A section with vocal ornamentation in its return. Because audiences found these vocal displays exciting, singers were encouraged to do more and more intricate passagework, often trying to outdo each other.

Opera seria began to fall out of fashion in the late eighteenth century; however, court theaters, which stood to gain from a continued belief in a noble hierarchy, staged them into the nineteenth century. Today, few *opere serie* remain in the international repertoire. In fact, Handel's operas are among the few heard regularly. Because today's audiences are familiar with what came after—Rossini, Verdi, and Puccini—the structure and predictability of *opera seria* can seem tiresome, but, when performed by singers who specialize in early music techniques, its *da capo* arias are sheer *tours de force*. Placed in their cultural context, these eighteenth-century works reflect a time when the cultured world rejected chaos in favor of a logical order upon which audiences could depend.

The history of *opera seria* can be divided into three periods:

1. The pre-reform period developed the *da capo* aria and in essence built on the foundations set by Francesco Cavalli and Antonio Cesto. The most significant composer of this period was Alessandro Scarlatti; today, though, one is likely to hear only *La Griselda* of Scarlatti's canon of more than fifty serious works. Other active *seria* composers included Handel's chief rival in London, Nicola Porpora; Giovanni Battista Pergolesi, remembered more for his comic works and the *intermezzo La serva padrona*; and Johann Hasse.

2. The age of the Metastasian libretto begins in the middle of the eighteenth century. Hasse had been joined by Tomasso Traetta, Niccolò Jommelli, and Baldassare Galuppi. The latter, paired with the librettist Carlo Goldoni, helped form the tradition of comic operas; hence, Galuppi's use of ensemble and scene complexes stemmed from his work in the comic style (see Chapter 9).

3. The end of the eighteenth century brought new composers with new ideas. The composers of this final phase of *opera seria* include Antonio Salieri, Giovanni Paisiello, and Domenico Cimarosa; foreigners but still able participants were Haydn and Mozart. The conventions of the Metastasian libretto were no longer the rule. The *da capo* aria, for instance, was becoming overshadowed by the *rondò* and through-composed aria forms (see Chapter 2); furthermore, as a result of Gluck's reforms, the chorus and ballet again were used actively in serious opera.

With the end of the eighteenth century came the end of the *lieto fine*, the happy ending requisite in Metastasian librettos (see Chapter 7). The novel, a new literary genre, depicted a darker side of life, often with introspective characters and gothic settings, and librettists borrowed these plots for the stage. Rather than portraying life as it should be, they presented it as it was. Composers working in this arena and who would influence all of those who followed included Niccolò Zingarelli (Bellini's teacher), Ferdinando Paer, Pietro Generali, and Simon Mayr.

Simon Mayr (1763–1845)

Born in Bavaria, Simon Mayr received his early musical training from his father, an organist. Although a patron offered to sponsor the young boy's musical studies in Vienna, Mayr's father insisted that he get a traditional education. Mayr did not leave music behind; while studying law and theology in university, he supported himself by playing the organ. His talent again was noticed and he was offered the possibility of studying in Italy. Within a decade, he was in the midst of an active and successful career composing operas for La Fenice and other theaters in Venice. His second work, *La Lodoiska*, which premiered at La Fenice in 1796 and was revised for Milan's La Scala three years later, brought him considerable fame.

Although Mayr's works are not in the repertory, he is a pivotal figure in the history of Italian opera because his life spanned more than eight decades (he was born in 1763, seven years after the birth of Mozart, and died in 1845, only three years before the death of his pupil Donizetti). His early works stem from the traditions of Gluck, especially in his recognition of the dramatic potential of ensembles and choruses. His later works foreshadow the nineteenth century; most important, he developed the multi-movement arias, duets, and finale patterns that would become standard by the time of Rossini (see Chapter 2). Although he composed with the lyricism of an Italian, he orchestrated with a vigor and harmonic brilliance that suggest his German heritage and training.

The importance of Mayr—and those of his generation—cannot be overestimated. To assume that there was no Italian opera between Mozart and Rossini (as some older histories would have had readers believe) is ingenuous. Recent scholarship has demonstrated that Mayr is responsible for pioneering many of the structures that would define early nineteenth-century Italian opera. Only by knowing his works and those of his generation can one understand what came before and after.

Serious opera in the nineteenth century saw the flowering of musical elements that had been introduced at the last century's close: inclusion of choruses and ensembles for dramatic purposes; the use of elaborate chain finales for dramatic climaxes; accompanied rather than "dry" recitative; and the pairing of arias to develop different emotions (see *cantabile* and *cabaletta* in Chapter 2). Composers also made more use of the orchestra, which had grown in size to include more strings, winds, and horns, trumpets, and trombones.

Fine examples of early nineteenth-century serious operas are Rossini's *Tancredi* (Venice, 1813) and *Elisabetta, regina d'Inghilterra* (Naples, 1815). Although touted as a comic composer, Rossini's serious works have been reevaluated; perhaps his most significant work in the genre was his last opera for the Italian stage: *Semiramide* (1823). Another important example of nineteenth-century serious opera is Bellini's *Il pirata*, a dark and brooding work that touches on emotion, oppression, and jealous passion, themes that would remain popular throughout the age.

Rather than a happy ending, these operas generally featured the death of one of the main characters (generally the female lead). Equally significant were the ubiquitous mad scenes that depicted the delicate psyche of the human mind (again, generally featuring the main female character). Various explanations have been suggested for the popularity of these dramatic episodes; feminist scholars feel that the killing of women onstage was a way for a male-dominated society to demonstrate control over women. Others describe these scenes as symbolic of current political oppression and liberation. Whatever the motive, plots with mad scenes remained commonplace from the 1820s into the 1840s.

Although Verdi began his career by writing mainstream works, his own brand of dramatic interpretation was quick to reveal itself. Employing popular literary and stage works as sources, he and his librettists created some of the century's most memorable characters. By the late 1840s, after a stay in Paris, he demonstrated the influence of *grand opéra* and of concerns for developing psychological portraits of the men and women who peopled his stage. This trend begins with *Luisa Miller* and *Stiffelio* and continues strongly through the trio of masterpieces of the early 1850s: *Rigoletto*, *Il trovatore*, and *La traviata*.

Nineteenth-century Italian composers and librettists used different terms to identify their serious operas. The terms *dramma lirico*, *tragedia lirica*, and *melodramma* seemed inspired by French operatic genres: *drame lyrique*, *tragédie lyrique*, and *melodrame*. The simple term, *dramma*, however, was reminiscent of the spoken stage. "Opera" was the sole designator that seemed to focus on the work as one for the musical stage. There often seems to be little rhyme or reason behind the choice of one term over another. This list classifies Verdi's serious works for the Italian stage as they are identified on their librettos.

Dramma
  Il trovatore
  Oberto, Conte di San Bonifacio
Dramma lirico
  Attila
  Ernani
  Giovanna d'Arco
  I lombardi alla prima crociata
  Nabucco
  Otello
Melodramma
  Un ballo in maschera
  Luisa Miller
  I masnadieri
  Rigoletto
Opera
  Aida
  Il corsaro
  La forza del destino
  La traviata
  Macbeth
  Simon Boccanegra
  Stiffelio (Aroldo)
Tragedia lirica
  Alzira
  Il battaglia di Legnano
  I due Foscari

Instead of a flourish of works from Italian composers after the unification of Italy in the 1860s, there was a flood of imports, including the *grand opéras* of Meyerbeer from France and the works of Wagner from Germany. The rise of movements like the *Scapigliatura* ("unkempt ones") criticized the musical establishment and vocally demonstrated disillusionment with the post-revolutionary world. *Scapigliati* such as Arrigo Boito and Franco Faccio attempted to create new operas that would point to the inadequacies of the traditions of the past. Their work *Amleto* (music by Faccio and libretto by Boito) and Boito's *Mefistofele* demonstrate the movement's attempts to renew Italian culture. Later, Boito would become the librettist for Verdi's *Otello* and *Falstaff*, and together they would strive to overcome what they perceived as an unfortunate German influence on Italian opera.

Stemming from the *Scapigliati*'s philosophies came *verismo*, made popular in works such as *Cavalleria rusticana* and *I pagliacci*.

VERISMO (FR., VÉRISME)

Verismo is often translated literally as "realism," but the origins of the term in late nineteenth-century Italian and French literature suggest that a more accurate definition is "naturalism" because these librettos are objective narratives of elements of the lowest classes of society in their own unique settings. The plots also demonstrate hints of determinism, for no matter how these characters struggle to overcome obstacles, they are trapped by their environment and are doomed to resort to violence or become its victims. One of the most significant literary influences on veristic opera was Giovanni Verga, who crafted tales of the harsh lives of Sicilian villagers. His short story "Cavalleria rusticana" inspired Mascagni to create the first acknowledged veristic opera.

Veristic works generally were narratives about the lower classes in Italy's *mezzogiorno* region (its poor South). Although the authors remained impersonal, they nonetheless took great care to create accurate pictures of their characters, often employing regional dialects and idioms. In *Cavalleria*, for instance, the characters Turiddu and Santuzza bear the Sicilian nicknames for Salvatore and Santina. When these portrayals of common passions reached the opera stage, their crudeness often displeased local audiences who saw them as embarrassing. Neapolitan audiences, for example, thought it far better to portray their city through its traditional dialect comedy than in a work as harsh as Giordano's *Mala vita*. Audiences outside of Italy, however, found this dramatic frankness impressive. In today's repertory, only two Italian works remain as representatives of *verismo*: *Cavalleria* and *I pagliacci*.

Although there is a tendency to limit the discussion of veristic opera to Italian works, composers elsewhere were influenced by naturalism. Perhaps the most significant example still performed today is the Czech masterpiece *Jenůfa* by Janáček. At the same time, some works traditionally called "veristic" do not warrant that designation. Because *Tosca* opened to threats of rioting in Rome, that work has been associated with the sensationalism of *verismo*. Given the necessary characteristics—lower-class characters driven by animal passions—*Tosca* simply does not fit the mold. Rather it must be seen as Puccini's attempt to lead Italian serious opera into yet another dramatic direction.

INTO THE TWENTIETH CENTURY

Far from the noble characters who trod the stage in the eighteenth century, Puccini's characters, he once said, were "little people with big sorrows." Puccini, who took Italian serious opera (often with a comic flair) into the twentieth century, toyed with different styles and subjects: whereas *Il tabarro* is veristic, *Suor Angelica* is sheer sentimentality. Never satisfied with the same type of dramatic theater, Puccini strove for something new in each of his works; *Madama Butterfly*, *La fanciulla del West*, and *Turandot* took him in different directions, and he even dabbled with the popular *operetta* in the score of *La Rondine* (see Chapter 9). Paralleling Puccini in his dramatic quest were Francesco Cilea with *L'Arlesiana* and Umberto Giordano in his historic drama *Andrea Chenier*.

For those who believe that there was no Italian opera after Puccini, a brief list of twentieth-century composers disproves this statement: Franco Alfano (who completed *Turandot* in addition to writing his own works), Ildebrando Pizzetti, Luigi Nono, Alfredo Casella, Luigi Dallapiccola, and Lucio Berio. Of these late works, Ermanno Wolf-Ferrari's opera *Sly* has recently been revived successfully as part of operatic seasons around the world.

OPERA SEMISERIA (IT., SEMI-SERIOUS OPERA)

By the end of the eighteenth century, comic elements were once again appearing in serious works. By the early nineteenth century, librettists had created a separate genre that shared elements of both *seria* and *buffa* works: *opera semiseria*. Not unlike works within the generic French *comédie*, these compositions have light subjects that are somehow tinged by a threat to the main hero or heroine (usually the latter). The comic element is often a traditional *basso buffo* role (see Chapter 5), but rather than the bumbling fool of *opera buffa*, this character is given power to control the main character's fate. *Buffo* elements also are tempered by a high degree of sentimentality in the plot. A happy ending is ensured, however, punctuated by a rousing finale in which the community celebrates the hero or heroine's salvation. Examples of *semiseria* works include *La gazza ladra*, *Linda di Chamounix*, and *La sonnambula*. The genre fell out of favor by the middle of the nineteenth century.

FRANCE

The first operas in France were Italian imports brought to Louis XIV's court in the 1640s at the urging of the Italian-born Prime Minister, Cardinal Jules Mazarin. Within a decade, the composer Robert Cambert and the librettist Pierre Perrin were presenting works that enhanced the Italian model with the drama, ballet, and spectacle of court performances called *divertissements*. With Louis XIV's permission, Perrin oversaw the inauguration of a national opera in 1671, but within a year, Jean-Baptiste Lully, the dominant figure in the French musical establishment, had gained control. His vision of opera—and his virtual monopoly of the musical stage—set the standard for French serious opera until the premiere of Jean-Philippe Rameau's *Hippolyte et Aricie* in 1733, forty-six years after Lully's death.

TRAGÉDIE LYRIQUE

Lully and the librettist Philippe Quinault superimposed existing French stage traditions on Italian opera; the *tragédie en musique* was sung throughout but mirrored stage plays by incorporating ballet and *"merveilleux,"* spectacular effects made possible by intricate stage machinery. As with their Italian counterparts, early French serious works contained the occasional comic scene, but these soon were removed at the order of the Academy of Letters. Control over librettos became standard in France, where texts needed the approval of a committee who judged their poetic and dramatic quality before they could be set. Lully retained an amazing amount of control himself, however, in essence, copyrighting his works through royal privilege and refusing to allow any cuts during performances. Musically, Lully's operas include an overture (see French overture, Chapter 2), *récitatifs*, *airs*, and, of course, the *divertissement* with its ballets and choruses. Because the emphasis was dramatic, both *récitatif* and air were sung in a declamatory style so that the music never obscured the text. More flexible rhythmically than Italian recitative, *récitatif* is in fact often difficult to differentiate from the *air* into which it might lead.

Lully's musical ensemble, the pride of the French court, came closer to the organization of a modern orchestra before those employed in Italian theaters did. At its core was the famed twenty-four-piece string ensemble, enhanced by a choir of wind instruments. Traditional in Lully's scoring was the division of strings into five parts (first and second violins; first and second violas; and cellos and basses), whereas non-French orchestral scoring leaves the violas together, resulting in a four-part texture. Lully employed his orchestra for more than mere accompaniment; instrumental interludes connecting to or foreshadowing elements of the plot formed a major part of his *tragédies en musique*.

The libretto, or *livret*, is divided into a prologue (which contained laudatory references to the King) and five acts. *Récitatif* propels the action while the *air* parallels the dramatic monologue of spoken *tragédies*. Subjects were drawn from mythology or French epic legends such as *Le chanson de Roland*. The plots generally center on the intrigue and conflicts that plague dignified nobles who are in the end saved by the intervention of supernatural forces (this permitted the spectacular arrival of gods and goddesses via the theater's stage machinery). Plots also include generous sections for chorus, another element that French critics found lacking in Italian works.

Lully, who composed court ballets and *comédies-ballets* with Molière (see Chapter 9), felt strongly that ballet was as much a dramatic expression as was vocal music; furthermore, a desire to please the King, who with his family often participated in dance presentations at court, ensured ample use of ballet. While the singers stood off to the side, dancers would take over the stage during the opera's *divertissements*. Representing priests or warriors, for instance, they actually were as much a part of the dramatic action as they were of the spectacle.

Composers such as Marc-Antoine Charpentier and André Campra wrote *tragédies lyriques* after the death of Lully, but even in death Lully held a monopoly on the French stage, having created a repertory of his own works during his lifetime. As well as milestones in the history of French serious opera, Lully's works are a mirror of the aesthetics of Louis XIV and his court. Although it may seem a strange tribute, Lully's works were so well-known that they inspired the first operatic parodies, performed as comic opera at the so-called Fair Theaters (see Chapter 9).

RAMEAU AND GLUCK

Rameau was in his mid-fifties when his first opera, *Hippolyte et Aricie*, was staged in 1733. Adopting Lully's model for the *tragédie lyrique*, Rameau's music, however, seemed more Italianate because it emphasized melody over dramatic declamation. In fact, whereas Lully had made the flexible *récitatif* the focus of his works, Rameau shifted the emphasis to the *air*. This change caused a rift in Parisian audiences not unlike the famous *Querelle des Bouffons* (see Chapter 9); one camp, the *Lullistes*, favored the traditional declamatory style made popular by a proven master while the other, the *Ramistes*, sided with a pioneer who put stress on melody.

Rameau maintained the five-act model; indeed, it would remain the structure of French opera throughout the nineteenth century. More than Lully, however, Rameau integrated the *divertissement* into the dramatic action of the libretto, where before the connection to the plot had often been slim. Rameau also composed more small ensembles, using the duet and trio effectively. Perhaps the most cited example is the "Trio des songes" from the fourth act of *Dardanus* (1739). In addition to operas, Rameau also wrote the *Traité de l'harmonie* (1722), a treatise on harmony that essentially set the ground rules for the system of functional harmony that still governs Western music.

In the past, scholars examined editions of Rameau's operas and, given the importance of his treatise and how it was applied in these scores, they dubbed him "the Father of Modern Orchestration." This judgment was made solely on *editions* of Rameau, however. Scholars in the 1990s returned to Rameau's original manuscripts and discovered that he scored just like everyone else in his day. During a period of intense French nationalism in the late nineteenth century, France's major composers planned editions of the works of early French masters; Rameau's music was given to Vincent D'Indy. In an effort to make Rameau's music even more novel, D'Indy touched up the orchestrations. Now, new editions that maintain the historical integrity of Rameau's music demonstrate that his operas stand on their own merits as masterpieces of the eighteenth century.

Gluck's mid-century reform works influenced opera in France (and elsewhere) well into the nineteenth century (see Chapter 4). His theories, in turn, were influenced by the work of other theorists, including Francesco Algarotti. Gluck believed that the overture should reflect the content of the work; that all elements, including dances and choruses, should relate to the plot; and that all unnecessary vocal excess should be eliminated. In essence, his aim was to simplify the French tradition. At the same time, the composer Niccolò Piccinni, together with his librettist Jean François Marmontel, proposed a more formal and expansive musical style in line with earlier traditions of the French stage. The Parisians once again divided into camps—the Gluckists and the Piccinnists—and, as usual, there was no winner but much spirited debate. Later composers of French serious opera, however, took their inspiration from Piccinni rather than from Gluck, perhaps because of the latter's perceived associations with *opéra comique*.

After the French Revolution, the strict social distinctions between styles of opera were loosened significantly and this fertile territory brought foreign composers to Paris, then the operatic center of the universe. Virtually all of the acknowledged greats of nineteenth century opera either visited Paris or chose to remain there. Without a doubt, the great compositions of Verdi and Wagner were inspired by their encounters with the Parisian stage.

OPÉRA COMIQUE

The greatest misunderstanding about French opera stems from the mistranslation of the term *comédie* as "comedy." The term actually refers to a theatrical work with a lighter or more sentimental subject than those in the lofty dramatic tradition of French tragedy. Moreover, a *comédie* (or work described as "*comique*") might be serious or humorous. Until the nineteenth century, there was a stringent division in French theater and opera, with pure tragedy in one category and all other subjects (including comedy) in the other.

In addition to contrasting subjects, an *opéra comique* differs from *tragédie lyrique* in that it has spoken dialogue rather than *récitatif*, a characteristic it shares with *Singspiel, zarzuela,* and ballad opera (see Chapter 10). Because of its serious and comic manifestations, *opéra comique* will be considered in this chapter and the next.

Opéra comique had its origins in the Fair Theaters of Paris (see Chapter 9). While the all-sung genres of serious opera remained linked to the court, *opéra comique* was under different government control. The only strict rule was that theaters that featured *opéras comiques* employ spoken dialogue rather than sung recitative. Also, its creators were freer to experiment with its structure. An *opéra* continued to feature five acts, but *comique* works might have three or four. Also, subjects could be serious or comic. The former, of course, never trod on the dramatic territory of the *tragedies lyriques*; rather, serious *comique* works featured subjects that were historical, didactic, or sentimental.

The main musical elements of the earliest *opéras comiques* were *vaudevilles*, popular songs with verses and a refrain. By the eighteenth century, however, composers such as André-Ernest-Modeste Grétry had ceased to employ the *vaudeville* in favor of newly composed music specially written for these works. Original music seemed especially important for works with serious subjects, perhaps to draw a distinction between them and those of *opéra comiques'* comic heritage. These serious works became extremely popular and were performed throughout Europe and America; one of the most important centers of *comique* production was New Orleans where a thriving French population dedicated its opera house to the latest works from France. These French exports also became a major influence on other vernacular traditions (see Chapter 10).

Important *comique* works in the nineteenth century include Gounod's *Roméo et Juliette* and *Faust*, Bizet's *Les pêcheurs des perles* and *Carmen*, and Massenet's *Werther* and *Manon*. As repertory works, these remained popular in Paris throughout the twentieth century.

When a comédie is not a comedy

One of the most famous composers of late eighteenth-century *opéra comique* was André-Ernest-Modeste Grétry. In 1784, his *comédie mise en musique*, *Richard Coeur-de-lion*, premiered in Paris. A brief summary of the plot demonstrates that its tale was not only serious but suggests why revolutionaries perceived it as a work of royalist propaganda.

Having come by information that his liege King Richard is being held prisoner in Linz Castle, Blondel arrives to rescue him. When he sees Marguerite of Flanders, Richard's love, Blondel plays a *romance* that Richard had written for her. She recognizes it but not Blondel, who is disguised as a blind man. The next day, Richard appears on the castle terrace. As he sings, he is answered in song by Blondel, and he rejoices that his liberation is near. After trapping the governor of the castle, Blondel successfully leads an attack. Richard is freed and united with Marguerite, thanks to Blondel's courage in battle.

Despite the politics associated with Blondel's rescue of a king when the monarchy was no longer popular, Grétry's score remained popular throughout the nineteenth century. Musically, it is united by the reappearance of Richard's *romance*; dramatically, its spectacle is a forerunner of *grand opéra*. Also, it serves as an excellent example of how a *comédie* in the French tradition is not always funny—as, of course, does Bizet's *Carmen*, perhaps the most famous *opéra comique* in opera history.

DRAME LYRIQUE (FR., LYRIC DRAMA)

In the late eighteenth and nineteenth centuries, a special manifestation of *opéra comique* linked especially to the spoken stage was mounted with frequency: the *drame lyrique*. Serious in tone, but also with a moral lesson, these works generally told the tale of a character whose life had been torn asunder by upturned fortunes. Happily, there is an eleventh-hour rescue or reprieve. Later, the term became associated with the works of French composers who were influenced by Wagner such as Massenet and Chabrier.

GRAND OPÉRA

Perhaps the most significant French serious genre of the nineteenth century was *grand opéra*. Written for the *Opéra*, these works retained the spectacle so important to French opera since the days of Lully. In addition to large choruses and impressive ballets, *grand opéra* demonstrated the latest in scenic design. In fact, these spectacular effects included the first employment of electricity on the operatic stage used to simulate a sunrise in *Le prophète* and the eerie moonlight of a deserted cloister in *Robert le diable*.

The first works that can be classified as *grand opéra* include Rossini's *Guillaume Tell*, Halévy's *La juive*, and Auber's *La muette de Portici*. The two who have become best associated with the genre are the composer Giacomo Meyerbeer and the librettist Eugène Scribe. Setting his subjects in locales that would exploit local color, Scribe wrote melodramatic works with tragic endings, that is, works that conformed to the aesthetics of the day. With an innate sense of what would please, Scribe molded his subjects to include scenes that would make the best use of large forces of performers; one of the most spectacular occurs in *Le prophète*, where dancers were fitted with roller skates so they could appear to be ice-skating. After Scribe wrote his libretto, Meyerbeer would create a score, combining his German flair at orchestration with the melodic lessons he had learned in Italy.

Meyerbeer and Scribe created four *grand opéras*: *Le prophète*, *Les Huguenots*, *Robert le diable* and *L'Africaine*. Although these are revived occasionally today, the forces needed to produce them seem to prohibit their entry into the international repertory.

TWENTIETH CENTURY

Opera composers in the twentieth century include Darius Milhaud and Arthur Honegger, both of the young progressive group called *Les Six*; another member, François Poulenc, composed *Dialogues des Carmélites*, seen frequently on the modern stage. Of the late twentieth-century French works, Messiaen's *Saint François d'Assise* (1983) is one of the best known. In addition to new compositions, French conductors and artists have recently begun to revive important masterpieces of the seventeeth century, thus keeping alive the tradition from which the line of French operas descends.

GERMANY

The French Revolution inspired composers of many nations to look within their own borders to define themselves musically. Cultural politics reached the German musical stage as early as the premiere of *Fidelio* in 1805. Such "rescue operas" (*Richard Coeur-de-lion* is another) featured plots in which one character liberates another. Their themes, however, were more universal: humans should be freed from all domination. Many German writers took up this cause by suggesting the liberation of the German musical culture from the Italian and French traditions that had long dominated its stages (even though this was often by popular demand). In response, German composers began to explore new techniques for composing opera, and the result was a specific strand of Romanticism.

One of the chief proponents of a new German musical culture was Carl Maria von Weber. In *Der Freischütz*, Weber musically portrayed a typical German setting; his use of the echo in the oft-cited Wolf Glen scene is just one example of how his score reflects the native landscape. In his writings, Weber proposed a new style of opera that would, in essence, unite all elements—poetry, music, text, and artistic design—to create a complete work of art that reflected German culture. This notion would have appealed to any nineteenth-century mind, but Weber, who himself was bitter from competition with Rossini, directed his argument specifically to his countrymen who shared a common language and sought a common artistic expression. He and others emphasized that music could be the voice of the German people, or the *Volkston*, a theory held in common with proponents of the *Lied*, or German song. Weber's writings influenced Wagner, who was drawn to Weber's notion that music could create a new world. This concept became an overriding theme in many of Wagner's works, but especially in the *Ring Cycle* and *Parsifal*.

A truly German opera would require German subjects; hence, Wagner turned to Teutonic myths and epics for his characters. Although he claimed to reject the Italian and French traditions by eschewing the term "opera" for *musikalisches Drama*, he nevertheless was inspired by the French theater, especially *grand opéra*, and by the music of Bellini, the only Italian whom he admired. By writing his own librettos and establishing his own theater at Bayreuth (see Chapter 6), Wagner essentially and purposefully isolated himself from established operatic traditions. Although he never achieved what he had hoped to in his lifetime, Wagner was one of the most significant influences on operatic music and production, influencing composers well into the twentieth century.

GESAMTKUNSTWERK (GER., TOTAL WORK OF ART)

In his prose writings, Wagner expounded on a "total art work" that would unify music, poetry, and dance, in essence returning to the principals of Greek theater. In addition, he proposed adding art and architecture to this mix, creating what he called "the artwork of the future." In his creation of the Bayreuth *Festspielhaus* (see Chapter 6), Wagner carefully considered the principles of *Gesamtkunstwerk*. Music and text (his own librettos) would unite to create something uniquely German, and the sets, the costumes, the singers, and even the theater structure would support the creation of the complete dramatic effect. The orchestra, too, would play an important role in this process, doing far more than simply accompanying singers. The orchestra is entrusted with the important *leitmotifs*, or musical signals that represent characters and settings. Hence, the orchestral ensemble participates on the level of a character, reminding the audience of an earlier event or an absent character by introducing the appropriate musical motive. Together, all elements work to create a unified effect.

In the nineteenth and twentieth centuries, Germany and Austria produced myriad *operettas* (see Chapter 10); those who continued to compose opera, however, all fell under the influence of Wagner. Significant were Wagner's son Siegfried, Englebert Humperdinck, Hans Pfitzner, and, of course, Richard Strauss. Many composers were hindered by the dictates of Nazi aesthetics (see Chapter 7), but many works that were suppressed during that regime have since been produced.

ENGLAND

As in Italy and France, Britain had a tradition of musical entertainment at court: the masque. After opera arrived in London in the seventeenth century, it immediately encountered resistance from those involved with the spoken stage. Among published attempts to dampen the public's interest in this new phenomenon were critiques that the English language could never provide singable texts for recitative and aria. Save for several short-lived vernacular genres (see Chapter 10), those who wished to see opera were generally forced to hear it in a foreign tongue.

Several examples of English operas exist. The earliest are *The Siege of Rhodes* (1656) and *Albion and Albanius* (1685), the latter with a text by John Dryden. John Blow's *Venus and Adonis,* written for the English court in 1682, served as the model for what is now heralded as the most important early English opera—indeed one which features frequently in the repertory: Henry Purcell's *Dido and Aeneas* (1689). Purcell went on to compose semi-operas (see Chapter 10) but after his death, no other composer picked up the thread of original all-sung works in English.

Although adaptations of Italian and French works in English became quite popular in the early nineteenth century, by the second half of the 1800s, theaters eventually returned to operas in the original language. In the late nineteenth century, attempts were made to establish an English Opera, but efforts were short-lived. Preferring the works of Gilbert and Sullivan and the popular musical, England would need to wait until the next century when Frederick Delius, Ralph Vaughan Williams, Michael Tippett, Maxwell Davies, and especially Benjamin Britten revived an English national opera. Indeed, several of Britten's works, most notably *Billy Budd,* have gained spots in the international repertory.

Just as the theater is symbolized by the masks of tragedy and comedy, opera has two faces as well. These traditions were kept distinct from each other, even to the point of dedicating certain theaters to one at the exclusion of the other. Cross-fertilization, however, was unavoidable. Chapter 9 considers the development of comic opera and demonstrates how it eventually influenced the direction of serious works as well.

9

COMIC OPERA AND OPERETTA

Renaissance dramatic theory equated the ruling class with tragedy and the lower class with comedy. In the seventeenth century, these preconceptions transferred easily to the operatic stage. While serious operas entertained noble audiences with stories of gods and heroes, comic ones delighted crowds with the escapades of characters based on ancient comic traditions, folklore, or real life. Designed to edify and instruct, serious works portrayed the world as it should be; comedy, on the other hand, mirrored the foibles of the world as it was. Most important, serious opera glorified the state, its characters symbolizing those in power. Meanwhile, comedy often targeted the flaws of the very social institutions serious opera held aloft; hence, it was perceived as a danger to the status quo. As a result, its texts were subject to censorship and its creators to censure.

Nevertheless, comic operas attracted crowds, so much so that new theaters were built to accommodate them. Their audiences were more likely to feature a democratic mix, for although venues producing serious operas were socially exclusive, anyone who could afford a ticket could attend comic performances. Even though the aesthetic pendulum would swing in favor of serious and sentimental subjects in the nineteenth century, the frequent inclusion of comic characters and allusions to early comic traditions demonstrate the genre's continued influence.

This chapter examines Italian and French comic opera, concluding with a brief discussion of the most significant descendant of the latter: operetta.

ITALY

Along with the serious opera tradition, Italy was a center of the development of *opera buffa*, the classic comic opera form. Its development is traced from early sources through its full flowering.

INTERMEZZO OR SCHERZO MUSICALE (PL., INTERMEZZI, SCHERZI MUSICALI; FR., INTERMÈDE; ENG., ENTR'ACTE)

Serious operas (*dramme per musica*) through the seventeenth century routinely included comic scenes. *Sant'Alessio* (1631–1632), for example, a narrative of the spiritual struggles of a popular Roman saint, featured comic numbers and satirical references. By the end of the century, such episodes were so widespread that some singers began to specialize in *buffa* or comic interpretation. Despite the popularity of comic elements, libretto reformers such as Zeno and Metastasio (see Chapters 3 and 4) deemed them crude and coarse, and, intent on returning opera to its lofty origins, called for their removal. Only in Naples—soon to become a major center of *opera buffa*—was comedy actively promoted; there, composers even added comic numbers to productions of *seria* works from other cities.

In the first decade of the eighteenth century, theaters in Venice devised a way to offer audiences both drama and comedy at the same performance without affecting the integrity of the *seria* work. Their solution was the *intermezzo* (pl., *intermezzi*), a short comic opera in two or three parts (*parti*) performed between the acts of an *opera seria*. *Frappolone e Florinetta*, believed to be the first *intermezzo*, premiered in 1706 at the S Cassiano, the theater that had begun Venice's venture into public opera sixty-nine years earlier. By the 1720s, *intermezzi* had been introduced in Naples, where perhaps the most famous example of the genre, Pergolesi's *La serva padrona*, premiered in 1733. This miniature masterpiece was performed throughout the century in Italian and in translation from London to St. Petersburg, even crossing the Atlantic to Baltimore in 1790. However, *La serva padrona* is most famous—indeed infamous—for sparking the *Querelle des Bouffons* in Paris.

Comparing French apples to Italian oranges: The Querelle des Bouffons

In August 1752, a troupe of Italian players known as Les Bouffons performed *La serva padrona* between the acts of Lully's *Acis et Galatée* at the Palais Royal (the Opéra). This vast venue placed the small troupe at a disadvantage; nevertheless, the singers quickly adapted to the theater and remained in Paris for the next two years, winning some supporters. Those in favor of these comic productions sat near the Queen's box, whereas opponents sat near the King's, designating a physical as well as a philosophical battle line for what came to be called the *Querelle des Bouffons* (War of the Buffoons).

The question was simple but inherently unanswerable: which was better, French *tragédie lyrique* or the Italian *buffa* style? Vociferous audiences expressed their opinions from their "side" of the theater; meanwhile, Parisian presses printed articles and pamphlets defending one side and attacking the other. Because of existing conditions in the theater administration (and in the kingdom), the underlying causes of the debate actually were economic as well as aesthetic, but at a time when the seeds of free thought were beginning to sprout, criticism of the royal theater was perceived as an attack on the throne. Many writers who strove for social change disguised their true objectives behind this musical argument.

Those defending French opera took Italians to task—as they had before—for their reliance on melody instead of dramatic content; their opponents questioned whether the French language was suitable for vocal settings. When the Bouffons left Paris in 1754, the quarrel ceased. They had left their mark, though, inspiring the first school of French comic composers and unwittingly sparking a veiled political debate that pulled an uneasy capital closer to revolution.

Intermezzi scores include the requisite recitative, arias, and duets of the formal eighteenth-century stage, but their librettos exhibit a strong connection to *commedia dell'arte* (see Chapter 1). As with the skits and plots in this tradition of improvised comedy, the two or three characters of the *intermezzi* often employ dialect, at times peppering it with comic sounds such as stuttering and sobbing. Pitted against one another in stereotypical conflicts are stock figures such as the bumbling old man, the cunning servant, the wily young girl, and the braggart soldier. The three characters in *La serva padrona* exemplify this link: Uberto, the old fool, is duped by sly Serpina, who engages the servant Vespone to disguise himself as a swaggering soldier. *Buffa* singers most likely learned their craft by watching the comedians of the spoken stage. That touring productions of *commedia dell'arte* plays often featured *intermezzi* between their acts even suggests that some comics also may have doubled as *buffa* singers.

By the middle of the eighteenth century, ballets had begun to replace *intermezzi* as entr'acte entertainment. Comedy had by no means fallen out of fashion, though. The *intermezzo's* international popularity had encouraged the maturation of the full-scale musical genre that was developing contemporaneously: *opera buffa*.

OPERA BUFFA (PL., OPERE BUFFE)

The Italian word "*buffa*" (as does the French *bouffe* and the English "buffoon") derives from the Latin *buffare*, meaning "to puff out the cheeks." This term, describing one of many characteristic facial expressions of actors performing Latin comedies, demonstrates the link to the masks and exaggerated gestures of the *commedia dell'arte* stage. This less-than-noble pedigree was one of the reasons reformers eventually would campaign to remove comedy from serious librettos.

Opere serie in the early seventeenth century generally included humorous scenes. Their popularity encouraged the composition of entire comic operas. One of the most important early examples of *opera buffa*, *Chi soffre speri* (1637), demonstrates Rome's initial acceptance of these works. Farther north, Florence and Bologna presented *buffa* works as well, and by the end of the century, comic opera, along with the *intermezzo*, found receptive audiences in Naples. There, noble patrons sponsored private performances of comedies, but the genre soon generated so much enthusiasm that it became a staple on local stages, even prompting the construction of new theaters. Whereas the S Bartolomeo offered *seria* works (the San Carlo would not be built until 1737), smaller houses such as the Fiorentini, Nuovo, and Pace produced *opere buffe*. Comic operas became so popular in that city that composers with established *seria* reputations began to write both genres for the Neapolitan stage. Among these were Scarlatti, Pergolesi, and Hasse (see Chapter 8).

Having introduced the *intermezzo*, Venice also cultivated a comic tradition, and new theaters accommodating *buffa* works opened there as well. Opera houses went in and out of business regularly in Venice, but several comic theaters enjoyed genuine commercial success. In fact, the S Angelo, S Cassiano, and S Moisè (which would later popularize one-act farces) remained in business into the early nineteenth century. Despite the ascendancy of Neapolitan comedy, it would be a Venetian, the librettist Carlo Goldoni, who would set a standard for *opera buffa* that in time challenged the supremacy of *opera seria*.

Carlo Goldoni: Master of Opera Buffa

Born in Venice in 1707, Carlo Goldoni was drawn to poetry as a young man. Although he chose law as a profession, he abandoned it to join a *commedia dell'arte* troupe for whom he penned scenarios and *intermezzi*. He next found employment as assistant to a theater poet, gaining experience in adapting and revising librettos. Although five of his own *seria* texts were produced successfully, financial woes in 1743 forced him to return to practicing law, this time in Tuscany. Within five years, he was back in Venice, though, writing full-scale *opere buffe*. In 1749, he began a seven-year collaboration with composer Baldassare Galuppi, creating for him some of the finest mid-century comic librettos. After his success in Venice with Galuppi and other composers, Goldoni went to Paris, where he remained until his death in 1793. His last comic libretto, *Il talismano*, was set by Salieri in 1779 (revised 1788).

Goldoni's comic texts became so popular that, as with those of Metastasio, they were reset by many composers, among them Haydn and Mozart. He had a talent for depicting comic characters and situations in tightly constructed texts, but his greatest contribution to the *buffa* genre was the so-called "chain" finale, a series of episodes that builds to a rollicking conclusion. Galuppi was particularly adept at setting these finales, employing continuous music with key and tempo changes to fit each segment. The possibilities of this musical construction were not lost on composers of *seria* works, who quickly appropriated the chain finale as well.

Goldoni also introduced the *mezzo carattere*, a "half" character type not wholly serious or comic. This bridge between the two genres helped to move comic opera from the world of broad comedy and burlesque into the realm of contemporary wit. Goldoni's well-crafted librettos and his overall design for *opera buffa* gave the genre prestige, making it not only a worthy competitor of *opera seria* but also an internationally respected art form.

The standard *opera buffa* model established by Goldoni and set by Galuppi opens with an ensemble. Throughout the work, all major characters are given arias, but, in contrast to most *seria* numbers of the period, they were not always *da capo* (see Chapter 2). Because action was considered a far more critical element in comedy than in drama (which centers on reflection and expression), the return of a *da capo* aria's A section was thought to disrupt the pace of the plot. Thus arias in Goldoni-Galuppi works are often strophic or bipartite with no return (A-B). As a result of his *commedia dell'arte* experience, Goldoni presented Galuppi with language that fit the *buffa* singing style. His writing suits *parlante* or syllabically set vocal lines—that is, one syllable or word of text per note. Unlike the florid settings of *seria* music that place one syllable or word on a group of notes, this "patter" style focuses on the text, permitting rapid delivery and repetition of words or syllables. It also allows the singer to interject comic sounds such as stuttering, sobbing, and hiccupping into the simple melodic line.

COMIC CHARACTERS

Many of *opera buffa*'s characters originated in the *commedia dell'arte*. However, librettists and composers molded them into people whom audiences would recognize from everyday life. Some of these descendants of folk comedy, to name but a very few, include Bartolo, Don Magnifico, Don Pasquale, Figaro, Susanna, Leporello, Despina, Norina, Belcore, and Falstaff. As *opera buffa* rose in stature, new comic types entered the repertory. Certain professionals such as physicians and notaries became the object of comic interpretation, but what really advanced comic opera beyond hackneyed plots and character types was Goldoni's introduction of the *mezzo carattere* role. A typical scenario casts these semi-serious characters as young lovers whose relationship is threatened by an older male, the stereotypical bumbler generally sung by a *basso buffo*. *Il barbiere di Siviglia* and *Don Pasquale* feature prime examples of this comic conflict.

BUFFA PERFORMERS

Singers with experience in *intermezzi* moved successfully into *opera buffa*. Unlike their *seria* colleagues, whose talents focused on the interpretation and ornamentation of melodies, *buffa* performers were given vocal lines that could be manipulated for comic delivery. Therefore, it was more important for a *buffa* artist to be a good comedian than a good singer. Some theaters offering both genres actually employed two casts of singers, one expert in the *seria* style and the other for *buffa* works. Occasionally, though, a singer successfully interpreted both, as did the bass Luigi Lablache, who created such diverse roles as Walton in *I puritani* and the lead in *Don Pasquale*. Although general *buffa* specialists might have had international careers, roles sung in dialect (basically incomprehensible outside of their own regions) required the linguistic expertise of local singers.

BEYOND THE GOLDEN AGE OF OPERA BUFFA

In the nineteenth century, composers began to turn to serious and semi-serious subjects. In many ways, the *buffa* tradition seemed to have crystallized, even retaining *recitativo secco*, which had been abandoned in *seria* works for the more expressive *recitativo accompagnato* (see Chapter 2). Therefore, when Donizetti used the latter in *Don Pasquale*, he was heralded for advancing Italian comic opera. Just a decade later, though, the Ricci brothers (Federico and Luigi) and Carlo Pedrotti, composers (respectively) of two of the century's last *buffa* works, *Crispino e la comare* (1850) and *Tutti in maschera* (1856), had returned to *recitativo secco*. Eventually, allusions to the early comic traditions came to serve different objectives. Although Leoncavallo set *I pagliacci* in the world of the *commedia dell'arte*, the reference was ironic and ominous, underscoring the opera's themes of jealousy and murder. It would not be until Verdi's *Falstaff* (1893) that Italy's comic genius would resurface, but here, too, the employment of Italianate Renaissance comic sources served a more serious end: nationalism (see Chapter 7).

Twentieth-century Italian comic opera includes Puccini's one-act masterpiece, *Gianni Schicchi* (1918). Significant, though, are operas that harkened to earlier comic models and traditions. Wolf-Ferrari's *Le donne curiose* (1903) and *I quattro rusteghi* (1906) take Goldoni works as their inspiration, and Busoni's *Turandot* (1917) and Malipiero's *Il capitan Spavento* (1958) summon themes and characters from the *commedia dell'arte*. Even the works of foreign composers such as Richard Strauss (*Ariadne auf Naxos*, 1912) and

Sergei Prokofiev (*The Love for Three Oranges*, 1921) demonstrate the lasting influence of *commedia dell'arte*.

DRAMMA GIOCOSO

Dramma giocoso is often incorrectly defined as dramatic opera with comic elements, a misinterpretation perhaps stemming from the Romantic portrayal of the best-known *dramma giocoso* in opera history: *Don Giovanni*. Early nineteenth-century aesthetics eschewed happy endings, so the opera's final fugue was often eliminated (as it was in the film *Amadeus*), leaving the audience with the sights and sounds of demons dragging Giovanni into the infernal abyss. Mozart conceived the work quite differently, however, labeling it on the score and in his personal works list as an *opera buffa*.

Some scholars maintain that usage of the terms *dramma giocoso* and *opera buffa* was regional; others propose that librettists preferred the former because of its literary connotations. For Goldoni, a comic libretto that included a *seria* character was a *dramma giocoso*. Da Ponte's *Don Giovanni* offers an example; its three nobles—Donna Anna, Donna Elvira, and Don Ottavio—are so obviously from the serious tradition that Mozart assigned them arias in the *seria* style. Nevertheless, *dramma giocoso* and *opera buffa* were synonymous in the eighteenth century and should be considered so today.

FARSA (PL., FARSE)

Through the 1700s, *farsa* referred to a comedy or *intermezzo*; by the end of the century, however, the term became associated with a genre made popular in Venice, particularly at the Teatro S Moisè. These *farse* condense the action of a full-length *opera buffa* into one act. Musically, they include recitative, arias, and, at their core, a comic ensemble. By the nineteenth-century, the *farsa*'s scope was extended to include the sentimental subjects that were replacing the broad comedy of the prior century.

Farse were economical to produce because they required simple sets and costumes and rarely featured a chorus. An evening's entertainment might include two *farse* programmed with a ballet or an orchestral selection. A young Rossini made his fame in Venice with *farse* such as *La cambiale di matrimonio* (1810), *La scala di seta* (1812), and *Il Signor*

Bruschino (1813). By the time Donizetti composed *Una follia* (1818), the genre was falling out of fashion.

FRANCE

Unlike the Italian tradition, French opera offers no facile categorization of serious and comic works. Although *tragédie lyrique* always signifies a serious opera, the terms *comédie* and *comique* refer to musical works with spoken dialogue rather than recitative (see Chapter 9). Often mistranslated as "comedies" and "comic operas," *comédies* and *opéras comiques* actually encompass a variety of subjects, both comic and serious (although lighter in tone than those of a *tragédie*). To be certain how to classify these works, one needs to consider each libretto individually. Only operas described as *bouffe* or *bouffon* (from the same root as *buffa*) are immediately identifiable as comedies.

ORIGINS OF FRENCH COMIC OPERA

When traveling Italian players introduced the *commedia dell'arte* to France in the late Middle Ages, the characters were quickly absorbed into the new culture: Arlecchino became Arlequin, Scaramuccia Scaramouche, and Colombina Colombine. Venues at which they were featured regularly were the two Parisian market fairs. Each fair, or *foire*, ran for several months, and French comics, in essence, were in residence there, improvising *commedia dell'arte* style skits that also included popular tune parodies called *vaudevilles*. Itinerant Italian players competed with these so-called Fair Theaters until one of their skits satirizing Louis XIV's mistress resulted in their expulsion. After the king's death, the more lenient government of the Regency granted Italian players royal permission to return as the *Comédiens Italiens Ordinaires du Roi*. Meanwhile, the *Théâtres de la Foire* also were brought under royal purview as the *Opéra-Comique*. In 1762, the Italians and the Fair Theaters were merged under that title with the stipulation that, in addition to musical selections and dance, their performances include spoken dialogue. Only the *tragédies lyriques* of the court theater could be sung throughout. This legitimization of *opéras comiques* was facilitated further by the new standard Charles-Simon Favart set for its librettos.

Charles-Simon Favart and Opéras Comiques

Charles-Simon Favart was born in Paris in 1710. The son of a pastry chef, his endeavors in the theater made him the most significant librettist of eighteenth-century *opéra comique*. In his first success, *La chercheuse d'esprit* (1741), Favart began to raise comedy above its coarse origins, shaping it into enjoyable but moral entertainment; indeed, Voltaire credited him with elevating comedy to polite society. Because Favart retained and exploited the double entendre, however, some accused him of making only veiled attempts at naiveté. One of the greatest literary talents in the French musical theater, Favart's true talent lay in parody. Perhaps his most famous, *Le siège de Cythère* (a parody of Lully's *Armide*), ushered him into a period of misfortune when he was urged to revise it as a military propaganda piece during the Seven Years' War. He and his wife, Justine Duronceray, survived their misadventures, including her temporary imprisonment, and returned to the theater at the end of hostilities.

In the midst of the *Querelles des Bouffons*, Favart began to insert Italianate *ariettes* into his works and to translate *intermezzi* into French. His popularity earned him the patronage of Madame de Pompadour, and, thanks to her influence, he was named director of the *Comédie-Italienne*. In this position, he also worked as an impresario, scouting French talent for Vienna's Burgtheater. By the end of his career, he had nurtured an impressive number of theatrical contacts throughout Europe.

COMIC OPERA AT COURT

Despite the supremacy of Lully's *tragédies*, comedy was also popular at the court of the "Sun King." In 1664, Molière began a fourteen-year collaboration with Lully that resulted in a series of works called *comédies-ballets* that merged dance, music, comedy, and, as always in French opera, spectacle. Molière structured the plots so that the ballet and vocal music were integral to the comedy. The most famous *comédie-ballet, Le bourgeois gentilhomme* (1670), offers an example of this strategy. In it, Molière demonstrates how a knowledge of music was critical to an aristocrat's success at court. Thus the dances and the masque are more than mere musical interludes; they are essential elements in the story of the social climbing Jourdain. The ambitious Lully, however, always was intent on having his music be more dominant than the text; therefore, despite their theatrical success, discord between the playwright and composer hastened the demise of *comédie-ballet*. Although in his serious works Lully would employ certain musical techniques learned from his projects with Molière, especially setting of recitative, other characteristics of this short-lived genre in time were absorbed into *opéra comique*.

Although not a product of the court musical establishment—but nonetheless linked to it by their subjects—were comic parodies of *tragédies lyriques* performed at the Fair Theaters. Enjoying great popularity for the first four decades of the eighteenth century, these parodies by *comique* performers took aim at the lofty style of Lully's serious operas. The government's attempts to prevent their staging resulted in extravagant and creative ways to circumvent legal controls, including paying claques to sit in the audience and sing the songs. Despite obstacles, the number of parodies produced demonstrates a lively tradition; it also suggests that the crowds included members of the noble audiences, because even though lower classes enjoyed laughing at the extravagant art forms that excluded them, only someone who knew the original work would appreciate all aspects of the parody. This element of satire would run through the history of French comic opera, later finding an outlet in *opéra bouffe*.

COMIC CHARACTERS

In addition to the French versions of *commedia dell'arte* personae, the burgeoning genre of *opéra comique* benefited from new characters, among these the priest, the dowager, the country bumpkin (whose origins can be traced to Molière), and a host of peasant types speaking in dialect. Another addition to comic casts was the naive young girl, a perfect target for the outrageous double entendres descended from the low comedy of the fair theaters. Favart was a master at employing these characters—indeed, he wrote most of the ingénue parts for his wife—in works such as *Les fêtes villageoises* and *Annette et Lubin*.

MUSICAL ELEMENTS

Eighteenth-century *opéras comiques* adopted certain musical forms. Among these was the "narrative" air, a number that, unlike a reflective aria, continues to move the story along. Narrative arias, like Italian *buffa* numbers, often were performed using humorous vocal techniques such as falsetto. Composers also began to employ the duet rather than spoken dialogue as a more effective means of communication between characters. As with Italian comedies, the French also incorporated ensembles at the ends of acts.

One of the most important changes in musical settings, however, involved composers such as François-André Danican Philidor (*Blaise le savetier*), André-Ernest-Modeste Grétry (*Les deux avares*), and Pierre-Alexandre Monsigny (*On ne s'avise jamais de tout*), who started to rely less on adapting song parodies and more on the composition of new music, raising the artistic status of comic opera. By the end of the eighteenth century, French comic librettos were set as *opéras comiques* and the related genres, *comédies mêlées d'ariettes* and *comédies lyriques*. Continuing the comic tradition in the nineteenth century were composers such as Adrien Boieldieu, Charles Lecocq, Hervé (Louis Auguste Ronger), and Jacques Offenbach. Ironically, one of the finest examples of French comic opera, *La fille du régiment*, was penned by the Italian Donizetti.

COMÉDIE-PARADE

One specifically comic manifestation of *opéra comique* in the eighteenth century was the *comédie-parade*, a one-act farce featuring stock characters and broad humor derived from the *commedia dell'arte* and fair theater traditions. Songs were either parodies or newly composed numbers. Despite its popularity, the *comédie-parade* fell out of fashion shortly before the turn of the century.

OPÉRA BOUFFE

By the mid-nineteenth century, more and more *opéras comiques* featured serious (and, some thought, pretentious) subjects. As a reaction, Jacques Offenbach (followed by other composers) created *opérettes*, one-act farcical sketches employing minimal musical forces and casts. Not unlike productions of Venetian *farse*, two or three *opérettes* would be presented as an evening's entertainment. Although they rarely had a true plot, their librettos' cutting social and political satire, most often aimed at the regime of Napoleon III, made them so popular that Offenbach expanded the concept to create full-length works. In 1855, he opened the *Théâtre des Bouffes Parisiens* to accommodate this new genre: *opéra bouffe*. Musically, the scores featured choral introductions and ensembles, large casts, and full orchestras; the librettos took aim at every aspect of Parisian life. The first (and most significant) *opéra bouffe* was Offenbach's *Orphée aux enfers*. Satirizing the oft-set Orpheus myth, the work parodied contemporary Parisian society, with the character *Opinion Publique* (Public Opinion) counseling Orpheus on how society would view his actions. Offenbach even made sport of Gluck's eighteenth-century setting of the tale by having his gods of the Underworld substitute a *cancan* for the ballet.

Playing on broad farce as well as intellect and wit, *opéra bouffe* was popular until 1879, marking the close of Offenbach's theater and the decline of his own fame (he would die a year later, his one serious opera, *Les contes d'Hoffmann*, unfinished). Taking its place as rival of the *opéra comique* was its most significant descendant: *opérette*.

OPERETTA (FR., OPÉRETTE; GER., OPERETTE)

Offenbach employed the term *opérette* for the one-act farces whose popularity inspired full-length *opéras bouffes*. Within several years of their debut on the Parisian stage, both genres (together with their composer) had traveled to Vienna. Although the French topical satire was of little interest to audiences there, they quickly warmed to the music. As Offenbach's popularity declined, *Operette* gained in stature in the hands of composers such as Franz von Suppé and, most notably, Johann Strauss, who molded the genre into something specifically Viennese by substituting romance for satire and emphasizing the rhythms of the waltz. In fact, even in Paris, *opérettes* favoring romantic subjects such as Lecocq's *La fille de Madame Angot* and Planquette's *Les cloches de Corneville* had begun to replace satires. In the end, it would be *Operettes* from the Viennese tradition such as Strauss' *Die Fledermaus* and *Der Zigeunerbaron* that would remain prominent in the nineteenth century. In the twentieth century, works by Franz Lehár, particularly *Die lustige Witwe*, proved so influential that even Puccini attempted *operetta* with *La rondine*.

BEYOND PARIS AND VIENNA

Offenbach's *opéras bouffes* also were performed on the international stage in translation or as parodies. Yet beyond these versions, the originals inspired new compositions. The genre would find fertile ground in England, where Arthur Sullivan set W.S. Gilbert's librettos for works such as *HMS Pinafore*, *The Mikado*, and *The Yeomen of the Guard*. These and works like them, in turn, became popular in the United States, inspiring American composers such as Reginald De Koven (*Robin Hood*) and Victor Herbert (*The Fortune Teller*). By the late nineteenth century, however, the British had moved on to a new genre they called musical comedy, to which the Americans in time also laid claim.

Although they stem from similar ancestry, the *operetta* and the musical are distinct entities. Productions of *operettas* such as *Fledermaus* and *Die lustige Witwe* remain in the province of the international opera repertory, whereas musicals are performed in theatrical seasons. On a technical level, both genres have different performance styles. Opera singers depend on their own natural vocal volume, whereas singers in musicals generally wear microphones. Also, the scores of operettas feature larger orchestral forces than are required in the pit of a musical. Some works, such as Gershwin's *Porgy and Bess*, seem to tread a fine line. Yet, even though it premiered at Broadway's Alvin Theatre on 52nd Street in New York, *Porgy* is an opera for one simple reason: its composer referred to it as one.

The development of the musical goes beyond the scope of this book; a full discussion of its diverse and rich heritage could well be the subject for another volume in this series. Our next chapter considers vernacular genres, operas outside of (but still influenced by) the Italian and French light opera and comic traditions.

10

VERNACULAR OPERA

Not long after their initial successes at home, early seventeenth-century Italian operas were taken abroad with singers who could perform them and often with the composers who had written them. By the eighteenth century, the genre had become so fashionable that it was almost *de rigueur* for European courts and theaters to have Italian composers and poets in residence. Hence, many Italian operas actually had their premieres outside of Italy; Paisiello's *Il barbiere di Siviglia*, for instance, was composed for the court of Russia's Catherine the Great. Only in France did the genre develop differently. When Italian opera was introduced there in the 1640s, the French court embraced the concept of all-sung theatrical works but distanced itself from the Italian style, creating its own musical dramas and merging them with the traditional court ballet (see Chapter 8). French operas were exported, too, often with the special stage machinery—requisite equipment in the royal theater—that could produce illusions such as making characters appear to fly. Because of the widespread presence of Italian composers and the strong influence of French dramatic music and spectacle, these two traditions dominated the international musical stage for nearly two centuries.

Developing contemporaneously in countries that hosted Italian and French productions were works now known as vernacular operas; performed in the languages of their countries of origin, they differed from the two prevailing traditions because they featured spoken dialogue instead of recitative (*opéra comique* is often considered a vernacular genre, but it is considered in this book along with other types of French opera in Chapters 8 and 9). Most areas of Europe, including Bohemia, Sweden, Poland, and Russia, boasted vernacular traditions. Although popular in their day, the scores of a majority of these works now reside in archives, awaiting rediscovery; productions of the few vernacular operas that have endured generally are intranational. The three traditions that have fared best internationally—English, German, and Spanish—are the focus of this chapter. In addition to spoken dialogue interspersed with musical numbers, the characteristics they share demonstrate a cross-fertilization suggesting notable fluidity and adaptability.

ENGLAND

England contributed two unique forms to the world of vernacular opera: semi-operas, which incorporated music, dance, and dialogue, most famously in the works of Henry Purcell, and ballad operas, the best known being *The Beggar's Opera* by John Gay.

SEMI-OPERA

Before Charles II was restored to the English throne in 1660, he spent part of his time in exile at the French court, where the musical establishment of his cousin Louis XIV was the envy of Europe. Hence, it was only natural that Charles, attempting to bolster the image of his impoverished court, hoped to emulate French music. His subjects were able to sample French opera when Lully's first *tragédie en musique*, *Cadmus et Hermione*, was produced in England soon after its premiere in 1673. To celebrate a political victory over Parliament, Charles himself requested a composition "like an Opera"; the result, *Albion and Albanius* (1685), was an opera in the style of Lully by the French composer Louis Grabu to a libretto by John Dryden.

Although influenced by the concept of opera, critics, many of them playwrights with their own self-interests at heart, strove to maintain the supremacy of spoken drama by challenging all-sung opera in English as unsuitable for their audiences' tastes. Within their own tradition, however, the court masque, an elaborate mixture of poetry, music, dance, and spectacle, proved a model for compromise: semi-opera. Popular from the 1670s to the early 1700s, semi-operas were plays that featured singing, dancing, instrumental music, and elaborate sets employing imported French stage machinery that created the spectacular illusions found in productions of *tragédies lyriques* (see Chapter 8) and *comédies ballets* (see Chapter 9). In addition to the expense of these scenographic effects, semi-operas were costly because they normally required two casts: one of actors who played the major characters and another of performers who sang the minor roles.

The most significant composer of semi-operas was Henry Purcell, who took up the genre after composing *Dido and Aeneas*, a work heralded as true English opera (see Chapter 8). Purcell's semi-operas include *The Prophetess, or The History of Dioclesian; King Arthur; The Fairy Queen*; and *The Indian Queen*, completed after his death by his brother, Daniel. (Purcell was formerly credited with *The Tempest*; now, only one song is traced to him and the rest of the score attributed to John Weldon). Generally, librettists would fashion the first four acts of a semi-opera to accommodate songs that were by and large peripheral to the plot. In the librettos for *King Arthur* and *The Indian Queen*, however, Dryden took unusual care to link musical episodes to the dramatic action. In *King Arthur*, for example, songs such as "Come if you dare, our trumpets sound" aptly characterize the Britons' boldness in battle against the Saxons, the main action of the first act. The greatest musical activity in a semi-opera occurred in the fifth act, which was set in the tradition of the masque, featuring extensive vocal, instrumental, and dance music; here again, though, a Purcell-Dryden work is an exception as *The Indian Queen* features a masque in the second act as well.

The popularity of the semi-opera continued after Purcell's death in 1695 as his brother and other composers continued to set them. Although by all accounts the genre would have remained popular into the next century, its death knell tolled with the arrival of Italian opera. Semi-opera required both actors and singers, but the expense of this fashionable new entertainment (especially the singers' salaries) prompted a royal decree that at least temporarily divided the musical and spoken stages. Although abandoned for other forms of entertainment in England, the semi-opera flourished in Spain into the eighteenth century (see the following section on Spain).

BALLAD OPERA

Even more short-lived than semi-opera was England's other significant vernacular genre, ballad opera, the first (and most famous) of which was John Gay's *The Beggar's Opera* (1728). Gay wrote the libretto, which included spoken dialogue and lyrics that were parodies of well-known songs arranged by Johann Christoph Pepusch, who also provided an overture for the work. In the repertory of vernacular English operas, Gay's work stands apart. Although there was nothing novel about the insertion of songs into plays (Shakespeare included texts for his characters to sing), the major portion of a ballad opera was dialogue. Gay, however, divided his libretto equally between spoken text and song. Even more significant was his approach to parody because he created texts that were not only relevant to the action but also contained recognizable allusions to the original lyrics.

Sources for The Beggar's Opera

John Gay plumbed a rich repertory for the parodies in *The Beggar's Opera*. From the folk tradition came Lucy Lockit's air, "Thus when a good huswife sees a rat," a parody of "A lovely lass to a friar came," a tune claimed by both the Scots and the Irish. Songs from popular published collections such as Thomas D'Urfey's *Pills to Purge Melancholy* also provided material. "Over the Hills and Far Away," parodied as well by George Farquhar in *The Recruiting Officer*, was transformed into a love song between Polly Peachum and Macheath that went on to become one of the most popular tunes in colonial America. Nor was the world of Italian opera spared: the Act III March from Handel's *Rinaldo* inspired the Air, "Let us take the road."

The wit of Gay's parodies can be seen by comparing the texts of "Oh London is a fine Town," from an original tune in *Pills to Purge Melancholy*, to "Our Polly is a sad slut," Mr. Peachum's Act I air:

> Oh London is a fine Town, and a gallant city.
> 'Tis Govern'd by the Scarlet Gown, come listen to my ditty;
> This City has a Mayor, this Mayor is a Lord
> He Governeth the Citizens upon his own accord.
> He boasteth his Gentility, and how Nobly he was Born,
> His Arms are three Ox-heads, and his Crest a Rampant Horn.
>
> Our Polly is a sad slut! nor heeds what we have taught her.

> I wonder any man alive will ever rear a Daughter!
> For she must have both hoods and gowns, and hoops to swell
>   her pride,
> With scarfs and stays, and gloves and lace; and she will have
>   men beside;
> And when she's drest with care and cost, all-tempting fine
>   and gay,
> As men should serve a Cowcumber, she flings herself away.

Gay's audiences would have connected the reference to Polly's "hoods and gowns" to the image of the Lord Mayor's "scarlet gown" in the original. Polly's pride, too, mirrors the Mayor's, a benefit of his noble birth; Polly, of course, acquires hers from the finery she insists on having. Gay's text also implies that both are fools. Polly, as Mr. Peachum points out, cultivates the image of a slattern so that she can attract men and "fling herself away." The Mayor's image is delightfully descriptive: a coat-of-arms bearing not one but three heads of the legendary dumb ox and a rampant (or raised) horn—a fitting allusion back to Polly's own sexual exploits.

It is unclear how familiar Gay was with contemporary French comic opera, but *The Beggar's Opera* clearly mirrors the parodies of the French fair theaters and rival Italian players (see Chapter 9) in several ways. Both portray shady characters, perfect opposites of those found on the genteel stage. Also, as with the *comique* theaters, Gay takes aim at opera. Not only are the characters of Lucy Lockit and Polly Peachum blatant allusions to Handel's rival stars, Faustina Bordoni and Francesca Cuzzoni, but the Beggar who speaks the Introduction expresses the English prejudices against Italian opera when he entreats the audience to forgive him because "I have not made my Opera throughout unnatural, like those in vogue; for I have no Recitative." Furthermore, only in parody would criminals and prostitutes be spared hanging to enjoy the requisite *lieto fine* (happy ending) of contemporary librettos. As with *comique* parodies, *The Beggar's Opera* is a commentary on audiences who would have needed to be familiar with the operatic stage to comprehend the nuances of the satire.

Among other ballad opera librettists was novelist Henry Fielding, who created several works that enjoyed successful runs, among them

The Mock Doctor (1732) and *Don Quixote in England* (1734). One other ballad opera deserves special note: Charles Coffey's *The Devil to Pay* (1731), which, as will be seen, was an important influence on the development of the German vernacular genre, *Singspiel*. Gay, Fielding, and others continued to compose ballad operas, but the success of *The Beggar's Opera* was never duplicated, and although it provided a lively outlet for English comedy, the genre died out after less than a decade. Thereafter, English audiences contented themselves with translations and adaptations of foreign works (many of which found their way to America). The operettas of Gilbert and Sullivan would revive their national musical stage in the nineteenth century, but true English opera awaited the pens of Ralph Vaughan Williams, Gustav Holst, and Benjamin Britten in the twentieth century (see Chapter 8).

GERMANY

Germany had its own form of partially sung, partially spoken dramas, known as *Singspiele*. This rich folk tradition was transformed into classic works by Mozart, Schubert, and many other composers in the eighteenth and nineteenth centuries.

SINGSPIEL (PL., SINGSPIELE)

Singspiel, as is ballad opera, is a play (Ger., *Spiel*) with songs. Until the genre was standardized in the mid-eighteenth century, however, the term was applied to various manifestations of theatrical music in Germany and Austria. Some of the earliest works called *Singspiele* were German-language productions akin to the Italian *dramme per musica*—that is, operas with recitative depicting serious secular and sacred subjects. Not yet solely associated with works in German, however, the term also was used for operas in Italian or even with macaronic (two-language) texts. Nor were composers consistent in their use of terms. In the eighteenth century, J.A. Hiller preferred *"komische Oper"* for works that today would be classified as *Singspiele*. Later, Franz Schubert employed it for one- or two-act works, differentiating them for the longer three-act *Oper*. Today, the accepted definition of *Singspiel* is any serious or comic work from Germany or Austria that features spoken dialogue interspersed with songs.

THE NORTHERN TRADITION

German folk comedy offered a font of tales and characters for the plots of early *Singspiele*, but trade with England provided one of its most influential models: ballad opera in the form of Coffey's *The Devil to Pay*, produced in German as *Der Teufel ist los* in Hamburg in 1743 and in Leipzig in 1753. Other foreign models were the French *opéra comique* and *comédie mêlée d'ariette* (see Chapter 8). In fact, some of the most significant eighteenth-century *Singspiel* librettos, the works of C.F. Weisse, demonstrate the influence of Charles-Simon Favart (see Chapter 9). As Favart had done for *comique* librettos, Weisse would set the standard for *Singspiel* texts just as his collaborator Hiller would do for its music.

Singspiele celebrated the rural lower middle class, generally satirizing upper-class characters and foreigners. Musically, this social divide was emphasized by assigning simple strophic songs to the former characters while depicting the others with arias, the music of urban high society. Often centering on a pair of lovers, the drama would move with spoken dialogue, while songs would be inserted at moments of reflection or emotion. Although rare in early works, some *Singspiele* featured brief sections of recitative in addition to dialogue, and choruses were sometimes included to depict the reactions of the townspeople.

Originally, the simplicity of *Singspiel* melodies was a practical matter because traveling troupes were generally composed of actors rather than singers. In time, the notion of simple melody, especially in the hands of composers such as Georg Benda and Johann Friedrich Reichardt, came to symbolize German musical culture as the antithesis of the daunting arias of Italian and French opera. Some numbers, especially from the *Singspiele* of Hiller and Weisse, actually were incorporated into the realm of published folk songs.

THE SOUTHERN TRADITION

The works of Weisse and Hiller belong to the northern and central *Singspiel* tradition. The southern tradition was based primarily in Vienna, where the popular songs and parodies performed by classic comic figures such as Hanswurst and Pickelhäring competed with an almost exclusive monopoly of Italian opera. In an effort to encourage German writers and composers in this bastion of Italian music, Emperor Joseph II founded the National-Singspiel in 1778, but the majority of works it generated turned out to be translations or adaptations of French and Italian operas. The most successful composition, Mozart's *Die Entführung aus dem Serail* (1782), failed to salvage this short-lived experiment, and the theater closed the following year. A second season several years later produced more significant *Singspiele*, many from the pen of the most important composer of the southern school: Carl Ditter von Dittersdorf. For a time, scholars thought that in works such as *Der Apotheker und der Doktor*, Dittersdorf appealed more to popular taste than did Mozart, but the recent discovery of a pastiche entitled *Der Stein der Weisen*, to which Mozart contributed, demonstrates that the composer of anomalies such as *Die Entführung* and *Die Zauberflöte* also could fit into the more generic style.

In general, Viennese *Singspiele*, with their comic, sentimental, and satiric plots, emphasized solo song, strophic duets, and the occasional simple chorus. Because of its popular appeal, houses such as the Theater auf den Wieden, managed by Emanuel Schikaneder, librettist of *Die Zauberflöte* and the work's first Papageno, did more for the *Singspiel* than the Emperor's theater ever could have. Yet even as Schubert contributed to the genre in the early 1800s with works such as *Der vierjährige Posten* and *Die Freunde von Salamanka*, he and other composers had begun seeking different expressions for German theatrical music. Schubert's contemporary Carl Maria von Weber wrestled with creating German opera that would garner equal status with Italian and French works (see Chapter 8). Thus, even though it has spoken dialogue, Weber's *Der Freischütz* is more aptly called a German Romantic opera, as is Schubert's *Fierrabras*.

Still performed through the first half of the nineteenth century, *Singspiel* nevertheless became less significant than the loftier new works that made greater demands on audiences and performers alike. By the emergence of Offenbach's creation, the *Operetta*, and its subsequent rise in the hands of Johann Strauss, the *Singspiel* had become a part of Vienna's musical past.

ZAUBEROPER (GER., MAGIC OPERA)

Zauberoper was linked primarily to popular theaters in the suburbs of Vienna in the late eighteenth and early nineteenth centuries, although "magic operas" such as Gaspare Spontini's *Alcidor* (Berlin, 1825) also were performed throughout Austria and Germany. Although the plots are connected to the tradition of folk tales, the works must be considered modern artistic enterprises because they exploited all the technical effects that the contemporary stage could produce to portray the fantasy in their plots. Mozart's *Die Zauberflöte* is the most famous example, but others include Schubert's *Die Zauberharfe* (*The Magic Harp*) and Ignaz von Seyfried's *Der Feenkönig* (*The Fairy King*).

SPAIN

During the reign of King Philip IV (1621–1665), the representative from the Vatican to the Spanish court was Giulio Rospigliosi (later Pope Clement IX), the librettist who had penned *Chi soffre speri* for the Roman stage. Named apostolic nuncio in 1644, Rospigliosi retained that post for ten years. During this time, the king not only developed an interest in theatrical music but also realized, along with his ministers, that fostering productions at court would enhance Spain's international prestige. Whether Rospigliosi or Italian scenographer Baccio di Bianco's work in the Madrid theater actually inspired this royal enthusiasm is unclear; scholars of the music of Juan Hidalgo, Spain's most influential composer of theater music at the time, are quick to note the absence of Italianate elements in his scores. What is apparent, however, is that important Spanish playwrights such as Miguel de Cervantes (author of *Don Quixote*), Tirso de Molina, and Pedro Calderón considered music a vital element in their dramas. Their works, including *comedias* and semi-operas, would inspire the development of Spain's vernacular genres.

SEMI-OPERAS

Pedro Calderón and Juan Hidalgo collaborated on several three-act plays highlighting the realm of mythological characters, which were symbols, of course, for the king and the Spanish court. Although mortal characters expressed themselves in strophic song, many of them parodies of popular tunes, the gods sang in recitative. Hidalgo also freely adapted dance rhythms into his music, producing scores that drew on the concept of Italian opera but exalted Spanish style.

Clearly Italianate, however, were Bianco's sets that made ample usage of the mechanical stage techniques so important in Italian court productions. Hidalgo-Calderón semi-operas, including *La estatua de Prometeo* (1670 or 1674), proved so popular that they were revived at court until the turn of the eighteenth century, a period that overlaps the popularity of the semi-opera in England. In addition to the participation of equally significant playwrights and composers willing to exploit the possibilities of dramas with music, the Spanish and English traditions may well be linked by the latter culture's interest in Calderón's plays, which had reached England in French translation.

ZARZUELA

In addition to encouraging productions at the Teatro del Buen Retiro in Madrid, Philip also attempted to have theatrical music performed at his hunting lodge, *La Zarzuela*. Large productions would have required casts from Madrid, which, in essence, would have closed the theater temporarily. So Philip settled for less complex fare at his country estate. Although some performances were sung throughout, the majority of works featured spoken dialogue, songs, and dances. Initially, theatrical compositions were identified by the venues at which they were performed: "de la Zarzuela" or "en el Buen Retiro." By the end of the seventeenth century, the shortened term "*zarzuela*" had come to signify a genre.

CHARACTERISTICS

During Philip's reign, *zarzuelas* featured monody, duets, and choruses (see Chapter 1). Similarly, they shared the mythological and pastoral subjects of the Spanish stage, as witnessed in works such as *El golfo de las sirenas* and *El laurel de Apolo* (*The Gulf of the Sirens* and *Apollo's Laurel*), both from 1657. When Hidalgo began composing *zarzuelas* in 1672, he, too, highlighted such subjects in works such as *Los juegos olímpicos* (*The Olympic Games*) and *Endimión y Diana* (*Endymion and Diana*).

Although *zarzuela* developed in the Spanish court and then in the theaters of Madrid and Barcelona, it drew inspiration from foreign models. The first influence was Italian opera, which arrived in Spain during hostilities between King Philip V in Madrid and King Charles III in Barcelona. It is perhaps significant that the rivals Philip, a Bourbon, and Charles, a Habsburg, both were descended from royal houses that cultivated a special dedication to Italian opera. During the eighteenth century, Spanish composers imitated Italian works, even in *zarzuelas* such as *La nuevas armas de amor*, a collaboration of composer Sebastián Durón and librettist José de Cañizare that included arias in its score. The cross-fertilization of Italian and Spanish music at this time was so intense that visiting Italian composers attempted to write *zarzuelas* and native composers translated and adapted Italian works into Spanish. Even though some *zarzuelas* were even labeled "*a la italiana*" for popular appeal, eventually the native genre could not compete with the grander productions of Italian opera.

THE TONADILLA

As a genre, the *zarzuela* was forgotten for the rest of eighteenth century, but native music found an outlet in a smaller theatrical form known as the *tonadilla*. Gaining notoriety mid-century, these one-act satirical sketches featured dances such as the *seguidilla* (which Bizet later would adopt for *Carmen*) and Spanish folk songs with accompaniments ranging from solo guitar to small orchestral ensembles. *Tonadillas* originally had small casts, but as the genre became more popular, its scope expanded. *La plaza de palacio de Barcelona* (1774), for instance, had a dozen roles. As with the early English ballad opera and French popular *comique* works, *tonadillas* told stories of lower class characters such as gypsies and peasants. One of the last composers to work in the genre was Manuel Garcia, the tenor who premiered the role of Almaviva in Rossini's *Il barbiere di Siviglia*; his works *El majo y la maja* and *La declaración* premiered in 1798 and 1799, respectively. The *tonadilla's* demise in the early nineteenth century made way for the return of the *zarzuela*.

NINETEENTH-CENTURY ZARZUELA

Although the return of the *zarzuela* with works such as *Colegiales y soldados*, performed in Madrid in 1849, might seem like a reaction to a century of Italian domination, native composers soon succumbed to another foreign influence. As a result of French invasions and the subsequent reaction of the *afrancesados*—influential Spanish who favored the social and artistic models of the French—*zarzuelas* assumed the characteristics of the *opéra comique*. As occurred with Italian works in the prior century, composers began to adapt *opéras comiques* for presentation as *zarzuelas*, among them Meyerbeer's *L'étoile du nord* (premiering as *Catalina* in 1854) and Auber's *Fra Diavolo* (under its original title in 1857). Further French influence came from Offenbach's *opéras bouffes* and translations of the newly popular *opérettes* (see Chapter 9).

GENERO CHICO

In the late 1860s, a new one-act manifestation of the *zarzuela*, the *genero chico*, appeared on Madrid stages. Featuring less music and more dialogue than the *opéra comique* adaptations, their plots centered on the city's working class with music derived from the Spanish folk repertory. Because of the popularity of these works more theaters began to offer them to an appreciative public. Among the composers who wrote in this genre were Federico Chueca, Joaquín Valverde, and Tomás Bretón, whose *La verbena e la paloma* (1894) remained popular into the next century.

TWENTIETH-CENTURY ZARZUELA

Running counter to the *genero chico* were composers who continued to compose large-scale *zarzuelas* that showed the influence of operetta (see Chapter 9). These works, particularly those inspired by Franz Lehár, defined the style of *zarzuela* in the twentieth century, although strategies to distance the genre from the Viennese model included the substitution of tangos for waltzes. A fine example is one of the few *zarzuelas* in the international repertory, Amadeo Vives' *Doña Francisquita*. As popular as these works were—and even with the participation of composers such as Falla, Albéniz and Granados—*zarzuela* composition ceased around the middle of the century. Nevertheless, continuing the work of the Sociedad Artistica formed in Madrid in the nineteenth century, the Teatro de la Zarzuela today remains an active center for the genre's production and preservation.

VERNACULAR TRADITIONS IN RETROSPECT

A brief look at only three vernacular genres demonstrates the varied issues involved in creating national culture in the shadow of dominant foreign traditions. In some cases, composers embraced musical elements from these reigning styles; others, however, strove to isolate and protect their own artistic expressions from outside influences. Contemporary politics often forced the imposition of foreign models and styles on genres that otherwise would have developed as a pure reflection of native culture. Some vernacular genres faltered because elitist audiences, prejudiced by class-conscious reactions to their popular origins, favored the loftier styles from abroad. On the other hand, many members of the rising middle class supported works that challenged musical establishments to which they had little or no access. Studied individually, these repertories offer rich sources for a fuller narrative of the role opera played in the development of national culture and aesthetics. Taken as a whole, the history of vernacular opera demonstrates how resilient and creative artistic expression can be in the face of political constraint and cultural models.

11

SCORES AND EDITIONS

A score is a handwritten or printed representation of a musical composition. In addition to staves with the vocal and instrumental parts, an opera score also includes the libretto's text, its words generally syllabicated and placed under the notes to which they are sung. The most obvious use for a score is as a guide that musicians and singers "read" to perform the music. However, scores also can be studied. For example, versions of the same opera can be examined and compared to piece together the work's composition or performance history. This type of research has received increasing attention recently because most composers rarely "authorized" a single version of an opera. In fact, many works went through numerous incarnations.

Opera scores were (and still are) revised for a variety of reasons. Some singers required arias to be transposed into other keys; indeed, entire roles have been rescored for different ranges. Although Rosina in Rossini's *Il barbiere di Siviglia* was originally a contralto part, it was quickly transposed upwards to become a lead role for sopranos. Less radical a change is the composition of substitute arias. Singers cast into new productions of previously premiered works often required something less (or more) demanding or simply something different from the original number. Verdi, for instance, composed new arias for two subsequent interpreters of Foresto in his opera *Attila*.

Instrumentation at times also needed to be altered; this was particularly true for the music played by a stage band (It., *banda sul palco*; Fr. *musique de scéne*), a prominent feature of works in the early nineteenth century. Because members of local town or military ensembles generally were employed to play these numbers, it was left up to the local bandmaster to flesh out these parts based on the players he had at his disposal.

Librettos also were changed, generally to placate censors or appeal to local aesthetics. Because Roman audiences preferred happy endings, Rossini provided one for the revival of *Otello* there in 1820. These few examples only touch on complex issues about which opera historians continue to uncover information. They prove, however, that it is naive to think of opera scores as monuments carved in stone; rather, various versions of scores reflect an extremely fluid theatrical tradition.

A Butterfly Collection

Giacomo Puccini completed the score of *Madama Butterfly* in 1903. The production employing that score had a disastrous premiere at La Scala in February 1904. The composer immediately withdrew the work from the stage and began to make revisions, the most significant of which was the division of the second act into two parts. This revised score was performed successfully in Brescia just three months later. When *Butterfly* opened in Paris in 1906, its score had been amended further; it is this version that is now often referred to as the "definitive edition." However, a fourth version, in which Puccini approved the reinsertion of material from the original Scala score, was performed in Milan in 1918. Productions after Puccini's death demonstrate further changes. So, which score is the real *Madama Butterfly*?

The four scores in which Puccini had a hand are all said to be "authorized" or authentic. No matter how noble the intentions of the editor or director, those changed without his approval or direct intervention cannot make this claim. Nevertheless, they are valid documents in the opera's stage history because they demonstrate how *Madama Butterfly* was (and continues to be) changed to suit singers, audiences, theaters, and directors' visions.

Full scores of operas feature the instrumental and vocal lines on the same page, with longer operas filling two or more volumes. A glance into the orchestra pit will reveal that the conductor has a full score, generously marked with notes and cues made during rehearsals. Members of the orchestra, on the other hand, play from music with only their parts. Singers, who must memorize their roles, learn from piano/vocal scores that include all the vocal parts and a "reduction" of the orchestral score into a piano accompaniment. Most singers will consult a full score as well, especially when preparing a role for the first time because it is important to see how the orchestral music interacts with the voices.

Until the recent advent of notation software such as Finale or Sibelius, composers handwrote scores. Sometimes, depending on the popularity of the work or the reputation of the composer, their operas were then typeset and sold in either full score or piano/vocal versions. The latter became extremely popular in the nineteenth century when the rising middle class could afford to own instruments and take music lessons (see Chapter 6). The resulting demand for piano/vocal scores created a boom market for music publishers and teachers; indeed, opera selections, both played and sung, were a major feature of parlor entertainment. The sheer number of published piano/vocal scores of entire operas and compilations of operatic selections demonstrates how significant this repertoire was. Indeed, the ability to perform these works and to claim knowledge of the most current operas became a symbol of status and culture.

While amateurs were singing and playing from printed editions at home, singers and orchestral musicians commonly played from scores and parts written out by copyists, musicians who themselves might have been budding composers. In addition to preparing scores and parts for performance, copyists usually created the piano/vocal reductions of operas for eventual publication. This type of work kept Wagner from starvation in Paris in the early 1840s.

HOLOGRAPH SCORES AND AUTOGRAPH SCORES

Libraries make a distinction between two types of manuscript scores. A holograph is written in the hand of the composer. Although many holographs are full scores, equally important are sketches in a composer's hand because these document the evolution of an opera's composition. Some sketches are so-called "short scores" in which the composer wrote out the vocal lines but gave only an indication of the orchestration intended to flesh out the piece.

Although still in handwriting (the literal meaning of "manu-script"), an autograph is in the hand of someone other than the composer, such as a student, family member, or copyist. Certain musicologists are as familiar with the handwriting of copyists as they are with those of the composers whose scores these copyists prepared. Because many of today's composers and those who assist them in the preparation of parts now use print-ready computer software, holographs and autographs will soon belong to the past.

CRITICAL EDITIONS

A critical edition is prepared by scholars and historically informed musicians who are experts in the music of the period in which the opera was composed or specialists in the works of specific composers. These scholarly editions follow strict methodology and editorial criteria. Necessary expertise includes the ability to resolve special problems found in scores from prior centuries. For example, seventeenth- and eighteenth-century orchestras included now-obsolete instruments such as theorbos, ophecleides, and horns pitched in a variety of keys. Although musicians in orchestras dedicated to "authenticity" in early music play these instruments, the average orchestra member does not. Therefore, editors must understand these early instruments as well as the disposition of early orchestras to make the music intelligible to students and performers. Although editors of critical scores often prepare modern performance materials of these older works, their primary purpose is to present a historically accurate representation of a work; thus, they consider all relevant primary sources, examining holograph, autograph, and published scores with which the composer was concerned. (A critical edition of *Madama Butterfly*, for example, would be based on the scores and librettos of the four versions with which Puccini was involved).

Although scholarly editions generally feature one score of a work, significant variant versions of one or more numbers may also be included, as might transcriptions of important sketch materials. Each decision an editor makes in preparing this type of score must be carefully annotated in a prose commentary, often a small volume published separately from the score. In principle, a critical edition is the most inclusive and scientifically produced version of a work. Among the critical editions available are those of the operas of Handel, Mozart, Rossini, Verdi, Musorgsky, Donizetti, Bellini, and Wagner. A word of caution, however: only publications under the supervision of a scholarly committee of specialists can promise true historical integrity.

FACSIMILE EDITIONS

A facsimile edition is a published photograph or photocopy of a holograph or manuscript. Because it is intended solely as reproduction of a composer's or copyist's original, it contains no added editorial markings or performance directions. As replicas of historical documents, facsimiles are invaluable aids for students and scholars unable to travel to the archives or libraries that house the originals. Pages of facsimiles are often included within critical editions because they provide examples of compositional strategies or support editorial decisions.

PERFORMING EDITIONS

Generally, critical editions can be employed for performance; indeed, some of the publishers also make parts available for opera companies that wish to use scores of the highest historical integrity. Other productions rely on performing editions rented from or sold by publishing houses that hold production rights or copyright. Directors of operas then decide how their individual productions will be performed, removing or inserting numbers to suit their vision of a work (see Chapter 4). Cuts often are taken to make lengthy works more palatable for contemporary audiences, or insertions or substitutions of numbers made to suit performers. As was the practice in prior centuries, virtuoso singers exert great control over what happens within a specific role in a given production. It is clearly fact that Maria Callas drew audiences to hear *Norma*, not its composer Bellini. For that reason, productions were tailored to suit her.

GENERAL EDITIONS

Music publishers often issue scores of operas for purchase by the general public. These are usually available in large bookstores or music shops. In essence, anyone who can read an orchestral score or who simply wishes to follow the vocal lines will find these editions useful in preparing to hear an opera. However, what one "reads" in these scores may not exactly match what is seen in a production or heard on a recording because, as has been noted, performing scores are manipulated and numbers can be moved or cut completely. Is this sacrilege? Not at all. It merely reflects the way operas have been produced throughout history after they left the eyes and ears of their creators.

RESOURCES

SELECTED BIBLIOGRAPHY

This volume has stressed the importance of reexamining opera history in light of recent research. To that end, this bibliography features literature published since 1990. Readers will find older authorities (as well as journal articles and research in foreign languages) cited in the bibliographies of the works listed. Entries in the online version of *The New Grove Dictionary of Music and Musicians* (www.grovemusic.com) also include bibliographies; this web site, accessible with a personal subscription or at participating public and university libraries, is updated routinely to include the latest publications. Relevant entries are marked OPERA.

GENERAL GUIDES TO REPERTORY OPERAS

Bourne, Joyce. *Who's Who in Opera: A Guide to Opera Characters*. Michael Kennedy, ed. New York: Oxford University Press, 1998.

Freeman, John W. *The Metropolitan Opera Stories of the Great Operas*. 2 vols. New York: Metropolitan Opera Guild and W.W. Norton, 1984–1997.

Lee, M. Owen. *The Operagoer's Guide: One Hundred Stories and Commentaries*. Portland, OR: Amadeus Press, 2001.

Lyric Opera of Chicago. *The Lyric Opera Companion: The History, Lore, and Stories of the World's Greatest Operas*. Kansas City, MO: Andrews and McMeel, 1991.

Peattie, Anthony, general ed. *The New Kobbé's Opera Book*. The Earl of Harewood, consultant ed. Revised edition of *The Definitive Kobbé's Opera Book*. New York: Putnam, 1997.

RECENT RESEARCH ON SPECIFIC TOPICS

Ahlquist, Karen. *Democracy at the Opera: Music, Theater, and Culture in New York, 1815–1860*. Urbana: University of Illinois Press, 1997.

Aikin, Judith Popovich. *A Language for German Opera: The Development of Forms and Formulas for Recitative and Aria in Seventeenth-Century German Libretti*. Wiesbaden: Harrassowitz, 2002.

Applegate, Celia, and Pamela Potter. *Music and German National Identity*. Chicago: University of Chicago Press, 2002.

Barbier, Patrick. *Opera in Paris, 1800–1850: A Lively History*. Translated by Robert Luoma. Portland, OR: Amadeus Press, 1995.

Borchmeyer, Dieter. *Drama and the World of Richard Wagner*. Translated by Daphne Ellis. Princeton, NJ: Princeton University Press, 2003.

Buckler, Julie A. *The Literary Lorgnette: Attending Opera in Imperial Russia*. Stanford, CA: Stanford University Press, 2000.

Budden, Julian. *Verdi*. New York: Schirmer Books, 1996.

Busch, Hans, ed. and trans. *Verdi's Falstaff in Letters and Contemporary Reviews*. Bloomington: Indiana University Press, 1997.

Campbell, Stuart, ed. and trans. *Russians on Russian Music, 1830–1880: An Anthology*. New York: Cambridge University Press, 1994.

Carter, Tim. *Monteverdi's Musical Theatre*. New Haven, CT: Yale University Press, 2002.

Celletti, Rodolfo. *A History of Bel Canto*. Frederick Fuller, trans. Oxford: Clarendon Press, 1996.

Citron, Marcia J. *Opera on Screen*. New Haven, CT: Yale University Press, 2000.

Chusid, Martin, ed. *Verdi's Middle Period, 1849–1859: Source Studies, Analysis, and Performance Practice*. Chicago: University of Chicago Press, 1997.

Conati, Marcello, and Mario Medici. *The Verdi-Boito Correspondence*. William Weaver, trans. Chicago: University of Chicago Press, 1994.

Crittenden, Camille. *Johann Strauss and Vienna: Operetta and the Politics of Popular Culture*. New York: Cambridge University Press, 2000.

Dizikes, John. *Opera in America: A Cultural History*. New Haven, CT: Yale University Press, 1993.

Drysdale, John D. *Louis Véron and the Finances of the Académie Royale de Musique*. New York: Peter Lang, 2003.

Edwards, Geoffrey. *The Verdi Baritone: Studies in the Development of Dramatic Character*. Bloomington: Indiana University Press, 1994.

———. *Verdi and Puccini Heroines: Dramatic Characterization in Great Soprano Roles*. Lanham, MD: Scarecrow Press, 2001.

Everist, Mark. *Giacomo Meyerbeer and Music Drama in Nineteenth-Century Paris*. Burlington, VT: Ashgate, 2004.

———. *Music Drama at the Paris Odéon, 1824–1828*. Berkeley: University of California Press, 2002.

Fenlon, Iain, and Tim Carter, eds. *Con che soavità: Studies in Italian Opera, Song, and Dance, 1580–1740*. New York: Oxford University Press, 1995.

Gasparov, Boris. *Five Operas and a Symphony: Word and Music in Russian Culture*. New Haven, CT: Yale University Press, 2005.

Goehring, Edmund J. *Three Modes of Perception in Mozart: The Philosophical, Pastoral, and Comic in Così fan tutte*. New York: Cambridge University Press, 2004.

Grey, Thomas S. *Wagner's Musical Prose: Texts and Contexts*. New York: Cambridge University Press, 1995.

Grout, Donald J., and Hermine Weigel Williams. *A Short History of Opera*, 4th ed. New York: Columbia University Press, 2003.

Hallman, Diana R. *Opera, Liberalism, and Antisemitism in Nineteenth-Century France: The Politics of Halévy's La Juive*. Cambridge: Cambridge University Press, 2002.

Hammond, Frederick. *Music and Spectacle in Baroque Rome: Barberini Patronage Under Urban VIII*. New Haven, CT: Yale University Press, 1994.

Heartz, Daniel, *Mozart's Operas*. Edited with contributing essays by Thomas Bauman. Berkeley: University of California Press, 1990.

———. *Music in European Capitals: The Galant Style, 1720–1780*. New York: W.W. Norton, 2003.

Huebner, Steven. *French Opera at the Fin de Siècle: Wagnerism, Nationalism, and Style*. New York: Oxford University Press, 1999.

Hunter, Mary Kathleen. *The Culture of Opera in Mozart's Vienna: A Poetics of Entertainment*. Princeton: Princeton University Press, 1999.

Hunter, Mary, and James Webster, eds. *Opera Buffa in Mozart's Vienna*. New York: Cambridge University Press, 1997.

Katz, Mark. *Capturing Sound: How Technology Has Changed Music*. Berkeley: University of California Press, 2004.

Kaufman, Thomas G. *Verdi and His Major Contemporaries: A Selected Chronology of Performances With Casts*. New York: Garland, 1990.

Kelly, Thomas Forrest. *First Nights at the Opera*. New Haven, CT: Yale University Press, 2004.

Kildea, Paul Francis. *Selling Britten: Music and the Marketplace*. New York: Oxford University Press, 2002.

Kimbell, David R.B. *Italian Opera*. New York: Cambridge University Press, 1991.

Kramer, Lawrence. *Opera and Modern Culture: Wagner and Strauss*. Berkeley: University of California Press, 2004.

LaRue, C. Steven. *Handel and His Singers: The Creation of the Royal Academy Operas, 1720–1728*. New York: Oxford University Press, 1995.

Latham, Alison, and Roger Parker, eds. *Verdi in Performance*. New York: Oxford University Press, 2001.

Letzter, Jacqueline, and Robert Adelson. *Women Writing Opera: Creativity and Controversy in the Age of the French Revolution*. Berkeley: University of California Press, 2001.

Levin, David J., ed. *Opera Through Other Eyes*. Stanford, CA: Stanford University Press, 1993.

Lindenberger, Herbert Samuel. *Opera in History: From Monteverdi to Cage*. Stanford, CA: Stanford University Press, 1998.

Marvin, Roberta Montemorra, and Downing A. Thomas, eds. *Operatic Migrations: Transforming Works and Crossing Boundaries*. Burlington, VT: Ashgate, 2005.

Meyer, Stephen C. *Carl Maria von Weber and the Search for a German Opera*. Bloomington: University of Indiana Press, 2003.

Millington, Barry, and Stewart Spencer, eds. *Wagner in Performance*. New Haven, CT: Yale University Press, 1992.

Morrison, Simon Alexander. *Russian Opera and the Symbolist Movement*. Berkeley: University of California Press, 2002.

Nicassio, Susan Vandiver. *Tosca's Rome: The Play and the Opera in Historical Perspective*. Chicago: University of Chicago Press, 2001.

Norman, Buford. *Touched by the Graces: The Libretti of Philippe Quinault in the Context of French Classicism*. Birmingham, AL: Summa Publications, 2001.

Parker, Roger. *Leonora's Last Act: Essays in Verdian Discourse*. Princeton, NJ: Princeton University Press, 1997.

———, ed. *The Oxford Illustrated History of Opera*. New York: Oxford University Press, 1994.

Parker, Roger, and Mary Ann Smart, eds. *Reading Critics Reading: Opera and Ballet Criticism in France From the Revolution to 1848*. New York: Oxford University Press, 2001.

Petrobelli, Pierluigi. *Music in the Theater: Essays on Verdi and Other Composers*. Translated by Roger Parker. Princeton: Princeton University Press, 1994.

Preston, Katherine K. *Opera on the Road: Traveling Opera Troupes in the United States, 1825–60*. Urbana: University of Illinois Press, 1993.

Price, Curtis A., Judith Milhous, and Robert. D. Hume. *Italian Opera in Eighteenth-Century London*. 2 vols. New York: Oxford University Press, 1995–2001.

Robinson, Paul A. *Opera, Sex, and Other Vital Matters*. Chicago: University of Chicago Press, 2002.

Rosselli, John. *Music and Musicians in Nineteenth-Century Italy*. London: B.T. Batsford, 1991.

———. *Singers of Italian Opera: The History of a Profession*. New York: Cambridge University Press, 1992.

———. *The Life of Bellini*. New York: Cambridge University Press, 1996.

———. *The Life of Mozart*. New York: Cambridge University Press, 1998.

———. *The Life of Verdi*. New York: Cambridge University Press, 2000.

Sadie, Stanley, ed. *History of Opera*. New York: W.W. Norton, 1990.

———, ed. *Verdi and His Operas*. Compiled by Roger Parker. New York: St. Martin's Press, 2000.

Salgado, Susana. *The Teatro Solís: 150 Years of Opera, Concert, and Ballet in Montevideo*. Middletown, CT: Wesleyan University Press, 2003.

Schmidgall, Gary. *Shakespeare and Opera*. New York: Oxford University Press, 1990.

Senici, Emanuele. *Landscape and Gender in Italian Opera: The Alpine Virgin from Bellini to Puccini*. New York: Cambridge University Press, 2005.

———, ed. *The Cambridge Companion to Rossini*. New York: Cambridge University Press, 2004.

Smart, Mary Ann. *Mimomania: Music and Gesture in Nineteenth-Century Opera*. Berkeley: University of California Press, 2004.

Spies, André Michael. *Opera, State, and Society in the Third Republic*. New York: P. Lang, 1998.

Steen, Michael. *The Life and Times of the Great Composers*. New York: Oxford University Press, 2004.

Stein, Louise K. *Songs of Mortals, Dialogues of the Gods: Music and Theatre in Seventeenth-Century Spain*. New York: Oxford University Press, 1993.

Sternfield, F.W. *The Birth of Opera*. New York: Oxford University Press, 1993.

Sturman, Janet Lynn. *Zarzuela: Spanish Operetta, American Stage*. Urbana: University of Illinois Press, 2000.

Taylor-Jay, Claire. *The Artist-Operas of Pfitzner, Krenek, and Hindemith: Politics and the Ideology of the Artist*. Burlington, VT: Ashgate, 2004.

Thomas, Downing A. *Aesthetics of Opera in the Ancien Régime, 1647–1785*. Cambridge: Cambridge University Press, 2002.

Till, Nicholas. *Mozart and the Enlightenment: Truth, Virtue, and Beauty in Mozart's Operas*. New York: W.W. Norton, 1993.

Traubner, Richard. *Operetta: A Theatrical History*. New York: Routledge, 2003.

Treadwell, James. *Interpreting Wagner*. New Haven, CT: Yale University Press, 2003.

Van, Gilles de. *Verdi's Theater: Creating Drama Through Music*. Translated by Gilda Roberts. Chicago: University of Chicago Press, 1998.

Vazsonyi, Nicholas, ed. *Wagner's Meistersinger: Performance, History, Representation*. Rochester, NY: University of Rochester Press, 2003.

Wade, Mara. *The German Pastoral Baroque "Singspiel."* New York: P. Lang, 1990.

Warrack, John. *German Opera: From the Beginnings to Wagner.* New York: Cambridge University Press, 2001.

Weiss, Piero, comp. *Opera: A History in Documents.* New York: Oxford University Press, 2002.

Williams, Simon. *Wagner and the Romantic Hero.* New York: Cambridge University Press, 2004.

Wlaschin, Ken. *Encyclopedia of Opera on Screen: A Guide to More Than 100 Years of Opera Films, Videos, and DVDs.* New Haven, CT: Yale University Press, 2004.

Woodfield, Ian. *Opera and Drama in Eighteenth-Century London: The King's Theatre, Garrick and the Business of Performance.* New York: Cambridge University Press, 2001.

DISCOGRAPHY AND VIDEOGRAPHY

Operas that are scheduled regularly are said to be in the "repertory." Compiling a precise list can be difficult, though, because the core of works can vary from country to country, reflecting national preferences. A survey of seasons for the past ten years at major US opera houses yields a list (arranged in alphabetical order by composer) of thirty of the most common productions in this country, listed as: Composer *Opera title* (librettist).

Bizet, Georges
   Carmen (Meilhac and Hálevy)
Donizetti, Gaetano
   Don Pasquale (Ruffini and Donizetti)
   Lucia di Lammermoor (Cammarano)
Gounod, Charles
   Faust (Barbier and Carré)
Handel, George Frideric
   Giulio Cesare in Egitto (Haym)
Lehár, Franz
   Die lustige Witwe (Léon and Stein)
Mascagni, Pietro/ Leoncavallo, Ruggiero
   Cavalleria rusticana (Targioni-Tozzetti and Menasci) performed with *I pagliacci* (Leoncavallo) as *Cav/Pag*
Mozart, Wolfgang Amadeus
   Così fan tutte (Da Ponte)

Die Zauberflöte (Schikaneder)
Don Giovanni (Da Ponte)
Le nozze di Figaro (Da Ponte)
Puccini, Giacomo
La bohème (Illica and Giocosa)
Madama Butterfly (Illica and Giocosa)
Tosca (Illica and Giocosa)
Rossini, Gioachino
Il barbiere di Siviglia (Sterbini)
Strauss, Johann
Die Fledermaus (Haffner and Genée)
Strauss, Richard
Ariadne auf Naxos (Hofmannsthal)
Der Rosenkavalier (Hofmannsthal)
Verdi, Giuseppe
Aida (Ghislanzoni)
Falstaff (Boito)
Il trovatore (Cammarano and Bardare)
La traviata (Piave)
Rigoletto (Piave)
Wagner, Richard
Das Rheingold (Wagner)
Die Walküre (Wagner)
Götterdämmerung (Wagner)
Lohengrin (Wagner)
Siegfried (Wagner)
Tannhäuser (Wagner)
Tristan und Isolde (Wagner)

Wagner dominates the list with seven works, followed by Verdi with five. Aside from Wagner's, however, there are only five other German operas. The Italian tradition emerges as the most popular, with eleven other works in addition to Verdi's (because they are generally performed together, *I pagliacci* and *Cavalleria rusticana* are counted as one production). The only French operas are *Carmen* and *Faust*. Although Gershwin's *Porgy and Bess* and other American works such as *A Streetcar Named Desire* and *Susannah* were mounted, none of those (or any English-language opera, for that matter) was scheduled enough times during the period surveyed to warrant entry on the list; neither did any Russian, Czech or Spanish work. Beyond national origin, it is clear that operas from the eighteenth and nineteenth centuries are programmed most frequently, obviously drawing the largest audiences. Only one Baroque work, *Giulio Cesare*, made the list. *Ariadne auf Naxos* (1912, second version, 1916) is the latest work from the twentieth century.

BEYOND THE COMMON REPERTORY

Audio and video recordings of common repertory works abound; indeed, one can choose by performer, conductor, or opera company. Beyond these are other significant operas that demonstrate the music of historical periods or of individual composer's styles. Following is a small sampling of CDs and DVDs of such works. Generally, many more recordings of these composers' works are available; space alone demanded the selection of one or two as examples. Furthermore, inclusion on this list is *not* a recommendation, for that is not within the scope of this book. The discography/videography is rather an aid for identifying recordings of significant works by composers and librettists mentioned in this book. The listings follow this format: Composer. *Opera title* (Librettist), label.

Adams, John. *Nixon in China* (Goodman), Nonesuch.

Auber, Daniel-François-Esprit. *La muette de Portici* (Scribe), EMI.

Barber, Samuel. *Antony and Cleopatra* (Zeffirelli), New World.

Bartók, Béla. *Bluebeard's Castle* (Balázs), EMI.

Berg, Alban. *Wozzeck* (Berg), EMI.

Bizet, Georges. *Les pêcheurs de perles* (Cormon and Carré), EMI.

Boieldieu, Adrien. *La dame blanche* (Scribe), EMI.

Britten, Benjamin. *Billy Budd* (Forster and Crozier), London.

Cavalli, Pier Francesco. *La Calisto* (Faustini), Harmonia Mundi.

Charpentier, Marc-Antoine. *Médée* (Corneille), Elektra.

Cherubini, Luigi. *Médée* (Hoffman), EMI.

Cilèa, Francesco. *Adriana Lecouvreur* (Colautti), VAI.

Cimarosa, Domenico. *Armida immaginaria* (Palomba), Dynamic.

Copland, Aaron. *The Tender Land* (Everett), Koch International.

Debussy, Claude. *Pelléas et Mélisande* (Maeterlinck), EMI.

Delibes, Leo. *Lakmé* (Gondinet and Gille), EMI.

Dittersdorf, Carl Ditter von. *Doktor und Apotheker* (Stephanie the Younger), Bayer.

Dvořák, Antonín. *Rusalka* (Kavpil), Decca.

Falla, Manuel de. *La vida breve* (Fernández Shaw), Telarc.

Flotow, Friedrich. *Martha* (Friedrich), EMI.

Floyd, Carlisle. *Of Mice and Men* (after Steinbeck), Albany.

Galuppi, Baldassare. *Il mondo alla roversa* (Goldoni), Chandos.

Gay, John (Johann Christoph Pepusch, arr.). *The Beggar's Opera* (Gay), Harmonia Mundi.

Glass, Philip. *Einstein on the Beach* (Knowles, Childs and Johnson), Nonesuch.

Glinka, Mikhail. *Ruslan and Lyudmila* (Shirkov), Philips.

Gounod, Charles. *Roméo et Juliette* (Barbier and Carré), EMI.

Grétry, André. *Richard Coeur-de-lion* (Sedaine), EMI.

Haydn, Josef. *Armida* (Porta), Elektra.

Humperdinck, Engelbert. *Hänsel und Gretel* (Wette), EMI.

Janáček, Leos. *Jenůfa* (Janáček), Elektra.

Jommelli, Niccolò. *Didone abbandonata* (Metastasio), Orfeo.

Joplin, Scott. *Treemonisha* (Joplin), Deutsche Grammophon.

Lecocq, Charles. *La fille de Madame Angot* (Clairville), EMI.

Lully, Jean-Baptiste. *Atys* (Quinault), Harmonia Mundi.

————. *Le bourgeois gentilhomme* (Molière), Harmonia Mundi.

Marschner, Heinrich. *Der Vampyr* (Wohlbruck), Capriccio.

Massenet, Jules. *Manon* (Meilhac and Gille), EMI.

Mayr, Giovanni Simone. *Medea in Corinto* (Romani), Opera Rara.

Menotti, Gian Carlo. *The Saint of Bleecker Street* (Menotti), Chandos.

Mercadante, Saverio. *Orazi e Curiazi* (Cammarano), Opera Rara.

Moore, Douglas. *The Ballad of Baby Doe* (Latouche), Deutsche Grammophon.

Mozart, Wolfgang Amadeus et al. *Der Stein der Weisen* (Schikaneder), Telarc.

Nicolai, Otto. *Die Lustigen Weiber Von Windsor* (Mosenthal), Lyrica.

Pacini, Giovanni. *Saffo* (Cammarano), Marco Polo .

Peri, Jacopo. *Euridice* (Rinuccini), Pavane.

Piccinni, Nicolò. *Roland* (Marmontel), Dynamic.

Planquette, Robert. *Les cloches de Corneville* (Clairville and Gabet), EMI.

Ponchielli, Amilcare. *La gioconda* (Gorrio [pseudonym for Boito]), EMI.

Poulenc, Francis. *Dialogues des Carmelites* (Poulenc), EMI.

Prokofiev, Sergei. *The Gambler* (Prokofiev), Philips.

Purcell, Henry. *Dido and Aeneas* (Tate), Harmonia Mundi.

Rameau, Jean-Philippe. *Castor et Pollux* (Bernard), Harmonia Mundi.

Ricci, Federico and Luigi. *Crispino e la comare* (Piave), Bongiovanni.

Rousseau, Jean-Jacques. *Le devin du village* (Rousseau), EMI.

Scarlatti, Alessandro. *Griselda* (Ruspoli), Harmonia Mundi.

Schubert, Franz. *Alfonso und Estrella* (Schober), Hyperion.

Smetana, Bedrich. *The Bartered Bride* (Sabina), Opera D'Oro.

Stravinsky, Igor. *The Rake's Progress* (Auden and Kallmen), Elektra.

Szymanowski, Karol. *King Roger* (Iwaszkiewicz), Naxos.

Traetta, Tommaso. *Antigona* (Coltellini), Decca.

Vaughan Williams, Ralph. *The Pilgrim's Progress* (Vaughan Williams), EMI.

Verdi, Giuseppe. *La forza del destino* (Piave), EMI.

⸻. *Les vêpres siciliennes* (Scribe and Duveyrier), Opera Rara.

Vivaldi, Antonio. *Orlando furioso* (Bracciolo), Naxos/Naive

Vives, Amadeo. *Doña Francisquita* (Romero and Shaw), Naive.

Wagner, Richard. *Die Feen* (Wagner), Orfeo.

⸻. *Rienzi* (Wagner), EMI.

Wolf-Ferrari, Ermanno. *Sly* (Forzano), Koch Schwann.

VIDEOS AND DVDs

DVDs purchased outside the United States or ordered from a foreign source need to be formatted for Region 1 to function on US players.

UK and European viewers should look for DVDs manufactured for Region 2.

The listings below follow this format: Composer, *Opera title* (Librettist), opera company, label.

Beethoven, Ludwig van. *Fidelio* (Sonnleithner), Metropolitan Opera, Deutsche Grammophon.

Bellini, Vincenzo. *La sonnambula* (Romani), RAI, VAI.

Berlioz, Hector. *Les Troyens* (Berlioz), Châtelet Opera, BBC/Opus Arte.

Boito, Arrigo. *Mefistofele* (Boito), San Francisco Opera, Kultur.

Borodin, Alexander. *Prince Igor* (Borodin), Kirov Opera, Philips.

Debussy, Claude. *Pelléas et Mélisande* (after Maeterlinck), Welsh National Opera, Deutsche Grammophon.

Donizetti, Gaetano. *La fille du regiment* (Saint-Georges and Bayard), La Scala, Naxos.

Gluck, Christoph von Willibad. *Orfeo ed Euridice* (Calzabigi), Glyndebourne Festival Opera, Kultur.

Halévy, Jacques-François Fromental. *La Juive.* (Scribe) Vienna State Opera, Deutsche Grammophon.

Korngold, Erich. *Die Tote Stadt* (Schott/Korngold), Opéra National du Rhin, Naxos.

Massanet, Jules. *Thaïs* (Gallet), Venice Opera, Qualiton Imports.

Meyerbeer, Giacomo. *Les Huguenots* (Scribe), Australian Opera, Kultur.

Monteverdi, Claudio. *L'incoronzaione di Poppea* (Busenello), Concerto Koln, Arthaus Musik.

Mussorgsky, Boris. *Boris Godunov* (Mussorgsky), Kirov Opera, Philips.

Offenbach, Jacques. *Orpheus in the Underworld* (Crémieux and Halévy), Théâtre de la Monnaie, Image Entertainment.

Paisiello, Giovanni. *Nina* (Lorenzi), Zurich Opera, Naxos.

Previn, André. *A Streetcar Named Desire* (Williams), San Francisco Opera, Image Entertainment.

Puccini, Giacomo. *Manon Lescaut* (Illica), Metropolitan Opera, Pioneer.

Rameau, Jean-Philippe. *Les Boréades* (Cahusac), Paris Opera, Naxos.

Rimsky-Korsakov, Nikolay. *Le Coq d'or* (Bel'sky) Châtelet Opera, Naxos.

Saint-Saëns, Camille. *Samson et Dalila* (Lemaire), Metropolitan Opera, Deutsche Grammophon.

Salieri, Antonio. *Falstaff* (Defranceschi), Schwetzingen Festspiele, Arthaus Musik.

Shostakovich, Dmitry. *Lady Macbeth of Mtsensk* (Shostakovich and Preys), Gran Teatre del Liceu, EMI.

Strauss, Johann. *Die Fledermaus* (Genée), Royal Opera, Image Entertainment.

Strauss, Richard. *Ariadne auf Naxos* (Hofmannsthal), Metropolitan Opera, Deutsche Grammophon.

Tchaikovsky, Pyotr Il'yich. *Mazeppa* (Burenin), Kirov Opera, Universal Music.

Thomas, Ambroise. *Hamlet* (Carré and Barbier), Barcelona Opera, EMI.

Verdi, Giuseppe. *Macbeth* (Piave and Maffei), Glyndebourne Opera, Arthaus.

————. *Nabucco* (Solera), Metropolitan Opera, Deutsche Grammophon.

Wagner, Richard. *Die Meistersinger von Nüremberg* (Wagner), Metropolitan Opera, Deutsche Grammophon.

Weber, Carl Maria von. *Der Freischütz* (Kind), Zurich Opera, Naxos.

Many of the recording labels listed maintain web sites through which their catalogs may be accessed. Readers are encouraged to check them because new issues are promoted regularly.

WEB SITES

The following is a sampling of web sites that contain information and links on opera topics. Some of these may require subscription. Topic searches will yield many more sites of interest.

Libretto translations: http://opera.stanford.edu/iu/librettim.html

Teacher resources: http://www.teachopera.net/

Broadcast and Web cast information: http://www.operaworld.com/special/broadcast.shtml

INFORMATION WEB SITES

http://www.operaam.org (Opera America)

http://www.metoperafamily.org/operanews/index.aspx (*Opera News* online) http://www.operatoday.com (*Opera Today*, an online journal)

THEATER WEB SITES

http://www.houstongrandopera.org (Houston Grand Opera)

http://www.teatroallascala.org/public/LaScala/EN/index.html (La Scala, Milan)

http://www.lyricopera.org/home.asp (The Lyric Opera, Chicago)

http://www.metoperafamily.org/metopera/home.aspx (The Metropolitan Opera, New York)

http://www.opera-de-paris.fr/ (Opéra National de Paris)

http://www.royalopera.org/ (The Royal Opera, London)

http://www.sfopera.com/ (The San Francisco Opera)

OPERA FESTIVAL WEB SITES

http://www.glimmerglass.org/ (Glimmerglass Festival, Cooperstown, NY)

http://www.rossinioperafestival.it/ (Rossini Festival, Pesaro, Italy)

http://www.bayreuther-festspiele.de/Anfangsseite/deutsch.htm (Wagner Bayreuth Festival, Germany)

http://www.wexfordopera.com/ (Wexford Festival, Wexford, Ireland)

SAMPLES OF SCHOLARLY RESEARCH PAGES:

http://www.nyu.edu/projects/verdi/ (American Institute of Verdi Studies, New York University)

http://humanities.uchicago.edu/orgs/ciao/ (Center for Italian Opera Studies, University of Chicago)

INDEX

1638

DISCARD